D1061290

HT

THE COSMIC CHRIST

THE
COSMIC
CHRIST

By

ALLAN D. GALLOWAY
B.D., Ph.D.

LONDON: NISBET & CO., LTD.
22 BERNERS STREET, W.1

First Published in 1951

Made and Printed in Great Britain.

TO

the Memory of

MY FATHER

INTRODUCTION

SOMETIMES the meaning of a word grows and is enhanced with the passing of the years. Sometimes it shrinks till it is only a dwarf of its former self. Most words exhibit both tendencies, flourishing and growing in one aspect of their meaning, while some other aspect becomes shrunken and dwarfed almost to extinction. In discussing the idea of salvation as it appears in the New Testament, Wheeler Robinson says :

> Salvation meant deliverance from any kind of ill, and the specific faith of the Christian increased the intensity, without limiting the extensity of the general experience of being " saved ", by whatever means. . . . The modern emphasis tends to fall on salvation from the power of moral evil in present experience. The New Testament, without, of course, denying or excluding this element as an accompaniment or even a condition of salvation, finds its centre of gravity in a cosmic event.[1]

That the term " salvation " had this wider connotation in the New Testament has been well known among Biblical scholars for some time. The emphasis now being accorded to this aspect of Biblical doctrine, along with the renewed interest in apocalyptic literature, coming at a time when the whole subject of man's relation to his material environment is very much in debate, has given wide currency to this odd phrase, " cosmic redemption ". This term is used in a vague and ill-defined way to refer to those aspects of the work of Christ which seem to go beyond the more restricted meaning which the word " salvation " or " redemption " bears in modern usage.

We are surely stating the obvious when we say that

[1] *Redemption and Revelation*, pp. 232–233.

" cosmic redemption " is a big subject. It is too big to be
competently handled in one volume or even by one man.
It leads us into a variety of fields of study which it is
beyond the powers of any one man to master completely.
But I propose no such Herculean task. Simply because
the problem is so large and undefined, there is a need for a
preliminary study such as is attempted here. I make no
attempt to formulate a complete doctrine of cosmic redemption. To discover what is the real problem at issue and
what kind of evidence is available for and relevant to its
solution, is a sufficient task.

This task falls naturally into two halves. Firstly, since
the ideas with which we are dealing have their origin in
Biblical and pre-Biblical times it is necessary to understand
them in the light of their history. It is in the historical
and linguistic researches of Biblical scholars that the idea
of cosmic redemption has received most attention. I have
found such works as W. L. Knox's *St Paul and the Church
of the Gentiles* and Hugo Gressmann's *Der Messias* immensely valuable in bringing together and ordering all this
mass of technical scholarship in such a way as to make its
results available to the mere theologian. I do not claim
to have brought any new facts to light in this field. But I
think I have done something to elucidate the theological
principles which governed the development of the doctrine.
With this end in view I have devoted Parts I and II of this
book to an outline survey of the theological development
of the idea of cosmic redemption in the Biblical and Patristic
periods respectively.

But here, unfortunately, the comparatively simple
method of historical treatment must end. Therefore the
second half of the book—Parts III and IV—is of quite a
different nature. After the great Patristic period the
idea of cosmic redemption never again featured significantly in official Christian theology. This is unfortunate,
because the cultural developments of the intervening

centuries now interpose themselves between us and a
proper understanding of these archaic formulations of this
doctrine.

This brings us to the second half of our task. Although
the doctrine of cosmic redemption may have fallen into
abeyance, the kind of existential experience which once
led men to formulate such a doctrine still has its modern
counterpart. The main problems which the early Church
solved by reference to the idea of cosmic redemption were
those of the relation of man as a religious and moral being
to an amoral environment. These problems appear in
modern thought. But the sharp transition from the ideas
and terminology of the primitive Church to those of post-
Renaissance Europe gives the impression of a serious hiatus
in the argument. This impression is confirmed by the fact
that when these problems do reappear, it is not in the field
of theology, but in the field of secular philosophy that they
are most prominent. We appear to launch out on an
entirely new and unrelated subject. We must somehow
relate these modern and entirely new formulations of the
problem to their counterpart in early Christian society. To
do this it is necessary to indulge in a considerable amount
of purely philosophical analysis.

Not so long ago there was a time when one could count
on the enthusiasm of theologians for any general philosophical question. But the more recent tendency has been
to receive any such digression from the substance of the
revealed Word with impatience. However, a subject such
as ours demands that we trespass fairly widely in the
philosophical field. If one were simply asking " What do
we mean by redemption ? " this could pass as a straightforward theological question. But when we qualify it
with the word " cosmic " a whole series of quite non-
theological questions are introduced. What precisely do
we mean by the word " cosmic " ? Its meaning is always
relative to a particular world-view which, in its turn is

conditioned by various scientific, philosophical and other cultural considerations. Its meaning for the early Christians whose minds were coloured by a background of Stoic philosophy, for instance, would be quite different from its meaning for us whose thinking is coloured by such views as the Kant-Laplace theory of the universe or any of its more recent rivals, by European Romanticism or by modern scientific positivism, and so on.

We cannot expect, therefore, to tackle a subject like this without becoming involved in a fair amount of rather technical philosophical discussion. The ridicule with which the idea of cosmic redemption is sometimes treated usually arises from the lack of a serious analysis of the fundamental concepts which the idea involves. On a superficial evaluation, the Biblical doctrine of cosmic redemption is a quaintly fantastic idea, attractive perhaps, but hardly credible. Yet it was the very heart of the primitive Gospel. It answered real problems of the human spirit and had a vital religious significance. We must not allow the archaic world-view with which it is allied to obscure its real existential import. Equally, we must not allow the sophistication of modern philosophies to obscure the fundamental identity of our own existential vexations with those of mankind in the first centuries of the Christian era. The language and concepts may differ widely, but human experience remains essentially the same.

There is, for instance, no obvious relationship at a superficial level between the cosmic speculations of the Gnostics of the second and third centuries and the philosophy of German Idealism. But at the level of the existential problems underlying their formal arguments we shall find quite a startling parallel. It is this task of digging our way through the mere verbiage to the level of existential understanding that is the most exacting one. All our philosophical analysis and argumentation is incidental to this end. Without such deep analysis of concepts the

Biblical doctrine of cosmic redemption with its angels and demons, its principalities and powers and all its curious views of elemental nature must remain a subject, perhaps of curious interest to anthropologists, but of no religious significance whatsoever.

The difficulties of negotiating this transition to a modern formulation of the problem are considerably increased by the lack of an adequate means of communication. Not only are our language, concepts and images quite different from those of the first centuries A.D. ; but such has been the development of our mainly technical civilisation that we are often quite inarticulate where our forefathers in the faith had a rich and subtly varied vocabulary of religious concepts to draw upon. Thus we find ourselves at a level where we have even to attempt to create new concepts or to rehabilitate old ones which have been long discarded. Modern theology is full of this difficulty, of course. Take the work of Nicholas Berdyaev, for instance, or Martin Buber or Karl Heim or any of the Existentialists. This kind of work makes heavy philosophical going. But it cannot be avoided.

What I have tried to say in my closing chapters is inherently simple. But it is the profound simplicity of the New Testament itself. It is like the simplicity of poetry. Once we try to subject it to analysis it becomes infinitely complex. This is my apology for the inevitable abstruseness of some of the latter parts of this work. If it makes exacting reading let the reader console himself with the thought that it was much more exacting in the writing. If it is clumsily said—as I know it is—perhaps the reader will sense my meaning behind the inadequate words and say it better for me. For in the last resort the meaning of what I have tried to say is not my private meaning. It is the Meaning of the imponderable Word in whom all things consist—a Meaning which is always beyond our grasp and yet is the light of our life.

My thanks are due to the many scholars who have from time to time advised and assisted me. Perhaps they will forgive me if I mention only Professor H. H. Farmer of Cambridge University and Professor Paul Tillich of Union Theological Seminary, New York, both of whom supervised my work as a research student. I am grateful, too, to the Iona Community in whose midst I first began to realise the importance of this aspect of Christian doctrine. My wife— bless her—has shown quite remarkable patience in typing my disorderly manuscript.

A.D.G.

TABLE OF CONTENTS

PART III

TRANSITION TO A NEW PHASE

PART IV

TOWARDS A MODERN FORMULATION

PART I

DEVELOPMENT TOWARDS
A DOCTRINE OF COSMIC
REDEMPTION IN THE BIBLE

THE COSMIC CHRIST

CHAPTER I

DEVELOPMENT IN THE OLD TESTAMENT

THERE are two problems which, however vaguely the unlettered mind may formulate them, must always vex everyone. It is true that they are recognised in the intellect by only a few. But for the mass of men they find expression in the vague sense of uneasiness and anxiety which they underlie. They are:

(1) the problem of evil, and
(2) the problem of particular existence.

The first demands that we separate the world sharply from God, to absolve Him from responsibility for evil. The second tends to be answered by uniting the world more closely to God, in order that the separateness of our existence may be overcome. Yet the answers must agree, for in the long run they are answers to the same question in its ethical and its ontological aspects respectively. Both answer the question : What is the relation of God to His creation ?

In developed religions three main types of answer are recognised :

(1) Cosmic Monism,
(2) Acosmic Monism, and
(3) Dualism.

Yet Christianity fits into none of these systems. The cross at its heart, as witnessing to the terrible reality of evil, makes Cosmic Monism impossible. The assertion of the absolute sovereignty of God excludes any ultimate dualism.

The principle of the Incarnation makes any form of acos-mism impossible. The answer which Christianity gives to the ontological question is to be understood in terms of the doctrine of Incarnation. The answer which it gives to the ethical question is to be understood in terms of the cross.

The World Outlook of Primitive Judaism. The roots of this lie in the Semitic religion out of which Christianity came and which it fulfilled. The involvement of God in the world, and His responsibility for it are asserted from the beginning—not merely in the creation myths, which, in the form we have them in the Old Testament are compara-tively late, but in the earliest forms of Semitic tribal religions.[1]

> The tribal or national societies of the ancient world were not strictly natural in the modern sense of the word, for the gods had their part and place in them equally with men. . . . Thus a man was born into a fixed relation to certain gods as surely as he was born into relation to his fellow men ; and his religion, that is, the part of his conduct which was determined by his relation to the gods, was simply one side of the general scheme of conduct prescribed for him by his position as a member of society. There was no separation between the spheres of religion and of ordinary life. Every social act had a reference to the gods as well as to men, for the social body was made up not of men only, but of gods and men.[2]

This seems to be true of all primitive religions.[3] It is certainly true of Semitic religion,[4] and its essential principle in its later development remains the same.[5]

As essentially non-speculative, Jewish religion never gives any systematic account of the relation of God to the world. But the implicit principle is that they recognised His universal presence and activity in the world without limiting His transcendence.

[1] W. Robertson Smith, *Religion of the Semites*, pp. 28–30. Notes by S. Cook, pp. 503–508.
[2] *Op. cit.*, pp. 29–30.
[3] *Ibid.*
[4] *Op. cit.*, pp. 48–50.
[5] *Op. cit.*, pp. 194–195.

The Problem Set by Primitive Judaism. Simply because the ontological question is answered in this way, by uniting the world so closely to God, the problem of evil becomes particularly acute. To trace its whole treatment in Jewish religion would be a departure from our main purpose. But two principles of the development of the Jewish treatment are to be noted :

(1) Because the ontological question is answered in the way indicated, the problem could be solved only in terms of redemption.

(2) As insight into the nature both of God and of evil deepens, the reference of God's redemptive act has to be widened continually. It grows along with their expanding horizon.

The Jewish treatment of the problem of evil will be considered only in so far as is necessary to exhibit the operation of these two principles. The essence of their answer is in two stages :

(1) It is essential to the righteousness of God that He should bring evil upon the ungodly—those who are unfaithful to Him.

(2) But though this is just and necessary, the continuation of such a state of affairs casts a slight upon God's righteous sovereignty ; therefore He makes a covenant with His people that one day this shall end. There shall be no more faithlessness and all shall be blessed.

Both points are illustrated in Jahweh's condemnation of the people of Israel and Moses' intercession for them in Exodus, Chapter 32, vv. 7-14. Having described the idolatry of the people, Jahweh says : " Now, therefore, let me alone that my wrath may wax hot against them, and that I may consume them." But Moses, in his intercession, points out the slight which this casts upon God's holy sovereignty :

" Wherefore should the Egyptians speak, and say, for mischief did He bring them out, to slay them in the mountains and to consume them from the face of the earth ? "

Moses then goes on to remind Jahweh of His promise to the fathers of Israel that He would bring the race to blessedness.

" Remember Abraham, Isaac, and Israel Thy servants, to whom Thou swarest by Thine own self, and saidst unto them, I will multiply your seed as the stars of heaven and all this land that I have spoken of will I give unto your seed, and they shall inherit it forever." Though it was at Sinai that the covenant was actually entered upon, the covenant principle seems to have been regarded as implicit in the promise to Abraham from the beginning.[1] This covenant principle constitutes the heart of their answer to the problem of evil.

The Restricted Reference of Primitive Eschatology. In the primitive religion of the early Jewish tribes the sovereignty of God was thought of only with reference to His own people. He was their God, and it was for them alone that He was responsible.[2] In accordance with the world-affirming nature of their religion they conceived of this as a responsibility for their life as a nation in this world, rather than for the transcendental destiny of their souls. Therefore it was the present hardships that they suffered as a nation that constituted for them the problem of evil. So the promise to Abraham is :

I will give unto thee, and thy seed after thee, the land wherein thou art a stranger, all the land of Canaan, for an everlasting possession ; and I will be their God.[3]

When they met with armed opposition in their attempts to grasp the fruit of this promise, there arose the concept of the *Day of Jahweh* as the occasion on which the Lord would drive out the enemies of the Hebrews before them.[4] At

---

[1] G. F. Moore, *Judaism*, Vol. I, pp. 535 ff.
[2] W. Robertson Smith, *op. cit.*, pp. 35–38.   [3] Genesis 17/8.
[4] R. H. Charles, *Eschatology : Hebrew, Jewish and Christian*, p. 87.

first the reference seems to have been to a purely local intervention. R. H. Charles says :

> Day amongst the Hebrews as amongst the Arabs, occasion-ally had the definite signification of " day of battle ". Thus in Is. 9/4 " the day of Midian " is the day of victory over Midian.[1]

Therefore the fulfilment of the promise consisted chiefly in a purely local manifestation of God's power.

The Extension of the Eschatological Reference. But already this contained the seeds of a wider eschatology. In terms of the first part of their answer to the problem of evil—namely the assertion of God's retributive justice—the re-verses which they suffered had to be regarded as an expres-sion of that justice. On the other hand, in terms of the second part of their answer to the problem of evil—namely the assertion of the covenant promise—God had to be regarded as having power over other nations and their armies. How the logic of this becomes explicit in Elijah[2] and his successors in the prophetic tradition is well known. In Amos, with reference to the fall of Samaria, the Assyrians are regarded quite unequivocally as the instruments of God's justice.[3] The same principle is even more clearly operative in First Isaiah.

This inevitably led to a drastic re-interpretation of the concept of the *Day of the Lord,* as the day on which Jahweh would manifest Himself in power. It had to become something far wider in its significance than a supreme act of " national service ". Thus Amos says :

> Woe unto you that desire the Day of the Lord ! To what end is it for you ? The Day of the Lord is darkness and not light.[4]

The Nature of the Prophetic Insight. What had once

---

[1] *Loc. cit.*
[2] Wellhausen, *History of Israel,* pp. 461 ff. Welch, *Religion of Israel,* pp. 57–58.
[3] Amos, 3/11–15 ; *cf.* Wellhausen, *op. cit.,* pp. 470–474.
[4] Amos, 5/18.

been conceived as a day of glorious victory was now thought
of as a day of doom.   A widely accepted explanation of
this reversal is that the prophets of Israel were the first
who truly understood the righteousness of Jahweh, and in
the light of this knowledge they realised that Israel must
suffer for her wickedness before she could be acceptable to
God.   One would not wish to deny this statement, but in
this form it is very liable to give a wrong impression.   It
suggests that the prophets reached their conclusions about
the concrete situation in the world by arguing *deductively*
from a knowledge of God's righteousness which they already
possessed through revelation.   Now there is no reason to
suppose that the mental processes of the prophets of Israel
were essentially different from those of other human beings.
Admittedly this type of deductive argument from the
principle of God's righteousness does sometimes occur, but
it is normally confined to academic theological treatises.
The writings of the prophets do not read like such treatises.
Despite the *ex cathedra* nature of their pronouncements,
they read like the fiery utterances of a man who has a
sudden insight into the actual situation.   This would suggest a complete reversal of the logic normally ascribed to
them, so that it becomes inductive rather than deductive.
That is to say, their inspiration took the form of an inspired
insight into the actual concrete situation.   They viewed
the political situation through the eyes of their own personal experience of shame and grace before the righteousness of God ; but this does not make their insight into that
situation any less immediate.   Therefore, instead of deduc-
ing the inevitability of Israel's sufferings from their
knowledge of the righteousness of God, it was their insight
into that inevitability that deepened their knowledge of
God and His justice.

This view has the advantage that it explains why pro-
phetism arose when it did.   The Jewish people had reached
a crisis in their national history.   This implied a crisis in

their relations with Jahweh, and it was because the prophets understood the historical situation that they were able to understand its religious meaning.

The Principle Behind the Extension of the Eschatological Reference. I make this examination of the nature of prophetic insight because, in analysing their reaction to the historical situation, we find the first clear instance of the operation of a principle of development which was to determine the whole growth of Jewish and early Christian eschatology. This principle is :

> *Once a community has accepted a redemptive faith, the impact of their environment upon them forces them either to narrow their concept of redemption by giving it an other-worldly interpretation, or to widen its reference so as to include the whole of their environment.*

Within the context of the limited horizon of the tribes in their first occupation of Palestine, the conception of the day of the Lord as a purely local manifestation of power was adequate to fulfil its function as theodicy.[1] This was because the impact of environment upon the nation was chiefly in the form of the armed resistance of those who sought to drive them out. But after the occupation, amid the political complexities of developed nationhood, an extension of their environmental horizon was inevitable. The problem of evil came to be felt primarily in the wider political insecurities which prevented them from enjoying the land which they possessed. The great insight of the prophets was their understanding of the meaning of this insecurity.

They perceived the organic unity of personal life with the totality of this wider environment. They perceived, for example, the organic relationship between evil (רַע) as the sufferings and disasters coming out of their total en-

---

[1] Though I treat Jewish eschatology as fulfilling the function of theodicy, I do not wish to suggest that this is in any sense its origin.

vironment, and evil as transgressions (פְּשָׁעִים). Thus, for instance, the recurring form in Amos, " For three transgressions of . . . and for four, I will not turn away the punishment thereof " represents also the inward form of his thought. The roots of evil run to the very foundations of man's social being, and therefore cannot be overcome in any mere local act of intervention by God. Therefore the Day of the Lord, as the occasion on which Jahweh triumphs finally over evil, had to be conceived as a day of judgment and doom. Its reference had to be extended to cover the whole social and political environment of Israel.

The Implied Extension of the Eschatological Reference to All Things. Once this extension of the reference of the judgment of God had been initiated, there was no point at which it could logically be limited. The idea of total world judgment is not present in the early prophets. Only those nations which constituted the political environment of Israel were mentioned. But the same principle by which the judgment was extended to them implied its farther extension to all nations.

Over and above this, there is a yet more extensive implication contained in the early prophets, though it does not become fully explicit till much later. The evils they had to reckon with were not only moral and political, but physical as well—e.g. drought and crop failure. These too belonged to the same organic totality of evil, and formed part of the pattern of judgment in terms of which they interpreted life. The distinction between moral and physical evil was not at all clearly drawn, as is witnessed to by the indiscriminate use of the word רַע to cover both types. Though we do find Judaism becoming conscious of the need for some such distinction (as, for instance, in the book of Job or in the book of Daniel) the clear-cut distinction which is so familiar to us is essentially of Greek origin and is dependent for its formulation partly on their philosophic spirit, and partly on their dualism of mind and matter.

Therefore for Amos, the whole realm of physical disaster —for us a purely contingent element disrupting the unity of history—is brought within the pattern of God's judgment. God, as the Lord of Hosts, expresses His will through all the forces of the natural and physical order :

> And I also have given you cleanness of teeth in all your cities, and want of bread in all your places; yet have ye not returned unto me, saith the Lord. And also I have withholden rain from you, when there were yet three months to the harvest : and I caused it to rain upon one city, and caused it not to rain upon another city : one piece was rained upon, and the piece whereon it rained not withered. So two or three cities wandered into one city, to drink water ; but they were not satisfied : yet have ye not returned unto me, saith the Lord. I have smitten you with blasting and mildew ; when your gardens and your vineyards and your fig trees and your olive trees increased, the palmerworm devoured them : yet have ye not returned unto me, saith the Lord. I have sent among you the pestilence after the manner of Egypt : your young men have I slain with the sword, and have taken away your horses ; and I have made the stink of your camps to come up unto your nostrils : yet have ye not returned unto me, saith the Lord. . . . For, lo, he that formeth the mountains, and createth the wind, and declareth unto man what is his thought, that maketh the morning darkness, and treadeth upon the high places of the earth, The Lord, The God of hosts, is his name.[1]

Here, we have set in motion a train of thought which could only lead logically to the cosmic imagery of apocalyptic.

However, this is all in terms of judgment, and not of redemption. And it is true that this is the main emphasis of the prophetic tradition. Most of the " comfortable "

[1] Amos, 4/6–13.

passages are now recognised as late additions to the text of
Amos.   But even in Amos, the redemptive aspect of the
covenant never disappears entirely.   There is still room for
the pleading note, " How shall Jacob arise, for he is small ? "
and for the promise, " Seek me and ye shall live."

The extension of the idea of judgment to cover the whole
of environment implied a corresponding extension of the
redemptive aspect of the covenant, and in this sense the
later insertions dealing with the " remnant " or the " kingdom " which we find in Amos and the other early prophets
are justified.   But the full development of this trend is
found in the apocalyptic writings of Daniel and the
Apocrypha.

CHAPTER II

THE APOCALYPTIC ATTITUDE TO THE WORLD

AT this point it is necessary to interrupt the continuity of our argument in order to meet the assertion that when Judaism came to adopt the apocalyptic form as an expression of its eschatological hopes, it abandoned the concern for the religious destiny of the life of this world which, as we have already seen, characterised its earlier development.

The Charge of Other-Worldliness. We have already noticed the emphasis which Amos placed on the idea of judgment. It has been maintained by some that this line of thought, coupled with the bitter experiences of the Exile, induced the Jewish people to abandon all hope for the redemption of their total environment. In terms of the principle of development which we have emphasised above[1] this would impel them to reformulate their idea of redemption in purely other-worldly terms. This is precisely how the apocalyptic tradition has often been interpreted. It is interpreted as abandoning this world entirely to judgment and destruction. Nothing of the goodness the world received from God remains in it. Montefiore refers to this interpretation in these terms :

> While in the period after Ezra it is allowed that the cruder anthropomorphisms of the pre-exilic religion have been overcome, it is asserted that God remained as much as ever a magnified, non-natural personality, on the mere human model, with all its imperfections removed and all its excellences infinitely increased. He ruled the

---

[1] *Supra*, p. 9 f.

world from without : His spirit was not conceived as immanent either in nature or in man.[1]

Coupled with this view of God as ruling the world from without, we are told, went the apocalyptic outlook of sheer despair for the world.   Bousset says :

Die judische Apocalyptik sei durchaus pessimistisch. Nach ihr verschlimmere der Weltzustand sich fortwahrend, bis durch Gottes absolut wunderbares Eingreifen der Weltverlauf aufgehoben und ein absolut neuer Anfang gesetzt wird.[2]

The Genuine Element of Pessimism in Jewish Apocalyptic. There clearly is such a pessimistic side to the later developments of Jewish eschatology—a tendency to take a seemingly negative attitude to current history, which contrasts sharply with the intensely historical attitude of the Pentateuch and the earlier prophets.   In the late apocalypse in Isaiah 24–27 we find the words : " Come, my people, enter into thy chambers, and shut thy doors about thee : hide thyself as it were for a little moment until the indignation is overpast."[3]   The same symptom appears in the closing words of the book of Daniel : " Blessed is he that waiteth and cometh to the thousand and three hundred and five and thirty days.   But go thou thy way till the end be : for thou shalt rest and stand in thy lot at the end of the days."[4] It cannot be denied that this kind of statement is typically apocalyptic, and can be duplicated in any of the apocalypses.

The Optimism of Jewish Apocalyptic.   On the other hand, the apocalyptic attitude to the present cannot be described as merely negative.   After all, the apocalyptic tradition arose as the logical implicate of the prophetic insight.   It may have had its formal origin in Persian and Babylonian

---

[1] *Hibbert Lectures,* p. 424.   For Montefiore's own refutation of this interpretation of Jewish theology, *vid. loc. cit.*

[2] *Religion des Judentums,* p. 581.

Isaiah, 26/20.   [4] Daniel, 12/13.

sources but it met an indigenous need in Judaism which was created by the prophetic teaching.[1] Now we have already analysed this prophetic insight as essentially an insight into the meaning of their contemporary history.[2] It would be a strange thing if the logical outcome of this insight was the denial of any meaning in the world.

Again, apocalyptic existed in the midst of a religious culture in which the dominant idea was that of the law.[3] The keeping of the law in the present world was the condition of inclusion in apocalyptic salvation. This, too, implied the meaningfulness of the present world and established its continuity with the New Heaven and the New Earth.

Thirdly, even when the idea of personal immortality had been introduced to Judaism by Greek and Oriental influences, the blessed life of the resurrection in the New Heaven and the New Earth was not removed to some transcendental sphere, but was conceived of as a life in the flesh, within this same space-time continuum. Very often the kingdom is thought of as being established on this earth, as in some sections of 1 Enoch.[4]

This implies an element of unbounded optimism which exists side by side with the pessimism which we have already recognised.

The Nature of the Apocalyptic Symbol. Ultimately, any attempt to determine whether Jewish apocalyptic writings are other-worldly in their import on the basis of such questions as whether the scene of the New Jerusalem is set in this world, or in a completely new creation, is entirely misleading. This is to approach apocalyptic as though it were not a symbol, but simply prediction, in the sense of history written before the event. Admittedly it seems to

---

[1] Manson, *The Teaching of Jesus*, p. 247. *Cf.* Wellhausen, *Zur apocalyptischen Literatur*, Skizzen u. Vorarbeiten, Heft 6, pp. 233 ff.
[2] *Supra*, p. 7 *ff.*
[3] *Cf.* Montefiore, *op. cit.*, p. 467 f.
[4] 1 Enoch, vi–xxxvi, lxxiii–xc, xci–civ.

have been regarded by its readers and writers in the centuries immediately before and after Our Lord's birth as something which would be more or less literally fulfilled within a finite period of time. But this does not in any way alter the fact that its real value lay in its meaning as a religious symbol. After all, the same people regarded the creation myth of Genesis as being literally true ; but it would be generally admitted that this did not necessarily destroy for them the deepest meaning of the myth as a religious symbol.

If this can be true of the myths about the beginning of the world, it can also be true of the myths about the end of the world. It is one of the strange misadventures of history that while the permanent value of the creation myth as a religious symbol has survived the rejection of its literal interpretation by modern culture, its counterpart in the apocalyptic imagery about the end of the world has suffered to the extent of becoming almost a total loss.

Just as we would no longer make deductions from the statement that God took six days to create the universe, so we should no longer criticise the apocalyptic symbol on the basis of a similar type of reasoning. Just as the doctrine of creation must be taken in its totality simply as symbolically asserting the divine ground of the world, so the apocalyptic symbol must be taken in its totality simply as asserting the divine destiny of the world.

The Apocalyptic Paradox and its Positive Meaning. Despite the recent popularity of the paradox among expositors of the Christian faith, the paradoxical meaning of apocalyptic has never received the same recognition as, for example, that of the prophetic ancestors of apocalyptic ; though it is essentially the same paradox which apocalyptic expresses in a more acute form. Even so great an authority as R. H. Charles, while he mentions both the optimistic and the pessimistic elements in apocalyptic, does not seem to be aware of any dialectical tension between them. In his small book, *Religious Development Between the Old and New Testaments*, he says :

> Thus, whereas prophecy incidentally dealt with the past and devoted itself to the present and the future as arising organically out of the past, apocalyptic, though its interests lay chiefly in the future as containing the solution of the problems of the past and the present, took within its purview things past, present and to come. It is no mere history of such things. While the ordinary man saw only the outside of things in all their incoherence and isolation, the apocalyptist sought to get behind the surface, and to penetrate to the essence of events, the spiritual purposes and forces that underlie them and give them their real significance. . . . Apocalyptic and not prophecy was the first to grasp the great idea that all history, alike human, cosmological and spiritual is a unity—a unity following naturally as a corollary of the unity of God, preached by the prophets.[1]

This is a magnificent description of the optimism of apocalyptic, and is well worth quoting for its own sake. But in the very same chapter we find also, without any recognition of the contradiction, the following words :

> At this period the earth came to be regarded as wholly unfit for this kingdom, and thus new conceptions of the kingdom arose, and it was taught by many that the messianic kingdom was to be merely of temporary duration, and the goal of the risen righteous was to be—not this temporary kingdom or millennium—but heaven itself. This conception, combined with kindred apocalyptic beliefs begat an attitude of detachment from this world.[2]

Charles does not seem to be aware of any tension between those two descriptions of the apocalyptic attitude to the world, but we cannot but wonder what has become of the unity of history, " human, cosmological and spiritual " when the earth is no longer regarded as a fit place for the

[1] pp. 23–24.   [2] p. 19.

kingdom, and the unity of history is interrupted by the cataclysmic imposition of a millennium.

The failure to recognise that these two elements are held together in the unity of paradox in apocalyptic is the cause of most of the misunderstanding. On the one hand there is a complete despair of any of the finite elements in history either constituting or realising its ultimate meaning. This is simply an extension of that which made the prophets say :

> Woe unto them that go down to Egypt for help ; and stay on horses and trust in chariots, because they are many ; and in horsemen because they are very strong ; but they look not unto the Holy One of Israel, neither seek they the Lord.[1]

On the other hand there is an absolute hope for history as a whole. It does assert the meaningfulness of all history, " human, cosmological and spiritual " in that its ultimate destiny is to be made conformable to the inner holiness of the One True God.

When apocalyptic is understood thus, as a religious symbol analogous to the correlative myth of the beginning of the world, we see that its attitude to the world is positive and affirmative, though it rejects the naturalistic affirmation of the world. But simply because it rejects all naturalistic affirmation, nothing is relegated to the sphere of the secular. The whole cosmos is brought within the redemptive aspect of the covenant.

The Apocalyptic Paradox in the New Testament. A great step in the rediscovery of the apocalyptic setting of the Synoptic Gospels is Schweitzer's *The Quest of the Historical Jesus.* I am not here concerned with his assertions about the mind of the historical Jesus, but rather with his interpretation of the Synoptic Gospels as documents. His assertion of their apocalyptic setting and intention is perfectly correct. Where he goes wrong is in his interpre-

[1] Isaiah 31/1.

tation of the apocalyptic symbol as such. It may well have been true that Jesus and His followers looked for a more or less literal fulfilment of the apocalyptic hope. But as I have already pointed out, they probably also interpreted the stories about the beginning of the world quite literally, yet we do not regard this as materially affecting their appreciation of the idea of creation as a religious symbol. When Schweitzer says : " Primitive theology is simply a theology of the future with no interest in history,"[1] he is interpreting apocalyptic as though it were simply what we have already called " history written before the event " and not a religious symbol. If this were a correct approach, then apocalyptic would have no cosmic significance whatsoever.

But Schweitzer has taken hold of only one side of the paradox. The result is that he is considerably embarrassed in his attempts to explain away all the historical realism of the Gospels as mere *Interimsethik*. On the other hand, a man like Von Dobschütz sees only the other side of the paradox. He makes the preposterous statement : " When we ask what is the kernel of early Christian religious feeling, we shall find that there is nothing eschatological about it."[2] and again he says of Jesus : " If we eliminate his eschatological ideas, his ethics remain unchanged."[3]

This contradiction between Schweitzer and Von Dobschütz corresponds exactly to the two contradictory elements within Charles' interpretation of apocalyptic, to which I have already drawn attention. One element negates the world and history. The other affirms it. The presence of neither element can be denied. C. H. Dodd states the position well when he says :

We seem to be confronted with two diverse strains in the teaching of Jesus, one of which seems to contemplate the indefinite continuance of human life under historical con-

[1] *The Quest of the Historical Jesus*, p. 342.
[2] *The Eschatology of the Gospels*, p. 17.
[3] *Op. cit.*, p. 13.

C

ditions, while the other appears to suggest a speedy end
of these conditions.   A drastic criticism might eliminate
one strain or the other, but both are deeply embedded in
the earliest form of the tradition known to us.   It would
be better to admit that we do not possess the key to their
reconciliation than to do such violence to our documents.

It may be possible to find a place for both strains if we
make full allowance for the symbolic character of the
apocalyptic sayings.   The symbolic method is inherent
in apocalyptic.[1]

Conclusion.   We have illustrated the principle by which
Judaism, since it rejected the dualistic implications of an
other-worldly eschatology, was forced to extend the
reference of the redemptive aspect of the covenant to cover
the whole of environment.   Now we have met the suggestion that when they expressed this in apocalyptic form,
they were in fact rejecting their own basic religious presuppositions, and adopting the other-worldly interpretation
of the idea of redemption which they had formerly rejected.
We have pointed out that apocalyptic is a paradoxical
symbol which, while it counters any naturalistic optimism
with an absolute despair, is so far from the despair of
dualism that it looks for the complete transformation of the
whole of creation.

This enables us to establish our thesis that since Judaism,
as a redemptive faith, rejected any dualistic solution to the
problem of evil, it was forced to develop towards a doctrine
of cosmic redemption, and that this doctrine found expression in the cosmic symbolism of apocalyptic.

[1] *The Parables of the Kingdom*, pp. 104–5.

CHAPTER III

THE COSMIC IMAGERY OF THE APOCALYPTIC BACKGROUND TO THE NEW TESTAMENT

SINCE the cosmic reference of apocalyptic imagery did not arise by chance, but was the logical result of the principle of development which we have exhibited in Jewish eschatology, it cannot be dismissed as a primitive irrelevance. It belongs to the historical structure and meaning of Christian theology. We have already attempted to describe the general attitude of apocalyptic to the world as being essentially positive, and not merely negative. We must now describe more fully this positive attitude to the whole cosmic order which prevailed in the religious thought of the time of Our Lord.

Just as the symbol of the creation of the world is the complement of the symbol of the end of the world, so the symbol of cosmic fall is the complement of the symbol of cosmic redemption. Therefore it is with the idea of the Fall that we must begin.

The Fall in Jewish Thought. As when we were dealing with the symbol of the creation and the end of the world, so it is again necessary to emphasise the distinction between the religious symbol and the concept. N. P. Williams, in speaking of the difficulties of finding the concept of the Fall in Genesis III, says :

These ideas—especially that of a hereditary bias towards evil—even when held in the vaguest and most popular form, and without any scholastic exactness of definition are yet of a somewhat artificial and abstract nature. They presuppose considerable powers of generalisation and induction from the facts of history and also of introspective self-analysis.[1]

From this he concludes that a tradition so primitive as that of Genesis III could not contain any such sophisticated thoughts.   From the point of view of the conceptual type of thought he describes, this is a perfectly correct statement. He does concede a certain meaningfulness to the symbol in that he later says, in this same connection :

> Recent study of the mind and its workings has taught us that, in the individual, the dream may be the source of interesting and important information as to the contents of the dim mysterious region of the unconscious ; for, in the fantastic imagery of the dream, impulses, instincts and wishes of which the conscious ego may be entirely ignorant find a symbolic expression through the partial relaxation in sleep of the censorship exercised by the higher self.   And myths are the dreams of the vast, slumberous, diffused race soul, embodying in symbolic and generalised form unmistakable testimony to the mutual affinities and interpretations of the most fundamental emotions of human nature.[2]

But we vastly underrate the significance of the religious symbol if we treat it as expressive of only emotion.   It expresses the orientation of the whole personality—thinking and willing as well as emotional—towards reality as a whole.   Williams himself, in the last chapter of his *Ideas of the Fall and Original Sin* expounds a doctrine of cosmic Fall which could be related to the traditional " Fall " stories only if we recognise the symbolic myth as capable of bearing much more than emotional meaning.

It is as a symbol in this sense that the story of the Fall is significant, not only in its primitive statements, but also in its more sophisticated formulations.   Any attempt to reduce it to scientific or pseudo-scientific statements—e.g.

---

[1] *Ideas of the Fall and Original Sin*, p. 12.
[2] *Op. cit.*, p. 34.

by the use of the idea of hereditary propensities—implies complete misunderstanding of the epistemological status of the myth.

If we approach the symbol of the Fall with this in mind, we find it symbolising two phases :

(1) the Fall as a psychological event, and
(2) the Fall as a universal event affecting the whole structure of the cosmos.

In each of the two main traditions of the Fall story— that represented by Genesis III, and that represented by Genesis VI—both elements are present. In the paradise story of Genesis III the main interest is in the Fall as a psychological event, as symbolised by the hesitation, weakness, and ultimate disobedience of Adam and Eve in eating of the tree of the knowledge of good and evil. But the universal, cosmic element is also represented as logically correlative with the Fall of Adam and Eve ; firstly in a causal relation in the serpent ; then in a consequential relation in the cursing of the ground because of Adam's sin. In the tradition of Genesis VI, the cosmic aspect of the Fall receives more emphasis. Here it is symbolised by the illicit intercourse of the בְּנֵי הָאֱלֹהִים, the sons of God—i.e. angels or " beings of a higher divine mould "[1]— with the daughters of men. This gave rise to a race of giants who spread evil abroad in the world.

For a long time this account of the Fall received preference. It occurs with variations in many of the late Apocrypha. In Ethiopic Enoch it is considerably expanded and developed. It is referred to in Jubilees 4/15 ff. and 5/1 ff. and in the Testament of the Twelve Patriarchs (Testament of Naphtali, 3/5 ; Testament of Reuben, 5/5–7). It occurs again in 2 Enoch 18. But in 2 Enoch 29 the cosmic Fall is not symbolised by the descent of heavenly beings to earthly levels, but by the attempt of Satanail and his angels to place his throne " higher than the clouds

---

[1] A. Dillman, *Genesis Critically and Exegetically Expounded*, p. 233.

above the earth". In 2 Enoch 31, this becomes related to the paradise story of Genesis III and takes the place of the symbol of the serpent within it. In the apocalypse of Ezra we find only the paradise story.

The Meaning of " Belief in Angels ". The symbol of the psychological Fall—the disobedience of Adam and Eve—is still sufficiently close to our own personal experience to have a vivid significance for us. But in an age which no longer " believes in angels " the story of a fallen angel loses all its symbolic power. It is therefore very difficult for us to recapture the full significance of the myth. The theological problem presented by angelology is not simply that of the existence of rosy-cheeked, aerial creatures with wings sprouting from their shoulder-blades. This in itself is no theological problem at all. Therefore we can lightly dismiss " belief in angels " in this sense, and even though the idea is so prominent in Biblical theology—both of the Old and New Testaments—the structure of Biblical faith remains essentially unaffected.

But the real question is not that of the existence of a certain type of being. This is a scientific question to be answered by empirical investigation. The real problem rests on the fact that the people who believed in angels in Biblical times believed in them and talked about them because they expressed something significant about the structure of existence. The symbol is no longer adequate for us. But what was once signified by the symbol still remains in one sense or another part of our experience.

We must ask ourselves what was the real meaning of belief in angels in and around the first Christian century. There is very little systematic unity in the interpretation of their significance. But a certain measure of general agreement does emerge from the chaos. Philo, commenting on Genesis VI, says :

It was Moses' custom to give the name of angels to those

whom other philosophers call demons (δαίμονας), souls, that is, which fly and hover in the air.[1]

These aerial beings may be either good in their offices or bad.[2] In 1 Enoch 15 and 2 Enoch 29/5, the fallen angels are again described as hovering in the lower air. This corresponds to the Stoic teaching about the location of demons. The Stoics developed the long tradition of demonology in Greek philosophy[3] into a systematic structure. It is probably them that Philo has in mind when he refers to " the philosophers ". 1 Enoch 15 identifies the demonic forces that threaten the welfare of men with the offspring of the fallen angels. Justin suggests a similar, though not identical idea when he identifies the fallen angels of the Genesis VI tradition with the pagan gods. From the early Christian point of view, this amounts to almost the same thing as identifying them with demons that threaten the welfare of men. And again, in 1 Enoch 18 we find the fallen angels closely associated with the seven stars—and therefore with all the fateful powers which these stars represent in terms of primitive astrology— though they are not actually identified with them.

This easy identification of the fallen angels with the demonic forces of paganism suggests a common meaning lying behind both which is more important than either of the symbols themselves. This common meaning which lies behind the whole of Jewish and pagan angelology and demonology may be expressed in these terms :

(1) Wherever there is vitality and movement, this tends to be explained in terms of, and related to an underlying spiritual force.

(2) When this vitality is expressed in terms of creative harmonious activity, it is associated with a good spirit (holy angel). When it is expressed in des-

---

[1] *On the Giants*, II (6), (Loeb translation).   [2] *Op. cit.*, IV (16).
[3] *Vid. Encyclopedia of Religion and Ethics* (Hastings) under " Demons ".

tructive, chaotic activity, it is associated with a
demonic or evil spirit—a fallen angel.

We can understand this more readily on its positive side
than on its negative. For example, when Dibelius refers
to the belief current in Talmudic Judaism, the classical
expression of which he translates as " *Es ist kein Ding in
der Welt, auch nicht ein Krautlein, über welches nicht ein
Engel gesetzt ist.*" (Jalkut Chadash 147d)[1], we can succeed
in recapturing just a little of the background which would
have made such a statement significant. The symbol of
the guardian angel over each thing suggests :

(1) The power of the thing to persist in time.
(2) The power which maintains the structural form
    against chaotic formlessness.
(3) In the case of living things, their power to maintain
    vitality and health in the face of disease.

It is the same insight as lies behind animistic beliefs in
general—the same thing as induced Thales to maintain that
" all things are full of gods[2]".

On its negative side, however, we have much more
difficulty in giving meaning to the Jewish belief in angels—
or its Gentile counterpart. That is to say, while we can
only just glimpse the meaning which lies behind the belief
in holy angels, we can scarcely even do this in the case of
fallen angels. In one sense, the work of redemption
wrought for us in Christ has been so complete in its destruction of the power of the demonic that we no longer
understand that power as a dynamic reality. Nicholas
Berdyaev says :

The greatest contribution of Christianity, although it is
not fully recognised by the Christian world, consisted in

[1] Martin Dibelius, *Die Geisterwelt im Glauben des Paulus*, p. 10.
[2] Aristotle, *De Anima*, 1 : 5, 411a 7.

that it liberated man from the power of the baser elemental nature and demons. It did so through the agency of Christ and the mystery of redemption. It rescued man forcibly from his immersion in elemental nature and revived his spirituality. It distinguished him from baser nature and set him up as an independent spiritual being, freeing him from submission to the natural world and exalting him to the heavens. Christianity alone restored the spiritual freedom of which man had been deprived by the power of the demons, the natural spirits and elemental forces of the pre-Christian world. The essential contribution of Christianity therefore lay in that it liberated man and offered a free solution for human destiny.[1]

But in this liberation from the power of the demonic there are two stages to be distinguished :

(1) that which overcomes the power of the demonic, and
(2) that which denies its existence.

The early church never denied the existence of the demonic. St. Paul denied the power of the demons, and their claim to receive worship. But he did not deny their existence.[2] But the overcoming of the power of the demons led to the masterful, controlling attitude to nature which made post-Renaissance science possible. This in its turn led to the denial of the reality of the demonic. This latter development is what Berdyaev calls " the reverse side of this process of liberation which has sometimes been bitterly described as ‘ the death of the Great Pan’ ". He goes on to say :

For it is in this period of the collapse of the ancient world and birth of Christianity that a divorce takes place between man and the mysterious depths of natural life. The Great Pan, who had been revealed to the natural man of antiquity, was driven to take refuge in the

[1] *Meaning of History*, pp. 113–114.
[2] I Corinthians 10/19–20 ; 8/5 ; Dibelius, *op. cit.*, p. 77.

uttermost depths of nature. A gulf separated the natural man from the man who had entered upon the path of redemption. The effect of Christianity was to divorce man from the inner life of nature, which as a result, became deanimated.[1]

This is why we can no longer understand the demonic. But those same forces which were once described in terms of the demonic still exist, and their existence is still recognised in a secular way by the sciences. The inexorable fate which was once expressed in terms of the influence of the stars, conceived as personal or semi-personal beings, is now expressed in terms of psychological, economic and physical determinism. What was once stated in terms of angelology is now stated in terms of the psychology of the unconscious and such half-psychical, half-physical terms as " light-energy ", " *élan vitale* ", and so on.

In the light of this consideration, we are now in a better position to state the real religious meaning symbolised by the myth of the fallen angels and their demonic associates that hover in the air. They symbolise all the distortion in the structure of existence. They signified all that was chaotic, discordant and deadly as against that which maintained structural integrity, harmony and life. They signified all the irrational forces of nature, the blind determinism of her physical laws, her storms, her famines and droughts, diseases of the body and of the mind, the enmity between man and beast, tyranny, social distress—all those natural structures which form the basis of human anxiety. All these were understood in terms of the demonic, i.e. as a direct result of the Fall in heavenly places.

Therefore the real significance of the myth of the fallen angels was that it described the fallen nature of the whole cosmos.[2]

---

[1] *Meaning of History*, p. 115.
[2] This is as much as need be said regarding the significance of the fallen angels or demons for the time being. The subject will receive fuller treatment at a later stage. *Infra*, pp. 228 ff.

The Restoration of Paradise. Just as the fallen status of all existence was symbolised in this way, so its former unfallen status was symbolised in the myth of the paradise from which Adam was evicted as a result of disobedience. Therefore the symbol of the restoration of all things to their essential nature takes the form of the myth of the restoration of paradise.

Long before the great period of apocalyptic literature we find this cosmic, paradise symbolism in the prophets and the Psalms. It seems probable that some such myth was current at the level of folk-lore as an expression of simple longing before it was incorporated by the prophets into an eschatological setting.[1] The overcoming of the demonic in nature found expression in a number of symbols which came to be more or less standardised. There was the symbol of the great peace between the animals :

> The wolf also shall dwell with the lamb, and the leopard shall lie down with the kid ; and the calf and the young lion and the fatling together : and the lion shall eat straw like an ox,[2]

and between the animals and man :

> And the suckling child shall play on the hole of the asp, and the weaned child shall put his hand on the cockatrice' den,[3]

and all this because of the reconciliation of the whole creation to God :

> They shall not hurt nor destroy in all my holy mountain, for the earth shall be full of the knowledge of the Lord as the waters cover the sea.[4]

Coupled with this there is the parallel symbol of the restoration of plant life to paradisiac splendour. In

---

[1] Hugo Gressmann, *Der Messias*, pp. 152 and 283.
[2] Isaiah 11/6–7.   [3] Isaiah 11/8.   [4] Isaiah 11/9.

Ezekiel 34 we find the two ideas together, first the restoration of animal life :

> And I will make with them a covenant of peace, and will cause evil beasts to cease out of the land : and they shall dwell safely in the wilderness, and sleep in the woods,[1]

then the land and its fruits :

> And I will make them and the places around my hill a blessing ; and I will cause the shower to come down in his season ; there shall be showers of blessing.   And the tree of the field shall yield her fruit and the earth shall yield her increase and they shall be safe in their land,[2]

and again the whole passage shows the same pattern in that it culminates in the restoration of the " knowledge of the Lord " :

> and shall know that I am the Lord when I have broken the bands of their yoke, and delivered them out of the hand of those that served themselves of them.[3]

The thirty-fifth chapter of Isaiah expresses the same hope.

The symbol of the land of milk and honey is also used with the same eschatological associations (e.g. Joel 3 : 18). Or where the symbolism of the agricultural ideal has superseded that of the nomadic ideal, it becomes interchangeable with the symbols of oil and wine (2 Enoch 8 : 5).

Again, just as the establishment of a new relationship between man and God was always inaugurated by a new covenant and the end of each historic age,[4] so the final restoration of all creation is to be inaugurated by a new covenant between God and nature. In Hosea 2 : 18–23 the great reconciliation of the animals and the fruitfulness of the ground is based upon a new covenant between

---

[1] Ezekiel 34/25.
[3] Ezekiel 34/27b.
[2] Ezekiel 34/26–27a.
[4] Gressmann, *op. cit.*, p. 162.

Jahweh and all nature. Gressmann says in this connection :

Der Begriff des Bundes ist hier erweitert und vom Leben der Menschen übertragen auf das der Tiere und dann vom Mikrokosmos auf den Makrokosmos. Der Gedanke des abstracten Naturgesetzes ist noch nicht erreicht; die Frage, Wie kommt es, dass Menschen, Tiere, ja die ganze Natur von bestimmten Ordnungen beherrscht sind ? wird antwortet durch die Idee des Bundes.[1]

It is difficult for us to understand such a view of nature. H. Wheeler Robinson begins his treatment of *Inspiration and Revelation in the Old Testament* with the words :

The Hebrew vocabulary includes no word equivalent to the word " Nature ". This is not surprising if by " Nature " we mean " The creative and regulative physical power which is conceived of as operating in the physical world and as the immediate cause of all its phenomena". (Definition in the Shorter Oxford English Dictionary.) The only way to render this idea into Hebrew would be to say simply " God ". We would have to describe a particular physical activity through anthropomorphic phrases such as the " voice " of God, heard in the thunder ; the " hand " of God felt in the pestilence; the " breath " of God animating the body of man ; the " wisdom " of God ultimately conceived as his instrument in Creation.[2]

The atmosphere of this type of world-outlook can be best illustrated by a passage from one of Enoch's visionary journeys through the universe. In 1 Enoch, Chapter 18, we read :

I saw the treasury of all the winds : I saw how He had furnished them with the whole creation and the firm foundations of the earth. And I saw the corner-stone of

[1] *Ibid.*, p. 163.
[2] *Inspiration and Revelation in the Old Testament*, p. 1. The words within parentheses are mine.

the earth : I saw the four winds which bear the earth and the firmament of the heaven, and have their station between heaven and earth : (these are the pillars of heaven). I saw the winds of heaven which turn and bring the circumference of the sun and all the stars to their setting. I saw the winds on the earth carrying their clouds. I saw the paths of the angels. I saw the end of the earth and the firmament of the heaven above. I proceeded and saw a place which burns day and night, where there are seven mountains of magnificent stones, three towards the east and three towards the south. And as for those towards the east one was of coloured stone, one of pearl, and one of Jacinth, and those towards the south of red stone. But the middle one reached to heaven like the throne of God, of alabaster, and the summit of the throne was of sapphire. And I saw a flaming fire. And beyond these mountains is a region the end of the great earth : there the heavens were completed. . . . I saw the seven stars like burning mountains and to me, when I enquired regarding them, the angel said : This is the end of heaven and earth : this has become a prison for the stars and the host of heaven. And the stars which roll over the fire are they which have transgressed the commandment of the Lord in the beginning of their rising, because they did not come forth at their appointed times. And he was wroth with them and has bound them till the time when their guilt should be consummated (even for ten thousand years).[1]

I have given this lengthy quotation for two reasons. Firstly, in the section before the hiatus, its beautiful, fantastic imagery gives us an impression of this view of nature as something which is not merely nature in our modern sense of the word (i.e. something sharply contrasted with the Divine) but as being capable of bearing the whole glory of God. Secondly, in the section after the hiatus, we see the other side of this—namely, that because nature is capable of bearing the divine image, it is also capable of the demonic. This is represented in the disobedience and

[1] 1 Enoch 18/1–10 and 13–16.

punishment of the stars.[1]   It is only that which is capable
of bearing the divine image that is capable of demonic
distortion.

The whole passage reminds me very much of my childhood
days when I found it much easier to think of the thunder
which scared me as the anger of God than to listen to my
father's contention that " It is only electricity ".   What
does that " only " imply ?   It implies a whole background
of post-Cartesian philosophy which my good father had
never read, but which had dominated the whole atmosphere
of the culture in which he lived.   It implies that electricity,
as belonging to the natural order, is no more than a thing
to be manipulated by man.

If we can get behind all this, either by the memory of our
childhood experience, or by the sympathetic appreciation
of the Jewish apocalypses, or the earlier, prophetic descriptions of the eschatological destiny of the whole of creation,
then we begin to appreciate something of the religious
meaning of the promise :

And I will transform the heaven and make it an eternal
blessing and light.
And I will transform the earth and make it a blessing.[2]

All these varied symbols of cosmic eschatology became
centred on the leading idea of later Jewish eschatology—
the Holy City, the New Jerusalem.[3]   For instance in
Ezekiel 28/13–14, we find paradise and the Holy Mountain,
the site of the New Jerusalem, identified.   In this conception was summed up the view of nature as that which was
ultimately destined to give complete expression to the glory
of God.   The apocalypse of St. John, which belongs to this
tradition, seems to suggest that the whole distinction

---

[1] *Supra*, pp. 25 f.   [2] 1 Enoch 45/4b–5a.
[3] The New Jerusalem is more central than even the idea of the Messiah,
which is not at all prominent in much of the later apocalyptic writing.
Cf. R. H. Charles, *Religion Between the Old and New Testaments*, p. 75.

between God and nature is ultimately to be overcome. In describing the New Jerusalem, the author says :

> And I saw no temple therein ; for the Lord God Almighty and the Lamb are the temple of it. And the city had no need of any sun, neither of the moon to shine in it : for the glory of God did lighten it, and the Lamb is the light thereof.[1]

The removal of the temple seems to symbolise the removal of the distinction between holy and secular. There is no longer any need of sun or moon because the distinction between the natural light and the divine light of God's glory has been overcome.[2] This was the substance of the apocalyptic hope for nature. Whether conceived of as of temporary duration (as in 1 Enoch xci–civ, the Psalms of Solomon, the Book of Jubilees, the Assumption of Moses, 2 Enoch, 2 Baruch, 4 Ezra) or as eternal (as in 1 Enoch vi–xc), the essential meaning of the symbol of the New Jerusalem is the same. The destiny of creation was that it should return to the paradisiac state from which it had fallen, so that the distinction between the things of heaven and the things of earth would be overcome.

The Apocalyptic Background to the Synoptic Gospels. This was the tradition which lay behind the apocalyptic setting of the Synoptic Gospels, to which we have already referred, and in this sense we are justified in saying that the scope of the redemptive work of Christ is cosmic in their presentation of it. But this is only in an implicit sense. There is no evidence that any doctrine of cosmic redemption ever became explicit at a *conceptual* level of thought. It is still present only by symbolic implication.

But the Synoptic Gospels do not merely repeat the earlier Jewish insight. Apart from any other considera-

---

[1] Revelation of St. John, 21/22–23.

[2] In Oriental religion the sun was thought of as the head of the universe in much the same way as a king is head of a state. W. L. Knox, *St. Paul and the Church of the Gentiles*, p. 161.

tions, there is this great difference that for the New Testament writers the great redeeming event was no longer a distant future hope, but had already occurred. It had not come fully or finally, but only partially and ambiguously ; yet it had become sufficiently actual to transfer their eschatological hopes from the realm of dreaming fantasy to that of present reality. The Messiah had come and already the eyes of the blind were opened and the ears of the deaf unstopped. The lame man leaped as an hart and the dumb sang, and the multitudes were fed on miraculous bread. Whatever the events which lay behind these stories in the early tradition of the church[1] they were sufficiently powerful in their significance to convince the first Christians that the new age had actually come, and only its final fulfilment was still lacking. Already in the Anointed One the things of heaven and the things of earth were joined together.

Something physical, as well as spiritual, had happened in the work of Christ. Indeed these two concepts are not held in the same kind of contrast as they would be now in the twentieth century. Our Lord made a sharp distinction between outward forms and personal faith ; but this is a different thing from the contrast between spirit and matter.[2]

The suggestion of the Gnostic Valentinus, that the miracles of Our Lord could be interpreted as the type of our salvation is in a sense quite correct, though Irenaeus was right in condemning the particular symbolic interpretation which Valentinus gives to the story of the woman healed of the issue of blood.[3]

In Mark 2 Our Lord acknowledges the connection be-

---

[1] I make the statement in this form simply to avoid raising questions of Biblical criticism which would be irrelevant here. I do not mean to imply any unduly radical position.

[2] The modern tendency to set " physical " and " spiritual " in metaphysical opposition to one another tends to misrepresent their meaning in the thought of the New Testament. Berdyaev, *Freedom and the Spirit*, p. 6 ff.

[3] Irenaeus, *Adversus Haereses*, Book I, Chapter 3.

D

tween His inward work of salvation and His physical work
of healing in the words :

> Whether is it easier to say to the sick of the palsy, Thy
> sins be forgiven thee ; or to say, Arise, and take up thy
> bed, and walk ?[1]

Again, when John the Baptist asks for an assurance of the
messianic vocation of Jesus, Our Lord points to His works
of healing as a sign that the new age has come.

The word σώζω as used in the New Testament does not
refer usually to a merely inward religious experience, as
modern Protestantism tends to believe.   It is used, in the
majority of cases, to signify the translation of some person
from a state of sickness to a state of health, or from a state
of physical danger to a state of safety.[2]   This is in line with
the characterisation of the new age in The Apocalypse of
Baruch, which says : " Health shall descend and sickness
shall be removed."[3]

Yet, in all this, Jesus is not a mere medical practitioner.
This is to be said not merely because He performed His
healing work by miraculous means, instead of using what
we today call scientific medicine.   The method of healing
by the casting out of demons and the invocation of divine
healing powers was quite the normal medical practice of
His day.   But it was as eschatological healing that these
acts were performed.   That is to say, they were performed
by One who claimed not merely to have some measure of
control over the demons, but who claimed *absolute* power
over them.   As W. Wagner has stated it, in his article
referred to above, on the meaning of σώζω in the New
Testament, Jesus is not merely a healer, but He has the
power of life and death itself.

---

[1] Mark 2/9.
[2] W. Wagner, *Über σώζω und seine Derivata im Neuen Testament*, Zeitschrift für die Neutestamentliche Wissenschaft, 1905, p. 211. *Cf.* H.
Wheeler Robinson, *Redemption and Revelation*, p. 232 f.
[3] *The Apocalypse of Baruch*, 73/2.

The ministry of Jesus begins, in all three of the Synoptic Gospels, with His complete victory over Satan, the leader of the demonic forces, in the temptation in the wilderness. From then on begins His ministry of thwarting and defeating these forces. Reading the Gospels as we do—and as we must do—in the light of our own religious experience, we tend, in accordance with the spirit of modern Protestantism, to see the temptation of Jesus simply as a testing of the moral and religious integrity of the Chosen One. But Branscomb, in his Moffat commentary on Mark says :

> A second thought is expressed in the story. Jesus had been designated as the divine agent for the overthrow of Satan and all his powers. The Prince of Evil immediately endeavours to conquer and destroy Him. Jesus does not yield. He faces the devil and defeats him. The victory is the prelude to the power which Jesus was to show over all spirits and demons.[1]

But I think the case can be stated much more strongly than this, so as to make this not a secondary meaning, but primary.

The sequence of ideas in the first chapter of Mark, the foundation Gospel, points very strongly to this view of the ministry of Jesus. The structure of the passage is as follows :

(1) Jesus is heralded as the Messiah by John the Baptist, in accordance with the tradition of Old Testament prophecy (vv. 1–8).
(2) The Messiahship of Jesus is acknowledged in a sign from God (vv. 8–11).
(3) He immediately joins battle with the demonic forces and overcomes Satan in the wilderness (vv. 12–13).
(4) The next step is to proclaim the meaning of the victory : " The time is fulfilled and the Kingdom of God is at hand." (vv. 14–15).

[1] *The Gospel of Mark*, p. 21.

(5) Then we encounter the practical conclusion to which
    all this leads. He returns to Capernaum (having
    called four disciples on the way—vv. 16–20) and
    there in the temple encounters a man with an
    unclean spirit (vv. 21–22). What follows is in
    three stages :

    (*a*) The unclean spirit recognises Jesus as the
    " Holy One of God " and therefore as his
    master, and as one who threatens his very
    existence (vv. 23–24).

    (*b*) Jesus, by His word of command drives the
    spirit out of him (vv. 24–26).

    (*c*) The whole incident culminates in the remark
    of the bystanders, who are represented as
    saying : " What is this ?—A new teaching !
    With authority he commandeth even un-
    clean spirits and they obey him " (v. 27).

How far this arrangement of the material by Mark was
deliberate, one cannot tell ; but I find it convincing
evidence that Mark saw the overcoming of the demonic
forces as the central activity of the ministry of Jesus.[1]
This impression is confirmed by the fact that from a merely
quantitative point of view, the main bulk of the Gospel of
Mark is devoted to accounts of healing of the sick and the
casting out of demons. And again, when the commission
is given to the twelve, the same view of the work of Christ
is shown. " He began to send them forth by two and two,
and he gave them authority over unclean spirits."[2] The
authority over the spirits is the first thought associated
with their mission and is its essential basis.[3] Burkitt seems
to confirm my view when he says :

It is when you study Matthew, Mark and Luke against
the background of the Books of Enoch that you see them
in their true perspective.[4]

[1] Foakes-Jackson and Lake, *The Beginnings of Christianity*, Vol. IV, p.
121.
[2] Mark 6/7.
[3] For the development of this view of the work of Christ in the Church
Fathers, see Gustav Aulen's *Christus Victor*.
[4] *Jewish and Christian Apocalypses*, p. 21.

He illustrates what he means by a reference to Matthew 12/43–45 (*cf.* Luke 11/24–26). Jesus says that an unclean spirit, when it has gone out of a man, passes through waterless places, seeking rest and finding none ; then it says, " To my house will I return from whence I came forth", and on coming finds it swept and garnished. Then it goes and takes seven others worse than itself and they enter and dwell there—and the last state of the man is worse than the first.

This illustrates the popular belief in demons—aerial beings that are the offspring of the fallen angels as set forth in 1 Enoch 15.[1] The whole passage, Matthew 12/22–45 (*cf.* Luke 11/14–36), is interpreted by him as the assertion by Jesus that

It is by no pact with the powers of evil that I exorcise unclean spirits from those you bring to me ; I am neither setting forth a new doctrine nor practising new and unlawful methods. If I can do good to men because the spirit that is in me is the spirit of God, it shows you the Kingdom of God at your doors before you were aware of it. ($\check{\epsilon}\phi\theta\alpha\sigma\epsilon\nu\ \dot{\epsilon}\phi\ \dot{\nu}\mu\hat{\alpha}\varsigma$).[2]

The signs of the immanence of this Kingdom were before the eyes of the followers of Jesus. He commanded the demons with authority and they appeared to obey Him. When seen against the background of apocalyptic teaching these isolated events took on a universal significance. It implied that the power with which the demons held the whole of nature enthralled had been broken.

[1] *Supra*, pp. 25 ff.
[2] Burkitt, *op. cit.*, p. 22. (For fuller exposition of this argument see also pp. 21–25.)

CHAPTER IV

THE DEVELOPMENT TOWARDS A CONCEPTUAL FORMULATION IN PAUL AND JOHN

A S St. Paul spread the gospel into a wider field, he found it necessary to translate the imagery of apocalyptic into more conceptual terms, partly in order to serve a homiletic need, and partly to preserve the faith from heretical distortion.

Basically his eschatology is the same as that of the synoptics, in that it rests in the same apocalyptic foundation. Schweitzer is correct in his assertion that the Epistles of St. Paul are dominated from first to last by the apocalyptic idea.[1] But while Schweitzer recognises the dual significance of apocalyptic as referring both to the present life and to the future life only in St. Paul, I have maintained that this double reference belongs to the meaning of the apocalyptic symbol as such. Therefore I am in a position to assert the unity of Synoptic and Pauline eschatology, while Schweitzer is not.

St. Paul's Attitude to the World. We found that the apocalyptic attitude to the world is one of despair that is continually being overcome by hope, in that it despairs of every element within history, yet its hope for history as a whole is absolute and unqualified. So in St. Paul we find the same ambiguous attitude to the world.

On the one hand, we find that the world, in terms of its existential distortion, is set in antithesis to the divine life (1 Corinthians 1/12) and ὁ κόσμος οὗτος is used synony-

---

[1] *The Mysticism of the Apostle Paul*, pp. 52 ff.

mously with ὁ αἰὼν οὗτος. In 1 Corinthians 3/18–19 the
two phrases are interchangeable (cf. 1 Corinthians 5/10 ;
7/31). That is to say, the idea of the created world becomes
so closely associated with the idea of its demonic distortion
that the two terms come to mean the same thing. The
frequency of such a usage in Paul is liable to give the
impression that he is indulging in a dualistic despair of the
world and retiring into a purely inward mysticism (cf. 1
Corinthians 1/26 ; 5/5 ; 2 Corinthians 5/16 ; 7/1 ; 11/18 ;
Philippians 3/3 ; Galatians 5/19 ; 6/8).

But on the other hand, the world, in terms of its essential
goodness reflects the image of God. " The invisible things
of him from the creation of the world are clearly seen, being
understood by the things that are made, even his eternal
power and Godhead."[1] The whole life of creation is an
expression of the eternal God-manhood of Christ.

> For by him all things were created, that are in heaven,
> and that are in earth, visible and invisible, whether they
> be thrones or dominions or principalities or powers : all
> things were created by him and for him. And he is
> before all things, and by him all things consist.[2]

Thus there is no fundamental dualism in Paul, though
J. Weiss thinks that there is, on the grounds of the pessimism about the world and the flesh to which we have
already referred.[3] But while to say that the world and the
flesh as such are evil is dualistic, to assert the existential
corruption of an essentially good creation is not dualistic—
though it does recognise the reality of evil, as any serious
theology must. If we make allowance for Paul's identification of the word κόσμος with the powers and forces which
distort the life of the natural order, then it is clear that he

[1] Romans 1/20.
[2] Colossians 1/16. It has been questioned whether this is really Paul's
own view, e.g. V. Porte, *The Mind of Christ in Paul*, pp. 179 ff. But I
have the support of the majority of scholars in attributing the view to
Paul himself.
[3] *History of Primitive Christianity*, p. 597.

is not making a dualistic assertion. In Ephesians 2/2 he says :

> ἐν αἷς ποτὲ περιεπατήσατε κατὰ τὸν αἰῶνα
> τοῦ κόσμου τούτου, κατὰ τὸν ἄρχοντα τῆς
> ἐξουσίας τοῦ ἀέρος.

Here κόσμος is equivalent to the whole army of demonic forces in the stars and in the lower air, which distort the goodness of creation, just as we encountered them in 1 Enoch, in Matthew 12/43 and elsewhere.[1] It is to be remembered, too, that this world-view is correlative with the paradise myth, and cannot be rightly interpreted apart from it.

Paul's View of the Demons. There is a much fuller exposition of this demonic distortion in Paul than in the Synoptic Gospels, though it remains largely unsystematic. Any attempt to force it into a system would be a misrepresentation. However, Paul does seem to be aware of the more systematic division of angels and spiritual powers into classes in late Judaism.[2] He seems to have recognised some kind of hierarchy of demonic forces, though we cannot say exactly what this hierarchy was.

Under a leadership, variously described as Sin, Death, Beliar, the Tempter or Satan, these angelic powers are in control of " this age ". They remain within the sovereignty of God in that they execute His judgment on the world ; yet they do this in a negative way as the destroyers of life and the body (1 Corinthians 5/5). They are the cause of evil in the world—both moral and physical. They bring temptation still (1 Corinthians 7/5) just as in the form of a serpent these powers first brought temptation to Eve (2 Corinthians 11/13). They obstruct good works (1 Thessalonians 2/16) and blind men to the way of their salvation (2 Corinthians 4/4). They are responsible for physical

---

[1] *Supra*, p. 25 f. and 39.
[2] Dibelius, *Die Geisterwelt im Glauben des Paulus*, pp. 181 ff.

suffering and disease (2 Corinthians 12/7). Their operations are essentially destructive (1 Corinthians 10/10). Through them not only sin, but death also entered the world (Romans 5/12) so that man became " corruptible " (*cf.* 1 Corinthians 15/51 ff.). Sin is represented as a personal or semi-personal demon which enters a man's body and expresses itself in the form of chaotic, uncontrolled vitality which disintegrates into death.

As the rulers of " this age ", these powers are identified with the half-divine, half-demonic gods of paganism (1 Corinthians 10/19 ff.).[1] They are identified with the powers of the stars (Romans 8/38)[2] or, indeed, with any of traditional symbols in which the demonic distortion of the world was recognised.

The World-Age. Paul himself was perfectly at home with strictly Jewish apocalyptic symbolism. But as a missionary teacher he had to interpret the idea of the kingdom of God to the Gentile world. The natural equivalent of this term, familiar both to Jew and Gentile[3] was that of the new " world-age ". This conception is one which we are only now beginning to understand, as a result of fairly recent historical research. It was widespread throughout the whole of Mediterranean culture at the time of St. Paul.[4] The Greeks, with their cyclical view of history were at home with it, and it became a highly developed system under the Stoics, being assimilated to the astronomical conception of the " Great Year " when all the stars would return to their original positions and there would be a new beginning to world history.

Many of these ideas had already been assimilated, in one form or another to syncretistic Judaism, so already there were bridges between the cosmic symbolism of the Hebrew and the Gentile world.[5] Burkitt has pointed out the close

---

[1] *Supra*, pp. 25 f.
[2] *Cf.* W. L. Knox, *St. Paul and the Church of the Gentiles*, pp. 100 ff.
[3] *Ibid.*, p. 92.
[4] *Ibid.*, Chapter I and *passim*.   [5] *Ibid.*, pp. 2 ff.

relationship between Posidonius and 1 Enoch.[1] Now
Posidonius, who lived in the second half of the second
century B.C.—a date contemporary with most sections of
1 Enoch—was the leading religious thinker of the pagan
world of his day, not so much as having a distinctive
philosophy of his own, but as " one who gathered up the
mass of beliefs which held the minds of men ".[2] Therefore
he may be taken as a typical representative of the type of
cosmic speculation current in pagan circles at that time.[3]

In this type of religious philosophy, represented by
Posidonius, each world age was taken to be under the
domination of the planets. They, conceived as semi-
personal powers, ruled the destinies of cosmic, social and
even personal history.[4] Associated with these κοσμοκράτορες,
as they were sometimes called,[5] and in some sense under
their direction, were the elements, στοιχεῖα, of the world.

It is difficult for us to represent, or even imagine what
these στοιχεῖα τοῦ κόσμου were. I think the religious
significance of the idea can best be understood in terms of
two statements. On the one hand, they tended to " make
men at home in the universe by personalising and spiritua-
lising all things ".[6] On the other hand, since those natural
forces could not become completely personal, they tend to
be in part sub-human, and in part super-human, thereby
assuming a demonic aspect similar to that represented by
the archaic Greek or Egyptian gods. They could therefore
represent either the divine glory or the demonic distortion
of the world. That is to say, these ideas fulfilled the same
function in typical pagan thought as the ideas of holy and
fallen angels represented in Judaism.

In syncretistic Judaism these ideas were assimilated to

[1] *Jewish and Christian Apocalypses*, pp. 30–31.
[2] E. Bevan, *Stoics and Sceptics*, p. 94.
[3] E. Bevan, *op. cit.*, gives an excellent account of the views of Posidonius
in Chapter III.
[4] J. Weiss, *op. cit.*, p. 600.
[5] For the use of this word, see Kittel's *Theologisches Worterbuch zum
Neuen Testament*.   [6] E. Bevan, *op. cit.*, p. 98.

the elaborate systems of angelology derived from Persian and Babylonian sources.   Dibelius says :

> Babylonische, persische, griechische Gedanken mögen sich hier getroffen haben, Rudimente längst überwunden Heidentums wiederaufgelebt sein—alles vereinte sich zu der Vorstellung, dass nichts in der Welt, anfangen vom Himmel, wo die Spekulation über den göttlichen Thronwagen diesen Ideen offenbar besonders Nahrung bot, bis herab zum Kraut auf der Wiese, ohne seinen Engel sei.[1]

Jubilees 2/2 refers to angels of fire, of the winds, of the clouds, of darkness, of the snow, of hail, of frost, of thunder and lightning, of cold and heat, of the four seasons, in fact " of all the spirits of his creatures which are in the heavens and on earth".[2]

These might be holy or fallen angels, but by the time of Paul the word " angel " had come to suffer a fate similar to that of the word κόσμος, which we have already noted ; i.e. it came to have a pejorative association, and to represent the fallen, demonic angel rather than the divine (*cf.* Romans 8/38).

These were the powers of this world-age which held the world and men in bondage to corruption in all senses of the word.

The Pagan Expectation of a New World-Age. This conception of our bondage to the elements of this world may be taken as the pagan counterpart to the Jewish myth of the Fall.   Corresponding to this " Fall " symbol, there was a widespread dream of a new age.

Vergil's Fourth Eclogue (40 B.C.) is in some ways the most striking instance of this.   It witnesses to a Roman tradition which is surprising in its similarity to the messianic hopes of Judaism (though there is no reason to believe that there is any direct connection).

---

[1] *Op. cit.*, p. 98.
[2] *Cf.* 1 Enoch 18/13–16 ; 43/1–3.

> The last age told by Cumae's seer is come,
> A mighty roll of generations new
> Is rising now.   Justice now returns
> And Saturn's realm, and from high heaven descends
> A worthier race of men.   Only do thou
> Smile, chaste Lucina, on the infant boy
> With whom the iron age will pass away,
> The golden age on all the earth be born.[1]

The similarity to the Hebrew symbols of the land flowing
with milk and honey, the peace with the animals, and the
restoration of paradise is clear in the following lines :

> Then earth shall haste to bring thee birthday gifts,
> Uncultured earth : the ivy's gadding curls
> The fox-glove and the water-lily twined
> With laughing bear's-breech.   Uncompelled thy goats
> Shall bring their udders heavy-laden home,
> And monstrous lions scare thy herds no more,
> Serpents shall cease, the treacherous poison-plant
> Shall fail, Assyrian balm shall fill the land.[2]

Again, the myth of the primordial paradise appears in
Georgics, Book I, 11.151 ff. (cf. Ovid, Metamorphoses 1.89
ff.; Horace, Epode 16).

In Persian religion there was the hope that Zoroaster
would come again as a heavenly saviour and establish
paradise on earth.   If there is any common source for the
tradition of the new age, other than a certain basic similarity
in the religious experience of mankind, it probably comes
from this Persian tradition.[3]   There are traces, too, of a
lively apocalyptic hope of a similar kind in Egypt.[4]   And
in Greece, nearly a century before Paul, apocalyptic hopes
had been entertained, though they came to be superseded
by the cyclical views of Stoicism.[5]

---

[1] Vergil, Eclogue iv, 11/4–11 (tr. T. F. Boyds).
[2] Ibid., 11/21–29.
[3] W. L. Knox, op. cit., pp. 8 f.
[4] Lietzmann, Der Weltheiland, pp. 20–25.
[5] W. L. Knox, op. cit., pp. 3 f.

Christ as the Bringer of the New World-Age in Paul. St. Paul was perfectly prepared, for homiletical purposes, to use any of these pagan ideas. He refers to man's unredeemed state in terms of bondage to the elements (Galatians 4/3, 9 ; Colossians 2/8). Our redemption from sin and death is redemption from the power of the forces indwelling in the physical universe. J. Weiss says :

> When Christ died upon the cross, not only did his body die, but in and with his flesh, " flesh " in particular was put to death, and with the flesh the indwelling sin (Romans 8/3). This is naturally only thinkable if flesh and sin are not merely abstract concepts, but realities, and so, for Paul, the flesh of humanity is a living organism into which Christ, by his becoming man, has entered and which in his crucifixion receives the destroying death-blow.[1]

I need hardly say, of course, that the " flesh " which is rejected and destroyed here, is not the body as such. Like the word κόσμος, σάρξ is used to refer to the demonic distortion of the material body.

The idea of resurrection for Paul is completely inseparable from that of the quickening of our mortal bodies by the life-giving spirit. This is something which occurs not merely after we are biologically dead, but actually delivers us from " the body of this death "—the living death of bondage to the elements of a universe into which sin and death have entered. The " glory which shall be revealed in us " is even here and now operative in our mortal bodies.

Now a man's body is his bond with the natural universe, and it cannot be restored without the restoration of the whole natural order. Therefore our redemption is immediately associated with the redemption, or restoration of the whole universe, i.e. the power of the elements is overcome. The spiritual powers of even the distant stars are brought within the orbit of the redeeming work of

[1] *Op. cit.*, p. 434,

Christ. In Romans 8/38 the words ἐνεστῶτα, μέλλοντα, ὕψωμα, βάθος are all technical astrological terms.[1] No part of the universe is left unaffected by what Christ has done.

Paul, however, was not interested in these ideas in any other than a homiletical way. He made no effort to formulate them into a systematic doctrine of cosmic redemption. However, as has so often happened in the history of the church, when his hand was forced by the growth of heretical systems, he formulated a more systematic presentation.

In his letter to the Colossians, Paul is combating a new teaching which had arisen (Colossians 2/8). It would be rash to describe this teaching in terms of later, more developed Gnostic systems of which we know much more. But it clearly has certain basic characteristics in common with later Gnostic developments.[2] This is particularly true in that it tends to " interpose certain spiritual agencies, intermediate beings, between God and man, as the instruments of communication and the objects of worship ".[3] The implication of this teaching places a limit on the work of Christ. It says in effect : Christ has redeemed us from Satan and the spirits of the lower air.[4] But we are still subject to the elemental powers beyond that. In other words, some doubt had arisen whether Christ's work really was cosmic in its scope. (Note the implication of this heresy : That if it was thus limited, then something further was required for our complete redemption.)

It is interesting to note, too, how the principle of eschatological development which we have already illustrated again comes into operation here. This principle was that when a faith is redemptive, it is forced by the

---

[1] W. L. Knox, op. cit., p. 106.

[2] Vid. J. B. Lightfoot, St. Paul's Epistles to the Colossians and Philemon, pp. 71–111.

[3] Ibid., p. 71.

[4] W. L. Knox, op. cit., p. 151, suggests it would be natural for this theory to limit the power of Christ to the sphere of the moon, where eternity begins.

problem of evil, either to extend the reference of redemption to the whole of environment, or else to become other-worldly and think of redemption as escape from environment. In the case of the Colossian heresy and the later Gnostic systems, we see it operating the other way. They circumscribed the area of the efficacy of the work of Christ and immediately were forced to reverse the Hebrew judgment about the world and to adopt dualistic presuppositions (Colossians 2/16–17) and an other-worldly interpretation of the idea of redemption. The whole aim of redemption in the Gnostics is to enable a man to escape from the world to beyond the powers of the seven spheres. The abstinences, observances, and self-abasement before angels, referred to in Colossians 2/18 constitute the preparation for such an escape.

This heresy at least did the service of raising the whole issue quite clearly, and some kind of systematic answer was demanded of Paul. The essence of Paul's answer is the assertion that the work of Christ is universally effective for all creation. The demonic powers in all parts of the universe have been " disarmed " by Him (Colossians 2/15).

The argument runs as follows : Christ is eternally pre-existent (Colossians 1/17), therefore He has power over the eternal spheres. He is the image of the Father (Colossians 1/15) and this ensures His supremacy over all angels and powers. He was actually the divine agent in the creation of all these things (Colossians 1/15–16). Therefore, His redeeming work which has been declared ἐν πάσῃ κτίσει τῇ ὑπὸ τὸν οὐρανόν is unlimited in its efficacy. In Him God " reconciles all things to himself, whether on earth or in heaven " (Colossians 1/20).

It was perfectly in accordance with the prevailing Stoic philosophy—aspects of which were in all probability incorporated in the heresy he was combating—for Paul to argue that since all things began in Christ (Colossians 1/16) and were sustained by Him (Colossians 1/17), it was also the ultimate destiny of all things to return to Him (Colossians 1/15–20)

> In current Stoic speculation, Zeus, as the one divine power manifested in the cosmos, was the beginning and the sustaining force and the end of the recurring world-ages, which made up the eternal circle of revolving time ; Jesus as the Messiah was not the end of one such system, but the end of the present age, in the sense of the close of history, and therefore the object which all creation had in view.[1]

This return of all things to Christ takes place in and through the Church, conceived as His body—a body of which He is the head (Colossians 2/19). This view of the church as a body of cosmic magnitude enabled Paul to relate the " powers " of the universe to Christ in the same way as human beings. Yet mankind still maintains its special status within the redemptive scheme. Paul's view of the special destiny of man within the work of cosmic redemption is shown, for example in 1 Corinthians 6/2–3, where he asserts that the saints shall judge not only the world, but even the angels. Again, in that very beautiful passage in which St. Paul transcends both Jewish and pagan symbols for the restoration of all things—Romans 8/19–24—it is as " waiting with eager longing for the revealing of the sons of God "[2] that the creation, which has been " subjected to futility "[3] has been " groaning in travail together until now ".[4] That is to say, the redemption of nature is conditional upon the redemption of man just as much as the redemption of man is conditional upon the redemption of nature.

Yet all this is not a matter of simple evolution towards the final perfection of the universe. It rests on the same

---

[1] W. L. Knox, *op. cit.*, p. 160.
[2] V. 19 (Revised Standard Version).
[3] V. 20 (Revised Standard Version).
[4] V. 22 (Revised Standard Version).

dialectical basis as we found in apocalyptic. Though it is a hope essential to the structure of the faith it can never be a matter of objective knowledge. "For we are saved by hope. Now hope that is seen is not hope. For who hopes for what he sees ? But if we hope for what we do not see, we wait for it with patience."[1]

Wisdom and Logos. When St. Paul argued in the Epistle to the Colossians that all creation was maintained by and subject to Jesus as the Christ, because "in him dwelt all the fulness of the Godhead bodily", he was simply identifying Jesus with the Divine Wisdom.[2]

The idea of the Word of God as an almost personal agent in creating and sustaining the world was of long standing in Judaism.[3] In the Old Testament, the Word means primarily a spoken word of God to the patriarch or the prophets. But it is used also in the sense of the Creator Word (e.g. Psalm 33/6, 9 ; 147/18 ; 148/8 ; 119/89) and also as the Word which executes judgment as a personal messenger and heals the world. (Isaiah 55/10 f.; *cf.* Wisdom 16/12 ; 18/14 ff.). In the Targums, the Word of God came to be that through which God has dealings with the world.[4]

In post-exilic Judaism, the personified figure of Wisdom came to be identified with the Word of God in this sense, partly under the influence of Gentile religions, and partly as a defensive measure against them.[5] In the syncretistic Judaism of the Diaspora, this figure of Wisdom was assimilated to the Stoic conception of Divine Reason. According to the Stoic conception, this Divine Reason was

---

[1] Romans 8/24–25. (Revised Standard Version).
[2] W. L. Knox, *op. cit.*, p. 159.
[3] E. Krebs, "Der Logos als Heiland im Ersten Jahrhundert," *Freiburg Theologische Studien*, 1910, pp. 57 ff.
[4] *Targum Genesis* 3/8 reads : "They heard the voice of the *memra* of the Lord walking in the Garden." (*Cf.* G. H. C. MacGregor, *St. John's Gospel*, p. xxxv). However, it must be recognised that no less an authority than G. F. Moore disputes this interpretation of the use of *memra* in the Targums. *Judaism*, p. 419.
[5] W. L. Knox, *op. cit.*, pp. 55 ff.

E

the pure fiery principle from which all things came and to which all things would return, and which, in the meantime, ordered all things in the world.[1] In Wisdom, Chapters 6–11, this union of Stoic and Jewish ideas is strongly in evidence. It is probable, too, that other aspects of the cosmic speculations of the pagan world were assimilated to this core of Jewish theology. W. L. Knox, for instance, suggests that the cult of the Egyptian god Isis influenced the syncretistic Judaism of Alexandria.[2] The god Isis represented the divine element in the cosmos which is always seeking to return to divinity.[3]

The evidence of this period is so confused that it is difficult for us to be certain just what was borrowed from whom and by whom in the course of the fashion of syncretism which was current throughout the whole Mediterranean basin during the first century. But it is sufficient for us to know that there was such coming and going between the theology of Judaism and the cosmic speculations of the pagan world. It was this syncretism which provided the ideological bridge that Paul required in order to translate the Jewish statement of the cosmic significance of the Messiah into terms which would be significant for the pagan world. This was what provided the basis for the first conceptual formulation of the cosmic significance of the work of Christ.

If we compare the following passage from the book of the Wisdom of Solomon with Colossians 1/15–27, we can see the force of W. L. Knox's assertion that Paul, in Colossians, is simply saying that Christ is nothing less than the Divine Wisdom of God immanent in the cosmos :

> For she is a breath of the power of God,   *Cf.* Col.
> And a clear effluence of the glory of the Almighty. 1/15, 19
> Therefore nothing defiled can enter into her.
> She is an effluence from everlasting light,

---

[1] E. Bevan, *op. cit.*, pp. 40 ff.
[2] W. L. Knox, *loc. cit.*   [3] *Cf.* Plutarch, *De Iside et Osiride*, 78, 383a.

An unspotted image of his goodness,
And she, though but one, hath power to do all things   *Cf.* Col. 1/16–17
And remaining in herself reneweth all things
And from generation to generation passing into holy souls   *Cf.* Col 1/9–14
She maketh them friends of God and prophets.
For nothing doth God love save him that dwelleth in Wisdom
For she is fairer than the sun,   *Cf.* Col. 1/17–18
And above all the constellations of the stars.
Being compared with the light she is found to be before it.   *Cf.* Col. 1/15
For the light of day succeedeth night,   *Cf.* Col. 1/13
But against Wisdom evil doth not prevail.[1]

Whether Paul was deliberately drawing on the Wisdom literature as a source or not, he must have known that his letter to the Colossians would be interpreted in the light of these speculations. Therefore in this sense he was deliberately using these concepts in which to express the cosmic significance of Christ. It is not elaborated into a precise system. But there can be no doubt of Paul's general intention, which was to assert that the work of Christ was of universal or cosmic significance.

When John introduced the Logos conception, the arrival on the field of a completely new word did not necessarily indicate the introduction of a startlingly new idea. Most of what is contained in the Logos conception is already implied in the Wisdom conception which lay in the background to Paul's thought. John makes it more explicit, only instead of using the more Hebrew term " Wisdom ", he uses the Greek term " Logos ". But against the background of the syncretism to which we have referred, this may well be regarded as a change in language rather than a fundamental alteration in material content. In Philo, for instance, Wisdom has no significant place. But in him

[1] The Wisdom of Solomon 7/25–30.

the term " Logos " is not so much a rival conception as one that fulfils the function of the Wisdom conception. John uses the term " Logos " in his prologue without definition or explanation.   But we may reasonably take it that he is not inaugurating a new and different line of thought from that which we find in Paul, but simply making more explicit what was implied in Paul.

It is unfortunate that modern theology has always regarded the Logos doctrine primarily as a doctrine of the person of Christ rather than as part of the doctrine of the work of Christ.   The two can never be completely separated, of course.   And the Logos doctrine is manifestly a doctrine of the person of Christ.   But if we interpret it against its background in Paul, we shall see that it is a doctrine of the person of Christ which arose in answer to the problems of interpreting the *work* of Christ to the Gentile world.   Therefore, in the long run, it is primarily as an assertion of the cosmic significance of the *work* of Christ that we should see it.

There is a great contrast between the philosophic opening of the Fourth Gospel and the naïve opening of Mark *in medias res*.   Yet if I have been correct in interpreting the first chapter of Mark as I have done,[1] then the similarity in their meaning is even more striking than the difference in the language and symbols which they employ.   The first chapter of Mark, the foundation Gospel of the Synoptics, describes the victory of Jesus over Satan in the wilderness and His resultant power and authority over the demons that infested the world.   When seen against its apocalyptic background this implied the beginning of a complete renewal of the fallen world.   John's Gospel begins with an assertion of the Logos doctrine.   When seen against its own syncretistic background this is tantamount to the assertion that in and through Christ the whole universe is reaching its maturity and returning to its perfection.   Both

[1] *Supra*, pp. 37 ff.

Mark and John, while using very different language and symbolism imply the same claim for the universal significance of the redeeming work of the Christ.

Conclusion.   This thought of the cosmic work of Christ, in one form or another, pervades the New Testament.   As is the case with the New Testament treatment of all aspects of the work of Christ, the variety of symbols employed precludes us from reducing it to a single, precise and systematic doctrine.   But there can be no doubt of the general currency of the notion that the Christ came not only to individuals, but to the whole universe, and that His work is significant for the whole of creation.   To try to describe it more exactly than we have done would be, I feel, to falsify the evidence of the New Testament.

That such ideas exist in the New Testament has been well known for some time.   I am saying nothing new in drawing attention to them.   I have unearthed no new historical facts.   What I have tried to show, however, is that these ideas are not peripheral and otiose speculations which surround the central doctrine of the redeeming work of Christ, but that they arose as a necessary implication of the fundamental insights of Jewish and Christian theology. The Jewish people were forced, by the impact of a harsh environment upon their lives, to choose between building their faith upon the firm despair of an other-worldly dualism or else on the hope of a redemption which would bring the whole of their environment within its scope. They chose the latter way, and herein lay the roots of the Christian doctrine of cosmic redemption.   Expanding horizons made it necessary to expand the scope of the hoped-for redeeming act of God.   When once this process had started there was no logical stopping place until the farthest parts of the universe were related in some positive way to the Redeeming Act.   Thus we find the idea pervasive in the New Testament that if Jesus is indeed the Christ, then He is a figure of cosmic significance.

No part of the doctrine of the work of Christ was precisely and systematically worked out in the New Testament. It was not until the great period of Patristic literature that it began to receive really systematic treatment. It is to that period that we must now turn to see how the church tried, and in the main failed, to interpret the doctrine of cosmic redemption implied in the New Testament.

PART II

THE PATRISTIC PERIOD

CHAPTER V

THE " CLASSICAL " VIEW OF THE ATONEMENT

THE manner in which the wider, cosmic background continued to be recognised as the setting of the drama of salvation in the centuries immediately after the writing of the New Testament has been recently emphasised by Gustav Aulen in his well-known book, *Christus Victor*. This conception of the work of Christ he calls the " Classic Idea of the Atonement ". He argues that it is to be distinguished from later views of the Atonement, firstly in that the redeeming event is conceived in dramatic rather than either forensic or exemplary terms. It is a story of divine conflict and victory. Secondly it is a cosmic victory. Christ—*Christus Victor*—fights against and triumphs over the evil powers of the world :

> The drama is a cosmic drama, and the victory over the hostile powers brings to pass a new relation, a relation of reconciliation between God and the world.[1]

Aulen is certainly right in condemning the tendency in modern theology to look at this so-called " classic " type of atonement theory, which was so widespread in the early centuries of Christendom, through the eyes of modern theological controversy instead of assessing it independently and interpreting it in its own light.[2] The tendency has been to regard it merely as the primitive beginnings of that objective type of view of the Atonement which found its

[1] P. 21.　　　　[2] Pp. 23 ff.

fuller and more mature expression in the writings of St.
Anselm.   But if we put the modern controversy between
the schools of the " orthodox " and the " liberal " views
of the Atonement out of our minds for the time being, then
the classic view appears as a third and quite independent
type of theory.

So far Aulen is correct.   But he is in some measure open
to the criticism that in his anxiety to assert the independence of the classic view, he is inclined to over-state his
case and to ignore the extent to which the Anselmic and
other later theories of the Atonement are in fact anticipated
in the New Testament and Patristic periods.   He chooses
Irenaeus as his main example, and I think successfully
establishes that Irenaeus does hold this " classical " view
of the Atonement.   But it is also possible to find in
Irenaeus a great many symbols which anticipate more
modern theories of the Atonement—theories which are
much less obviously cosmic in their reference and background.   The complex intertwining of a number of different conceptions of the work of Christ in the early
Christian centuries becomes obvious in that well-known
passage from Irenaeus which is often quoted with reference
to the formation of the Canon of the New Testament.
Irenaeus gives a number of rather fantastic reasons why
there should be four and only four Gospels.   Then he goes
on to say that each of the four Gospels corresponds to a
particular aspect of the person and work of the Christ.
As the Divine Word He has a royal nature and a kingly
office.   As offering the perfect sacrifice He has a priestly
office.   As being truly incarnate He has a human office.
And as the One on whom the Spirit descended, He has a
prophetic office.   John's is the Gospel of the kingly Word ;
Luke's the Gospel of His priestly character ; Matthew's
the Gospel of His humanity ; and Mark's the Gospel of
His prophetic character.[1]   Here, in the very writer that

[1] *Adversus Haereses*, 3/11/8.

Aulen uses as his test case, we have a recognition of the four main conceptions of the person and work of Christ which, in various permutations and combinations have formed the central concepts of most modern theories of the Atonement.

However, while this leaves Aulen open to the criticism that he has over-stated his case, it does not seriously affect his main contention. For though such anticipations of modern theories of the Atonement do occur in Irenaeus, they are not advanced as theories independent of his main conception, which is undoubtedly of this " classic " type. They are not offered as alternatives to it. Rather they are subsumed under it, and contained within it as in a matrix. The dominant idea throughout is that of a cosmic drama such as Aulen describes.

Where Aulen seems to me to go more seriously astray is in his tendency to treat this " classical " view as though it were a definite and fairly clearly defined conception, comparable to any of the modern views of the Atonement. This gives rather a distorted picture of what seems to have been the actual historical situation. If Aulen had gone back into the purely apocalyptic tradition which we have already described, he would have found a much more specific and definite conception of the cosmic drama of salvation. It is true that within the apocalyptic tradition there are wide differences of opinion over such questions as what shall be the time and the manner of the coming of the kingdom, and what classes of people shall be saved, and so on. But behind all this there lies a recognisable unity of thought and of religious experience. But in the theological literature of the second and third centuries this is no longer the case.

Even in Irenaeus, whom Aulen singles out from among the other Patristic writers as presenting " a clear and comprehensive doctrine of the atonement and redemption,"[1]

---

[1] Gustav Aulen, *op. cit.*, p. 33.

this " classical " view of the Atonement is not so clear and
definite as one would like to believe. That the basic conception is one of some kind of cosmic drama is beyond
question. But it is not at all a definite and clear concept.
There are at least two rather unrelated strains of thought
running through the work of Irenaeus. On the one hand
there is the conception of the saviour, derived from the
more strictly Jewish type of apocalyptic, as the one who
wins the final victory over the devil and all his ministering
powers. On the other hand there is a sequence of ideas
which are much more Greek or at least Graeco-Judaic in
flavour.[1] Here the central concepts are corruption, incorruption, Incarnation, recapitulation, and so on. The
result is that in reading Irenaeus, we are left in no doubt as
to his faith in the work of Christ as a victory over the
powers of evil on a cosmic scale ; but this mixture of Greek
and Jewish symbols leaves a very vague and ill-defined
picture when we try to ascertain just how this cosmic
victory was won, and what its total effect was.[2] And
Irenaeus was, by Aulen's own confession, more " clear " on
the subject than most of the other Patristic writers.

Thus, while Aulen is right in drawing our attention to
this *Christus Victor* conception as constituting the typical
form of atonement doctrine in the Patristic period, he is
inclined to mislead us by giving the impression that it had
a more definite content than in fact it did, and also that
there was more widespread agreement as to its meaning
and content than in fact there was.

The position can best be understood if we look back for
a moment to the difficulty of interpretation which faced
Paul and John. Christianity was born, so to speak, out
of the womb of the Judaism which it fulfilled, and it was

---

[1] I say Graeco-Judaic because many of these ideas had already been
incorporated in certain of the apocalypses which came under Greek
influence, e.g. Baruch 40/3 " Donec finiatur mundus corruptionis."
[2] Irenaeus' conception of the work of Christ as a victory won on a cosmic
scale receives fuller treatment below, pp. 99 ff.

presented in the Gospels in a thoroughly apocalyptic setting. It is in the apocalyptic conception of the Son of Man coming in power and glory that the later *Christus Victor* conception has its roots. We have already referred to the hope which seems to have been entertained in various forms by different elements of Mediterranean culture, that a new world-age was about to be born.[1] But in spite of the familiarity of the Gentile world with this idea, the task of interpreting the strictly Jewish apocalyptic ideas which formed the background and setting of the Gospel message was extreme, difficult. Paul and John attempted this task in a manner, the brilliance and daring of which tends to be veiled from us by our familiarity with it. But their successors in this work, while they may have been their equals in intellectual ability, had not the same depth of religious insight, and therefore this work of interpreting the cosmic symbolism of Jewish apocalyptic was never really successfully completed.

The noticeable falling away from the spiritual intensity of the New Testament which occurred in the Patristic period has often been remarked upon.[2] The great drama in which our salvation was achieved had always been a μυστήριον— a secret thing. But in the New Testament it is very much an open secret for those who have eyes to see. Though the saving event remains mysterious in its nature, we sense in the confident utterances of the New Testament writers that they know exactly what they are talking about, though frequently they can give it only a symbolic expression. But in the sub-New Testament period it becomes at once something less of a mystery, and at the same time something less definite. It becomes more something to be wondered about, and less something to be wondered at. One of the main reasons for this lapse of spiritual insight is just this fact to which we have been referring—that the

[1] *Supra*, pp. 45 ff.
[2] *Cf.* Sidney Cave, *The Doctrine of the Work of Christ*, pp. 69-70.

Gentile world was not entirely at home with the cosmic symbolism of Jewish apocalyptic.

On the personal and moral aspect of the Christian message, the Fathers speak with a confident earnestness and conviction equal to that of the New Testament. But in their treatment of the wider reference of Christian eschatology they speak neither with the same confidence nor with the same degree of unanimity. Thus, while this element of Biblical teaching continued to be represented in the theology of the early centuries of Christendom, it was not entertained as a single, generally agreed theory, but rather as an extremely vague and ill-defined conception which pervaded and formed a background to the thought of almost all the Christian writers of that period. The question of the correct interpretation and exact significance of the victory which Christ had won over the powers of this world was one of the major problems of the day, and the answers that were given to it varied widely.

Therefore, while we may say that Aulen is correct in asserting that the *Christus Victor* conception was the dominant idea in the thought of this period about the Atonement, he was wrong in treating it as constituting in itself a specific doctrine of the Atonement. It was the basic conception in a number of widely different theories of the Atonement, ranging from the wild speculations of certain of the Gnostic schools to the extremely cautious conservatism of one such as Irenaeus. I think Canon Raven gives a fair picture of the widespread and bewildering differences of opinion which must have existed within the common faith that Christ was victorious over the powers of this world, when he says of the earliest days of Christianity :

Parthians and Medes and Elamites, strangers from Rome, Jews and proselytes, all had striven to tell in their own tongues this wonderful work of God ; and the result was much more like Babel than Pentecost.

This state of chaos is by no means faithfully mirrored in the literary remains of the time ; for with few exceptions those alone have survived which commended themselves to the orthodox of later centuries. And the superficial student of doctrine may easily obtain a wholly false impression. For him the church of the Synagogue, the sects of Ophites, of Valentinus and Basilides, Marcion and the Montanists, the authors of the apocryphal gospels and of the Clemintine literature are mere shadows to be classified and docketed and dismissed as unimportant. Looking back upon the period he sees nothing but the triumphant succession of the Greek Apologists and imagines their work to be the expression of the *communis sensus fidelium*. In reality, of course, such a picture is purely fictitious. A contemporary would have seen a number of isolated pioneers gathering knots of disciples around them in their own neighbourhood, in some cases in communion with the churches of their own province, in others forming schismatic congregations of their own. Amid the welter of speculation he would have found it difficult to forecast what would be the lines of future development or even to discover which of these varying sects represented the true faith most adequately. For although the majority of Christians were no doubt uninfluenced by experiments in doctrine and united rather by membership in the Church than by agreement in reasoned belief, this was due rather to lack of interest in theology than to the possession of fixed formularies or definite knowledge.[1]

[1] C. E. Raven, *Apollinarianism*, pp. 5–6.

CHAPTER VI

THE GNOSTIC SCHOOLS AND COSMIC REDEMPTION

IT was in this situation that the schools of thought that have come to be classed under the general head of Gnosticism began to flourish and became a real menace to orthodoxy. The failure of the church to arrive at a really successful interpretation of the cosmic symbolism of Jewish apocalyptic not only contributed largely to the chaotic situation which Canon Raven describes, but it left open the way for the formulation of what were alternatives to the central ideas of Biblical eschatology rather than re-interpretations of them.

We have already observed how some of the objections with which Paul had to contend, particularly in his letter to the Colossians, contain ideas which, if they do not in themselves represent a primitive Gnosticism, are at least closely similar to the ideas which play a central part in the Gnosticism of the second and third centuries. These ideas are concerned with the operation of intermediary powers or angels set in the heavens between God and man. They are associated with the influence which the stars were thought to exercise over man, and the Colossian heretics appear to have treated them as a factor to be reckoned with by the man who was anxious that he or his soul, should make his way past them into heaven. Paul's answer was to assert, as best he could, the total cosmic significance of the work of Christ as victor over all the powers and principalities of this world.

This illustrates the direct relationship which there is

between the failure of the church to interpret the cosmic aspects of the Jewish apocalyptic elements in Christian eschatology and the rise of certain ideas which were particularly widespread in the Gnostic schools. These same ideas, that the soul which wishes to be saved must reckon with the powers which are associated with the spheres of the stars as well as making the simple act of faith in Christ, provide yet another instance of the principle that, unless the reference of the Redemptive Act includes the whole of environment right to man's farthest horizon, then the redemption is incomplete, for there yet remains something of evil to be overcome.

If such incompleteness in the Redemptive Act of God be recognised, then the old problem of theodicy returns if we are at the same time to continue to believe in the absolute righteousness of God. It is the same dilemma as that to which we have already referred as facing Judaism. Either we accept the fact that environment is not capable of redemption and interpret the redemption of souls entirely in terms of escape from environment—thereby accepting a dualism which we must explain as best we may—or else we must, as St. Paul tended to do when faced with the same problem, find means of showing how the whole of environment is included within the reference of the Redemptive Act. Within Gnosticism elements of both these solutions appear, but by far the main emphasis was on the dualistic solution.

I do not suggest that this problem of theodicy which was raised by the failure of the church to interpret the cosmic aspect of salvation was the historical origin of Gnosticism. The vast complexity of Gnostic origins defies any such simple description. But it did constitute one of the major problems which most of the Gnostic schools tried to meet in one way or another, and is one of the reasons why the Gnostic speculations along these lines were welcomed by so many.

F

It is difficult to deal with Gnosticism in relation to the main problem which we have on hand without either becoming involved in all the well-known historical difficulties which are attached to any study of Gnosticsm, or else presupposing some felicitous answer to these problems without justifying the presupposition. The obscure complexity of Gnostic origins, the dearth of original Gnostic documents, the contradictory and unreliable nature of the Patristic evidences on the subject, the extreme diversity of the Gnostic schools themselves, and the vast complexity of their inter-relationships and their relationship to Christianity itself—all these factors raise difficulties which we must bear in mind but with which we cannot hope to deal directly. There are dangers involved in discussing any subject against such a background of obscurity, but they are dangers which we must face.

One of these dangers meets us right at the start. In this general treatment we are dealing with the Gnostic movement as a whole, yet it is becoming increasingly doubtful if it can be rightly regarded as a whole. It may well be that we ought to speak of " the Gnosticisms " rather than simply of Gnosticism.[1] Therefore, when I speak of the widespread concern of Gnosticism with the problem of evil in relation to the problems of theodicy and salvation, I do not mean that this is a unitary thread which runs through all Gnosticism, and which can be regarded as the essence of Gnosticism, binding all the schools into a unity. The point I wish to make involves no such sweeping generalisation. It is simply that in the group of speculative schools of religious thought of the second and third centuries A.D., which have come to be grouped under the general name of Gnosticism, we do in fact find that the problem of evil tends to occupy a fairly prominent place, particularly evil in its total cosmic aspect. Bigg, Mansel and Burkitt all witness to the centrality of this problem in

[1] Eugène de Faye, *Gnostiques et Gnosticism*, pp. 417 ff.

the Gnostic schools.[1] Tertullian, in a well-known passage, says that the origin of all heresies—by which he means, of course, all Gnostic heresies—lies in an over-curious pressing of the questions : " Unde malum et quare ? Unde homo et quomodo ? "[2]

However, as has been pointed out by Eugène de Faye, this statement of Tertullian's does not quite represent the sense in which the Gnostics approached the problem. He points out that it was a tendency of the ecclesiastical opponents of Gnosticism, who are our main sources of information on the subject, to present Gnosticism in this rather unfavourable light as arising essentially from an over-curious concern with the purely speculative problem of the origin of evil. If, as he tries to do, we base our view of Gnosticism primarily on the few original Gnostic fragments which we possess, inadequate as these may be, rather than upon the second-hand evidence of the anti-Gnostic fathers, we do not find this to be quite true. He finds that it is true neither of Valentinus nor of Marcion, though there is a sense in which it might be said of Basilides, though even he is concerned not so much to know simply what is the origin of evil, but rather where the responsibility for evil lies.[3]

De Faye's criticism here is correct in denying that the problem of evil considered in and for itself is the central concern of the Gnostic schools. Disinterested curiosity such as that with which we have become familiar under the influence of Renaissance humanism is as untypical of the Gnostics as it was of all the speculation of the second and third centuries A.D. The primary concern of the main Gnostic schools was not simply to solve certain theological problems. Their primary concern was salvation, and it

---

[1] Bigg, *Christian Platonists of Alexandria*, p. 28. Mansel, *Gnostic Heresies of the Second and Third Centuries*, pp. 11 ff. Burkitt, *The Church and Gnosis*, pp. 48 ff.

[2] *De Praescriptione Haereticorum*, 7 ; *cf.* Epiphanius, *Contra Haereses*, 24.6.72.

[3] *Op. cit.*, p. 418.

was for this purpose that they sought knowledge. By the way of knowledge they sought

(a) to have the assurance of salvation, and

(b) to know the way of salvation.

It is as incidental to the solving of these practical problems of the spiritual life that the problem of evil and of theodicy arises. Unless we can be assured that God is not responsible for evil and that in Him there is nothing but goodness, there can be no certainty of final salvation. And again, it is important to know how evil came into existence and how its forces operate if we are going to avoid its snares and make our way into the realm of light and salvation. In the main, it was within this context and as incidental to it that the problem of evil arose in the Gnostic schools.

In the face of what appears to have been the failure of orthodoxy to interpret effectively the cosmic aspects of Biblical eschatology the Gnostic schools were forced

(a) to reformulate the symbol of the Fall in such a way as to make its cosmic significance more apparent, thereby removing the responsibility for cosmic as well as personal evils from God, and

(b) to relate the redemptive work of Christ to this total fallen situation.

These problems hold a prominent place in all the main Gnostic writers, whether we judge them by the fragments of their own work which have come to us through more or less reliable channels, or by the fuller, if less reliable, accounts of them which we have in the anti-Gnostic Fathers. The citations of the work of Basilides which occur in the writings of Clement and Origen, and which constitute the only original sources on his thought, show him to be concerned first of all with the problem of evil in its immediate and acute form in the persecutions.[1] However, he finds that he cannot solve the problems raised on

[1] *Stromateis*, 4/12.

this level except in terms of the wider cosmic problem. If God is righteous, he appears to think, then all suffering must be an expiation for sin. Therefore in all those who appear to suffer innocently there must lurk some sin committed before they entered this life—a sin which they are now expiating.

Then again we find him concerned with the problem of the origin of the animal passions in man which appear to be the cause of his sin.[1] He is anxious to show that these do not properly belong to the soul which God has created, but that they are accidental adjuncts ($\pi\rho\sigma\alpha\rho\tau\dot{\eta}\mu\alpha\tau\alpha$). He thought of them as forces or essences which were at large in the world and which attached themselves to the souls of men.

These views, however, did not solve the problem of evil. They merely referred the personal and individual problem to the more fundamental cosmic problem. The questions of how and where the soul had previously sinned and of how these animal passions which attached themselves to the souls of men came into existence, still remained.

Exactly how Basilides dealt with these wider problems which he raised is not at all clear. But that he did deal with them is certain. He seems to have entertained some form of that hierarchical conception of creation which is so common in the Gnostic schools. Irenaeus attributes to him a theory of successive emanations from God resulting finally in the creation of the material world,[2] though in Hippolytus' account of his teaching, the creation of the whole hierarchy, including the material universe, is ascribed directly to God.[3] There may have been some connection between his theory of the passions as distinct powers operative in the world and the hierarchical system of spiritual beings associated with the different spheres of

[1] *Ibid.*, 2/20. This passage witnesses also to the presence of the same ideas in Valentinus.

[2] *Adversus Haereses*, 1.24.3–4.

[3] *Philosophoumena*, 7.10.

the world. Either he ascribed the fallen status of the
world to the progressive weakening of the divine wisdom
and power in each successive emanation, so that the last
one, the physical world, was depraved ;[1] or else he ascribed
it to the fact that though the whole hierarchy was created
by God, certain of the elements in it had wandered out of
their proper sphere, so that, for instance, the animal
passions could fix themselves to the soul of man, where
they did not belong, the spiritual thus becoming confused
with the material.[2] Our view of these alternatives will
depend largely on whether we place more trust in the
account of Irenaeus or that of Hippolytus. Probably both
elements played a part in the thought of Basilides, or at
least in that of his followers.

Corresponding to those two cosmic views of the Fall, we
have evidence of two views of redemption. Corresponding
to the account of the fallen status of the world which
Irenaeus ascribes to him, there is a view of redemption
which, though cosmic in its scale, consists only in the
redemption of the spiritual. The physical cosmos, as the
creation of a lesser power, is beyond redemption and given
over to corruption.[3] Corresponding to the view of the
Fall ascribed to him by Hippolytus, there is a view of the
redemption of the cosmos which involves not merely the
liberation of the spiritual seed from its material environment, but also the restoration of all the various elements
of the created hierarchy, including matter, to their proper
place and making them content to stay there. Thus all
creation is restored to its proper order and its original state
of goodness.[4] Man would presumably thus be set free from
the animal passions which attach themselves to his soul and
cause him to sin and bring suffering upon him as a punishment. As in the case of the two accounts of the fallen
status of the world which we have observed to be associated

[1] Irenaeus, *loc. cit.*   [2] *Philosophoumena*, 7.15.
[3] Irenaeus, *loc. cit.*   [4] Hippolytus, *loc. cit.*

with his name, it is not improbable that both these views of a cosmic redemption played some part in his thought and in that of his followers.

We need not pursue the inquiry into his thought any further. From our standpoint, the interesting thing is that the same dilemma to which we have had to refer again and again occurs once more—either cosmic redemption or dualism. The same problem appears in one form or another in almost all forms of Gnosticism, and in the main, their choice was in favour of dualism. The respect for the physical which was so characteristic of Judaism, and which Biblical Christianity inherited, had excluded the possibility of this preference for dualism in Biblical writings. But in the prevailing Platonism of the second and third centuries, with its glorification of mind at the expense of matter, the way was left open for any theory of the dualism of spirit and matter to receive popular acceptance, both among scholarly people and among the rank and file of educated or semi-educated classes.

The same problem arises for Valentinus, and he has no hesitation whatever in adopting a dualistic solution. His problem is essentially the same as that to which we have referred in Basilides. His first interest is to be assured of salvation and to know the way of salvation ; therefore, like Basilides he must find a way of exonerating God for evil and of showing how evil is to be overcome. And again, like Basilides, while his primary problem is moral and personal, he cannot solve it on this level. Both these writers, like Paul before them, found themselves forced to refer the personal problem to its wider cosmic setting. Eugène de Faye says of Valentinus :

Il semble certain que le problème du mal et de la rédemption a été le premier objet de ses méditations. Il est parti de là, et c'est de là que s'est élancée sa pensée. Le problème s'est sans cesse élargi devant lui ; il a fini par embrasser l'Univers. C'est ainsi que sa pensée s'est élancée de la sphère purement psychologique à la sphère métaphysique. A ce point de vue, Valentin rappelle l'apôtre Paul. Celui-ci a commencé par un problème d'ordre psychologique qui s'est transformé en problème métaphysique. Il a debaté par l'épître aux Galates, pour finir, si l'on en admet l'authenticité, par l'épître aux Colossiens. La marche de l'esprit est la même de part et d'autre.[1]

If we make some slight corrections and reservations, this statement is correct and points to the conclusion that I am trying to establish. When de Faye contrasts the psychological with the metaphysical approach, it is clear from the context to what he is referring. But the choice of these words is rather unfortunate. The contrast is really between the personal and the cosmic approach to the subject, and it is better to hold to these terms. For even Paul's cosmic treatment of the idea of redemption cannot be said to involve metaphysical speculation in the normal sense of that term, and even when Valentinus confines himself to the psychological approach, his three-fold psychology of spirit, soul and body already involves a whole background of metaphysical thought. The real parallel between these two writers to which de Faye's statement points us is that :

(1) Both St. Paul and Valentinus are interested primarily in the redemption of persons, and this is in line with the whole tradition of Biblical Christianity.

(2) In the face of the problem of evil as it exists in the total cosmic environment of man, both were eventually forced to approach the problem of redemption in terms of this wider cosmic issue.

(3) Both were faced with the alternative either of formulating a doctrine of cosmic redemption, or else of resorting to dualism.

The great difference between them is that Paul, remaining

[1] *Op. cit.*, p. 50.

faithful to the Judaism of which Christianity was the fulfilment, avoided dualism and confidently asserted a doctrine
of cosmic redemption, in however rudimentary a form.
On the other hand, Valentinus, being Greek and not Jewish
in his religious and cultural background, was perfectly
happy to accept a dualism of spirit and matter.

In the evidences which we possess on Valentinianism it
is difficult to distinguish between the ideas of Valentinus
himself and those of his followers. But we need not set
ourselves this task. It will suffice for the present purpose
simply to observe the kind of solution to the problems of
the Fall and redemption which is associated with the name
of Valentinus. He seems to have accounted for the
existence and present condition of the actual world in
terms of a fairly elaborately worked-out theory of emanations. First of all, two Aeons—beings of an essential,
spiritual nature—emanated from God. From these there
emanated another pair, and so on through a long series.[1]
They all dwelt within the Pleroma, the realm of light and
the fulness of the Godhead. But Sophia, the youngest of
the Aeons, fell away from perfection, either through giving
expression to a passionate desire to know the Father of all
the Aeons,[2] or through an attempt to emulate the spon-
taneous generation by which the Father alone produced
the first pair of Aeons.[3] In any case, as a result of this fall
in the spiritual realm, she gave birth to the Demiurge, who
was outside the Pleroma, and with her help became the
creator and ruler of the material world.

Thus the material world was thought of not merely as
having been corrupted by a fall in spiritual places, but as
being entirely the result of such a fall, and therefore
essentially evil and beyond redemption. But the supreme
God, unbeknown to the Demiurge, put a germ of spirit
into a certain class of men. This made them capable of

---

[1] Irenaeus, *op. cit.*, 1.1–2.   *Cf.* Hippolytus, *op. cit.* 6.24–25.
[2] Irenaeus, *op. cit.* 1.2.2.   [3] Hippolytus, *op. cit.*, 6.25.

rising above the material world and the power of those who created it—a fact which terrified the Demiurge and his angels so that they became the enemies of man.[1]

In this situation of complete enmity between man on the one hand and this world and the powers of this world on the other, the central theme of the idea of redemption inevitably became that of the liberation of those men in whom the spiritual germ implanted by God had taken root, from the realm of this world and transporting them into the heavenly spheres within the Pleroma. The only fit destiny for material creation was that it should be dissolved. It appears that Valentinus believed that when the spiritual men had finally been given the power which was theirs by right in virtue of their spirituality, they would themselves be the agents who would dissolve the whole material universe.[2]

Because of their inability to understand the cosmic aspect of Biblical eschatology, and because of the failure of the church to interpret it to them in a form which could be integrated with the rest of their cultural background, they substituted instead a dualistic view of the world. Without a doctrine of cosmic redemption this was the logical conclusion. But it denied everything in Judaism of which the Incarnation and crucifixion of Christ were the fulfilment. Therefore the essential contradiction between the theology of Valentinus and Biblical Christianity becomes most obviously manifest at just this point in the docetic view which the Valentinians take of the Incarnation and sufferings of Christ.

Essentially the same kind of problem lies in the background of the dualism of Marcion. There is justification for Harnack's contention that Marcion should be treated more as a religious genius than as a speculative thinker such as Basilides or Valentinus. But the problem of evil exists for him just as for the others, and it is of considerable

---

[1] Clement, *op. cit.*, 2.8.   [2] *Ibid.*, 4.13.

moment in determining the outcome of his thought.[1] His modified dualism, which is represented by the opposition between a supreme God who is over all and an inferior God who is the creator of this world (the God of the Jews and of the Old Testament), fulfils the same speculative function as that of Valentinus ; namely, that of filling the gap which is left in the system of Biblical theology when the cosmic aspect of apocalyptic eschatology is omitted or is misunderstood. The apocalyptic eschatology provided an answer to the problem of evil in its cosmic as well as in its personal aspect. When it was not given due emphasis, the problem demanded another answer, and some form of dualism was the only alternative.

This shows the sense in which it is true to say that the failure of the church to interpret adequately to the Gentile world the apocalyptic eschatology of the Bible contributed largely to the rise of Gnosticism. The foregoing references to the speculations of these men, Basilides, Valentinus and Marcion, the three greatest of the Gnostics, show the influence which this failure on the part of the church had upon their thought. Until orthodoxy could succeed in making its own solution to these problems more plain, the Gnostics had a very strong case in their favour. This is true, at least, of the more intellectually respectable aspects of Gnosticism, such as those with which we have been dealing.

In its later and more popular manifestations, such as we have in the *Pistis Sophia*, these serious problems tend to become lost in the fantastic complexity of an ever-increasing number of Aeons. Here the interest is directed more towards knowing the names of the various powers, and the various formulas which were believed to contain the saving knowledge, rather than towards the serious problems which the idea of salvation involves. But in and behind Gnosticism there remained this problem of the cosmic implications

[1] Bousset, *Hauptprobleme der Gnosis*, pp. 109–113.

of the idea of salvation and the failure of the pagan world
to understand the full meaning of the Biblical symbols.
The church's answer to Gnosticism could be complete only
when she herself had produced an alternative answer to
these problems, and if she was to remain faithful to the
tradition of Biblical Christianity, this answer would have
to depend largely on a continuation of the work of interpreting Jewish apocalyptic which had been undertaken by
Paul and John.

The Attempts of the Church to Refute Gnostic Dualism.
This task of refuting Gnostic Dualism fell to the Fathers of
the second and third centuries.   Primarily the church gave
her answer simply by proclaiming the resurrection of the
body and anathematising the dualism of the Gnostics.
But when this was done, she still owed the Gnostics an
explanation of how she, in her turn, overcame the problem
of evil.   In this task the Fathers did not always show quite
the profundity of thought that they did in some others,
either in grasping the full seriousness of the problem or in
answering it.   In their treatment of it they fall into two
groups.   The first and larger group consisted of those who,
having seen the errors into which philosophy had led the
Gnostics, shied clear of all attempts to solve the philosophic
problems which Christianity raised, and clung steadfastly
to a degenerate chiliastic form of Jewish apocalyptic, with
which alone they were content to meet the cosmic speculations of the Gnostics.   The second group, represented
chiefly by the Alexandrine school, not only used the methods
of philosophy, but were so fascinated by the actual content
of the Greek tradition that they allowed it to obscure their
interpretation of the Christian Gospel ;   and, particularly
in their acceptance of the Platonic depreciation of matter,
they fell to some extent at least into the very error which
they were combating.   Thus, at a time when the menace
of heresy might have forced the church to formulate more
definitely the doctrine of cosmic redemption, the beginnings

of which we have found in the Scriptures, her efforts were frustrated by an over-cautious conservatism on the one hand, and by an over-daring acceptance of certain Greek conceptions on the other. Thus it was that the doctrine of cosmic redemption, which like most of the central doctrines of the church had found only its primitive beginnings in the Bible, failed to reach maturity. From now on, it is the decline rather than the development of this doctrine that we are tracing.

CHAPTER VII

THE SCHOOL OF ALEXANDRIA

T*HE Problem of Evil in Clement of Alexandria.* To Clement goes the credit of being the first of the great thinkers of the church to meet the Gnostics on their own ground and to attempt to formulate the orthodox answer to the problem of evil as it was raised by them. But he was not a likely man to formulate the doctrine of cosmic redemption which, as I have suggested, was what the situation really called for. He was a man of first-rate philosophic ability, but his interest was much too moral and individualistic for him to be drawn to such a task. Rather he tends to argue that the problem which the Gnostics raise does not really exist at all. What we take to be the evils in our environment are not ultimately such at all, but serve a perfectly just and wholesome function as corrective and punitive measures within the providence of God.

This becomes very clear in his treatment of suffering. He adopts a pedagogic view of suffering which one cannot but feel is derived as much from Plato as from the Christian Gospel.[1] On this basis he is prepared to argue that every-

---

[1] There is a superficial similarity between the pedagogic view of suffering which Clement adopts and the view which we find in the prophets of the Old Testament when they treat national disasters, and sometimes even personal suffering, as the just punishment of sin. But, in reality, the similarity is only formal. The prophetic teaching about suffering is the immediate expression of an intense religious experience. It is an interpretation of the world as seen through the eyes of their own personal guilt-consciousness on the one hand, and their consciousness of the redeeming love of God on the other. Clement gives ample evidence that he shared a very similar personal experience. But it does not find expression in his philosophic treatment of the problem of suffering. To use what has recently become a rather over-worked word, he does not write, as the prophets did, from an existential standpoint. Rather, he is conducting an objective moral argument.

thing exists by the will of God, and therefore is good and beloved by Him.[1]   If we suffer it is because we have sinned, and He, who is our wise Instructor, must punish us from time to time for our own good.

> Thus also He who is our great General, the Word, the Commander-in-Chief of the universe, by admonishing those who throw off the restraints of His law, that He may effect their release from slavery, error, and captivity of the adversary, brings them peacefully to the sacred concord of citizenship.[2]

Such a view as this tends to remind us of Leibnitz' *Theodicy* : that " this is the best of all possible worlds ". This impression is confirmed by other statements that Clement makes from time to time, such as when he says of " perfect peacemaking " that it

> calls Providence holy and good ; and has its being in the knowledge of divine and human affairs, by which it deems the opposites that are in the world to be the fairest harmony of creation.[3]

Clement betrays that he would have liked very much to believe that the world, just as it is, is the best of all possible worlds ; though he never quite succeeds in reconciling this view with all the facts.

If such a view of the world could be maintained, then clearly there would be no need either for dualism or for a doctrine of cosmic redemption. But Clement found himself in serious difficulties with it. In the first place, if we are to defend the justice of God on the grounds that each man merits the sufferings that overtake him because of his own sin, this requires a doctrine of the unrestricted freedom of the will. Bigg treats Clement as having simply asserted what Tertullian later called " liberum arbitrium ".[4] But

---

[1] *Paedagogus*, 1.8.   [2] *Ibid.*
[3] *Stromateis*, 4.6.   [4] Bigg, *Christian Platonists of Alexandria*, p. 79.

this is an over-simplification.   Clement certainly begins by
saying that only what is a matter of choice can be a matter
of judgment and punishment.   But he is unable to maintain the issue in this clear-cut form, and all kinds of am-
biguities and contradictions creep into his treatment of
moral choice.[1]   He is at once too profound and too honest
a thinker to treat the question of the freedom of the will
in simple terms of sheer indeterminism.   When he tries to
clear matters up by drawing distinctions between what is
done by " desire ", what is done by " choice " and what is
done by " intention " ;   or between different types of sin,
such as ἀνομία, ἀδικία and ἁμαρτία, he simply makes confusion worse confounded.   Even when one makes allowance
for the fact that the Greek of this passage[2] is both difficult
and corrupt, it still remains obvious that there is serious
confusion of thought behind it.

His position remains self-contradictory.   On the one
hand, his theodicy leads him to say :

Each one of us, who sins, with his own free will chooses
punishment, and the blame lies with him who chooses.
God is without blame.[3]

Yet his honesty and his psychological insight lead him to
say also :

Sinning arises from being unable to determine what
ought to be done, or being unable to do it ; as doubtless
one falls into a ditch either through not knowing, or
through inability to leap across through feebleness of
body.[4]

For our present purpose, the important word in this sen-
tence is " unable ".   If there are occasions on which men
are unable to avoid sin either through weakness or ignor-

[1] *Stromateis*, 2.14–15.   [2] *Loc. cit.*
[3] *Paedagogus*, 1.8.   *Cf.* Plato, *Republic*, Book 10 (617).
[4] *Stromateis*, 2.15.

ance, and yet none the less their sins are visited upon them in the form of suffering, then the whole system of equitable justice by which Clement seeks to justify God falls to the ground. It is true that the difficulty is to some extent eased when Clement points out that our being " unable " often arises from the fact that we do not train ourselves properly. But this can never entirely solve the problem.

When Clement is brought face to face with evil in a very stark form in the persecutions, he has to adopt a very different approach. Basilides had already tried to include the sufferings of the persecutions within a scheme of corrective punishment by hypostatising sins in a previous life, for which the Christian might have to atone in this life by martyrdom or some other form of suffering. Clement rejected this argument, chiefly because he saw in it the implication that Christ Himself, who suffered on the cross, must also be guilty.[1] In the last resort, Clement's answer to the problem of suffering as raised by the persecutions is simply to say :

> What wrong is done us, as far as we are concerned, in being released by death to go to the Lord, and so undergoing a change of life, as if a change from one time of life to another ? Did we think rightly, we would feel obliged to those who have afforded the means for speedy departure. . . .[2]

Ultimately, this implies that it is not in terms of this life, but in terms of the life to come, that the equitable justice of God's providence becomes manifest. This may well be true, but if it is, then it denies what is the main argument of the *Paedagogus* in relation to suffering, which is that suffering can be seen in terms of this life as being the just correction and punishment of personal sin.

In Clement we have a noble attempt to meet the Gnostic challenge by arguing that there really is no cosmic problem

---

[1] *Ibid.*, 4.12.   [2] *Ibid.*, 4.11.

G

at all, that the whole issue can be settled at the level of personal morality. But it was only by leaving many loose ends and unanswered questions that he was able to confine the argument to this field. It was his great successor, Origen, who took up the problem where he left it and extended it to its full scope. Origen recognised that there really was a cosmic as well as a personal problem involved, and that the answer to Gnostic dualism must ultimately be in terms of a doctrine of cosmic redemption.

Origen's Attempt to Formulate a Christian Doctrine of Cosmic Redemption. Like Clement, Origen takes his main stand against the Gnostics on the issue of free will. We have seen how Clement failed to establish his point firmly because he tended to confine the scope of his argument to the sphere of personal morality. But Origen meets the Gnostics on their own ground of cosmic speculation. He takes the concept of free will, which Clement had used in dealing with the problem at a personal level, and makes it a basic concept in interpreting the whole cosmos.

In the second and third centuries the problem of evil was conceived mainly as the problem of imperfection.[1] The central questions were : Why are some beings inferior to others ? What has made man such an inferior creature that he continually fights a losing battle in the moral struggle ? Why are his material environment and his own physical constitution so inimical to the moral life ?

In the face of these questions, it was necessary to show :

(a) that God is not responsible for the imperfections of creation, and

(b) that these imperfections are overcome in the work of redemption.

Of these two problems, Origen seeks to answer the first in his doctrine of the Fall, and the second in his doctrine of redemption.

Origen's Doctrine of the Fall. Origen adopts the generally

[1] René Cadiou, *Introduction au Système d'Origène*, p. 15 f.

accepted view of his times, that the various orders of
creatures in the universe corresponded to various degrees
of perfection or imperfection. The various classes of
spiritual beings and " powers ", mentioned by St. Paul,
are interpreted by Origen as referring to an orderly hierarchy of both supra-mundane and infra-mundane creatures.[1]
Now these various powers, some of which are good and
some of which are evil, cannot be regarded as having been
created thus, for if God had created a universe in which
some creatures were set above others and some were less
perfect than others, He would be either unjust or lacking
in power. For Origen, both the perfections and the imperfections of the creature are not essential to its nature,
but acquired.

To say that any creature was created with a goodness
which was not contingent upon the right exercise of free
will, would be to make that creature equal with God, for
it is a property of God alone to be essentially good.[2]   On
the other hand, to say that God created the evil powers as
essentially evil, and not merely as free to act well or ill,
would mean calling God evil.[3]   This is impossible.   Therefore, we must say that those creatures, which now constitute
the whole hierarchy of creation, were originally created
equal and free,[4] and have received their present status as
rewards or punishments for the manner in which they used
their free will.[5]

There was once a time when there was no evil at all in
God's creation. " *Serpens fuit aliquando non serpens.*"[6]
All creation enjoyed the blessings of a heavenly existence.
It consisted of rational beings who were all equal and
incorporeal, according to their proper nature.[7]   But some
of those blessed creatures, led by him who is now known
as Satan, Lucifer, or the Prince of Darkness, fell away from

---

[1] *De Principiis*, 1.5.1.   [2] *Ibid.*, 1.6.2.
[3] *Ibid.*, 1.5.3.   [4] *Cf.* Plato, *Phaedrus*, 246 A.
[5] *De Principiis*, 1.5.3.   [6] *Hom. in Ezech.*, 1.3.
[7] *De Principiis*, 1.7.1.

their original state by their own act of defection.[1] They
did this by the free will with which every creature is
endowed.[2] Their falling away consisted in a kind of wilful
negligence,[3] comparable to that of a student of geometry,
who wilfully neglects his subject and so forgets it.[4] These
heavenly beings, which were not essentially good, but
derived their goodness only from willing participation in
the essential goodness of the Holy Trinity, wilfully neglected this contemplative participation, and so fell away.
In some, this falling away was more serious than in others ;
therefore the punishment and correction which they
received had to be appropriate to the degree of their fault,
according to the justice of God.[5] Certain parts of this
spiritual creation became the gross substance that we
know as matter, and so the physical world was formed as
an inferior copy of the heavenly. This gross matter
became the domain of Satan, the chief of the defaulters,
so that " his glory was turned into dust".[6]

Since the Fall, each being has been set in a place according to its merit. There is a ladder of existence from the
holiest angel right down to Satan himself. All these
different orders of being fall into three main classes.[7]

(1) There are those who did not fall away from their
primal state of blessedness. They have been set over the
whole spiritual and physical universe to rule it for its good.

(2) Those who have fallen away, but who, so to speak,
looked back as they did so, and so are not entirely depraved,
and have an opportunity of regaining their former blessedness by means of a process of moral education, form the
second class. In this class men belong, and they have been
set in the physical world not only as a punishment for their
sin, but also that they may have a place suited to their
moral education.

---

[1] *Ibid.*, 1.5.3–5.
[2] *Ibid.*, cf. *Contra Celsum*, 5.10.
[3] *De Principiis*, 1.6.2.
[4] *Ibid.*, 1.4.1.
[5] *Ibid.*, 1.6.2. and 2.9.3–8.
[6] *Ibid.*, 1.5.5.
[7] *Ibid.*, 5.6.2.

(3) There are those that have fallen away completely and therefore have not even deserved the moral education of life in this world of matter.   These are in obedience to Satan and have become the tempters and tormentors of men.   Whether they will ever be restored to their place remains a doubtful question.[1]

This hierarchical scheme of things applied itself easily to the then widely held conception of the universe as consisting of seven or eight spheres, each sphere being delimited by the orbit of the various planets, and each higher sphere being more refined and purer than that below it.   This view of the physical universe seems to have enjoyed almost universal acceptance in the early centuries of Christendom in a manner much like that in which the theories of modern physics or of evolutionary biology are today vaguely conceived by the popular mind in half-scientific, half-metaphysical terms.   Origen accepted this view of the universe and identified its hierarchical structure with the hierarchy of the various degrees of punishment which resulted from the Fall.   Thus for Origen, the whole universe, both personal and impersonal, physical as well as psychical, becomes a vast moral structure.

Those beings which have not been set in the physical universe in accordance with the degree of their defection, have been set there for the sake of the moral re-education of mankind.   He argues from the regularity with which the luminaries of the skies proceed on their various courses that they must in reality be rational creatures.[2]   They have been set in their various luminous bodies, some shining with more brightness than others according as their sin in the Fall was lesser or greater.[3]   In the case of some of the most glorious of the heavenly bodies, it may be that they have been made " subject to the vanity of the flesh ", not because they have sinned, but simply for the sake of the redemption of other fallen creatures.   They thus pro-

[1] *Ibid.*, 5.6.3.   [2] *Ibid.*, 1.7.3.   [3] *Ibid.*, 1.7.2.

vide light (both literal and metaphorical) in a universe whose whole history is that of the redemption of a fallen spiritual creation.[1]

This enables Origen to give a very definite exegesis to St. Paul's words :

> The creature has been made subject to vanity, not willingly, but by reason of him who subjected the same in hope, because the creature itself shall be delivered from the bondage of corruption into the glorious liberty of the children of God.[2]

Thus, in Origen's view, the reason for the sufferings and moral difficulties of the present life is that the whole of creation is involved in the Fall, and the physical universe as we know it is entirely the result of the Fall.

Origen's Doctrine of Redemption. It is true at any time that the view we take of the Fall determines to a large extent the view which we take of redemption. This becomes especially true of Origen, when he adopts without question the maxim which was universally accepted by the Stoic eclecticism so widely current in his day—the maxim that " the end is always like the beginning ".[3] According to this statement, the whole process of redemption should be simply a reversal of the process by which fallen creatures were set in the realm of gross visible matter, so that they are all restored to their original state. This, in the main, is the view which Origen adopts, though he does not hold to it with complete consistency throughout.

As in Clement, the role of Christ is essentially that of παιδαγωγός or teacher. From Him all creation learns again the obedience which it has forgotten,[4] and as it learns, it becomes worthy to be restored to a higher and more heavenly state, until at last it becomes worthy of the blessedness of the invisible realm of heaven. Logically

---

[1] *Ibid.*, 1.7.5.
[2] *Loc. cit.* and *op. cit.*, 3.5.4.   *Cf. Contra Celsum* 10–13.
[3] *De Principiis*, 1.6.2.   [4] *Ibid.*, 3.5.6.

this would seem to imply the eventual disappearance of all forms of bodily existence. But in fidelity to Christian orthodoxy, Origen retains the dogma of the resurrection of the body, insisting that creatures so magnificent as these redeemed rational natures must be capable of moving about in space. If they are to be capable of having the property of motion, he argues, they will require to retain some kind of bodily form. But it will not be a body of gross matter such as we know in this world.

The idea of a more refined type of matter would already be both familiar and acceptable to most of Origen's readers, in view of the generally held belief that the planets were composed of a finer type of matter than this gross earth. This belief goes back at least as far as Aristotle, and had been incorporated by the Stoics into their system. Fire, they contended, was the most refined of all kinds of matter. That is why the heavenly bodies shine so brightly. They regarded the Divine Reason, the origin of all things, as being an ethereal kind of fire which had " condensed " into the various material bodies of this universe and would eventually return to its original form of pure ethereal fire. The widespread knowledge and acceptance of this view of matter made it easy for Origen to compromise by describing the final stage of the salvation of creation as one in which bodies survive ; but they are bodies so refined that they have lost all corporeality.[1]

This applies not only to human bodies, but to the luminaries of the skies as well. They, too, at the final consummation, will cast off corruptible visible matter and enter into an eternal, invisible and glorious existence.[2]

The logic of Origen's argument should lead to a universalism in which the whole physical cosmos casts off gross matter and enters into this ethereal existence. Such a universalism is indeed suggested by him when he argues that the words, " The Lord said unto my Lord, Sit thou at

[1] *Ibid.*, 1.6.4. and 2.10.   [2] *Ibid.*, 1.7.1–5 and 2.3.6.

my right hand and I will make thine enemies thy footstool "[1],
are to be interpreted as implying the salvation of all.   For
to be " put under " Christ, he argues, means to be made
subject to Him in obedience, and what is this but to be
saved ?   But he is very doubtful about this, and leaves it
an open question.[2]

For him, the redemptive process is gradual rather than
cataclysmic.   It takes place throughout not merely one
world-age, but many.[3]   There have been many worlds
before this one, and there will be others to follow it before
the final consummation.[4]   Though the process is gradual,
the climax will come in a great conflagration—but not a
destructive conflagration.   Rather it will be a purifying
fire, which will take away all grossness from matter and
restore those rational creatures which have learned obedience to Christ, to their original heavenly state.[5]   Thus all
the evils of suffering and temptation to which we are
subjected in this world because of its material grossness
and the dominion of demonic forces over it, will be no more.
Then God will be all in all.

The Difficulties of Origen's View.   When stated thus in
broad outline, Origen's account of the cosmic aspect of the
Fall and redemption forms an impressive and even attractive system.   Whether or not it is a correct interpretation
of Biblical eschatology, it hangs together sufficiently well
to appear as a possible one.   But when we try to work it
out more systematically and in detail, its difficulties become
more apparent.   In this respect, it is more like a Platonic
myth than a precise work of philosophy, though Origen
does not appear to present it as such.   Cadiou says :

> A vrai dire, ce n'est pas une philosophie.   Origène
> composait ainsi son mythe platonicien de l'âme autour
> de quelques idées claires, inspirées par des considérations
> chrétiennes.[6]

[1] Psalm 110/1.   [2] *De Principiis*, 1.6.1–3.   [3] *Ibid.*, 4.6.6.
[4] *Ibid.*, 2.3.4–5.   [5] *Contra Celsum*, 5.14–17.   [6] *Op. cit.*, p. 23.

When one treats his system otherwise than as a myth, and attempts to give a precise account of the manner in which the redemptive process operates, innumerable difficulties and obscurities come to light. The main feature of Origen's system, which distinguishes it from the Gnostic heresies, is his assertion of the universal reign of moral freedom and moral justice in the whole created order. The unity and consistency of his system depends on his being able to maintain this principle throughout. One cannot but admire the extent to which he does succeed in bringing the whole natural order within such a magnificent scheme. But in the long run he fails in that he admits that there are some parts of the physical cosmos which have been made subject to the vanity of the flesh, not according to their merits, but simply because it is necessary for the salvation of man. This, he says, is true of certain of the heavenly bodies, and possibly of some of the lower orders of nature as well.

Again, when we try to determine the relation of the gross matter of the world to the rational natures of which it is supposed to be the embodiment, the confusion becomes deeper the more we search into Origen's views and comments about it. In the case of human bodies, the application of his thesis is fairly clear. Individual spiritual creatures have been set in these bodies according to their merits or demerits. If we accept his hypothesis that the heavenly bodies are inhabited by rational natures similar to human beings, only of a higher order, we can understand how his thesis might apply in their case, too. But when we come to consider lower animal nature and mineral bodies of this world, the difficulty becomes acute. The scheme of redemption which Origen outlines would naturally suggest that at this level of the material hierarchy, as well as at others, these things are the physical embodiment of rational natures which have sunk to a still lower level than human beings. If he is going to bring all of creation within his moral scheme, this is the conclusion which he must draw. I think Origen would gladly have done this in quite an unequivocal way, but he was rather embarrassed by this side of his own teaching in that it brought him dangerously near to the Pythagorean conception of metempsychosis which some of the Gnostics embraced.

It is very difficult to know exactly how Origen meant to deal with this point, especially since it is on questions such as this, where Origen's orthodoxy was suspect, that Rufinus was most inclined to tamper with the text of the original in the Latin version of the *De Principiis* which he has left us, and which is still our main source. In the last paragraph of the first book of the *De Principiis*, Rufinus makes Origen say :

> We think that those opinions which some are accustomed unnecessarily to inquire into and uphold, to the effect that souls depart so far from their true selves as to forget their rational nature and dignity and to sink down into the condition of irrational animals, like beasts or cattle, ought certainly not to be accepted.[1]

This definitely excludes the lower orders of creation from his moral scheme. But according to the original Greek text of this passage as Paul Koetschau reconstructs it from various quotations and fragments, Origen said exactly the opposite.

> When the soul falls away from good and inclines toward evil, it becomes more and more involved in this. Then, unless it turns back it is rendered brutish by its folly and bestial by its wickedness . . . and it is carried towards the condition of unreason and, so to speak, of the watery

---

[1] " Illa sane quos nequamquam recipienda censemus, quae a quibusdam superfluo vel perquiri vel adstrui solent, id est quod animae in tantum sui discessum veniant, ut naturae rationabilis ac dignitatis oblitae etiam in ordinem inrationabilium animantium vel bestiarum vel pecudum devolvantur." Koetschau, *Die Griechischen Christlichen Schriftsteller der Ersten Drei Jahrhunderte*, V, p. 105.

life. Then, as befits the degree of its fall into evil it is
clothed with the body of this or that irrational animal.[1]

There can be no doubt that the latter statement is nearer
to the true text of Origen and that he did include the lower
animal orders within his moral system.[2] But though the
logic of his system forced him to adopt this position, he is
clearly not altogether happy about it and prefers to lay very
little stress upon it. He also speaks at times of a total
world soul.[3] How this world soul is related to the universal
moral individualism on which his system is based is very
difficult to conceive.

What Origen has, in fact, done, is to take the main
outlines of the most widely accepted ideas of the current
Stoic eclecticism and to try to interpret Christian doctrine
in terms of them. Whatever may have been the similarities
between certain aspects of Stoic belief and the Christian
faith, this task was ultimately an impossible one. Stoicism
had succeeded, after its fashion, in bringing the whole
universe within a moral system. But there are two good
reasons why the Stoics could succeed here, while Origen
failed.

(1) They thought of the Divine Reason primarily, if not
entirely, in terms of immanence, and thought of it also as
being essentially material in its nature, however refined
that matter might be. From this position it was easy for
them to treat the whole physical universe as being essentially rational in its nature. But Origen as a Christian
could not adopt quite this position.

(2) The Stoics also conceived human nature primarily
in terms of impersonal rationality. Their morality was
one in which the universal law of reason must over-rule

[1] Ἡ ψυχὴ ἀπορρέουσα τοῦ καλοῦ καὶ τῇ κακίᾳ προσκλινομένη καὶ ἐπὶ πλεῖον ἐν
ταύτῃ γινομένη, εἰ μὴ ὑποστρέψοι, ὑπὸ τῆς ἀνοίας ἀποκτηνοῦται καὶ ὑπὸ τῆς
πονηρίας ἀποθηριοῦται . . . . καὶ αἱρεῖται πρὸς τὸ ἀλογωθῆναι καὶ τὸν ἔνυδρανον,
ἵν οὕτως εἴπω, βίον. καὶ τάξα κατ᾽ ἀξίαν τῆς ἐπὶ πλεῖον ἀποπτώσεως τῆς κακίας
ἐνδύεται σῶμα ⟨τοι⟩ ὅδε ἢ τοιοῦδε ἀλόγου ζῴου. Ibid., p. 104.
[2] Cf. De Principiis, 2.7.1.   [3] De Principiis, 2.1.3.

unique individuality. The value of a human person for them lay not in his unique personality, but in his participation in the Divine Reason immanent in the universe. It was a comparatively easy matter for them to integrate an ethic based on this conception of personality with their cosmology. But the Christian ethic with which Origen had to deal, though there are many parallels between it and the Stoic morality, rested on a completely different conception of the nature and significance of human personality. It placed an ultimate value on personality as such, and did this in terms of love rather than in terms of mere respect for Reason. One cannot take this intensely personal morality, which is at the core of Christianity, and introduce it into the Stoic system, substituting it for their more impersonal morality, without disrupting the relation which existed within Stoicism between cosmology and morality.

It is mainly on these two difficulties that Origen's attempt to formulate a doctrine of cosmic redemption in terms of the philosophy of his day finally comes to grief. It is only through an ambiguity in his use of the word " soul " that he is able to hold together the Stoic and Christian elements in his philosophy. When he speaks of the rational creatures whom God created in the beginning, and who stood equally before Him in the blessedness of heaven, we can think of them as enjoying a relationship of personal communion with their Creator. At this stage in the argument, we can interpret his meaning in terms of the Christian conception of personality. But when he comes to describe the descent of these heavenly creatures into the bodies of irrational animals, he has to switch over to a purely Stoic conception of personality. It is only by defining the soul in such a way as to exclude any reference to the truly personal, that he is able to preserve some semblance of continued identity in the soul that has sunk to the level of the irrational animal. For this purpose he adopts the Aristotelian definition of the soul: " The power

of imagination and desire, or of feeling and motion ".[1] It
is not unreasonable to suggest that every living animal has
a soul in this sense. But it is a far cry from this to the
Christian conception of the soul as personality.

Having accepted this very impersonal definition of the
soul, Origen goes on to describe the manner of its descent
into irrational animal nature in terms obviously derived
from Stoic cosmology.[2] God, he says, is often spoken of
in Scriptures as a consuming fire[3] or as having in some
sense the properties of fire. This property would naturally
be shared by the rational creatures which he created in the
beginning. But the association between the word $\psi\nu\chi\eta$
and the verb $\psi\dot{\nu}\chi\epsilon\sigma\theta\alpha\iota$ (to grow cold) suggests to us what
has happened. The process by which a rational creature
loses the divine fire of reason and becomes a mere animal,
is that, when it turns away from God, the fire begins to
cool. In this, Origen is borrowing directly from Stoicism.

If we take into account Origen's view of animal nature,
this is a very profound degradation for any rational creature. Origen was not sufficient of a romanticist to see
anything of personality in the lower animals. As J. M.
Denis has pointed out,[4] his view of sub-human animals is
very like that of Descartes, who regarded them as mere
machines and nothing more. The seemingly constructive
behaviour of animals, says Origen, is entirely the product
of a blind impulse which is put into them by God. They
exist purely as part of the equipment of a universe designed
for the moral re-education of men.[5]

Now it might be possible to think of a soul which had
once enjoyed communion with God as sinking to such a
level of sheer impersonality as this, if one thought of that
soul in purely Stoic terms, and of its communion purely in
terms of impersonal participation in the Divine Reason ;

---

[1] *Ibid.*, 2.8. *Cf.* Aristotle, *De Anima*, 3.9.1.
[2] *De Principiis, loc. cit.*
[3] Hebrews 12/29 ; Deuteronomy 4/24 and 9/3.
[4] *La Philosophie D'Origène*, pp. 105 ff. [5] *Contra Celsum*, 4.81–89.

though, in fact, the Stoics excluded the animals from the great city of men and gods.[1] But if we begin by thinking of the rational creatures whom God first created in terms of the Christian conception of personality, then the view that such a personality can be condemned to become a mere animal and yet retain its identity as a soul, becomes quite untenable.

But Origen himself was by no means oblivious to the difficulties which his system involved. He betrays this in the hesitant and often contradictory way in which he tries to relate the natural world to his moral scheme of things. Regarded as a myth expressing his intuition of the ultimate justice of God in His dealings with the world in creation and providence, the system which he works out in the *De Principiis* has real value. But it cannot be regarded as a successful interpretation of Christian eschatology in a systematic doctrine of cosmic redemption.

His preoccupation with the content as well as the methods of current philosophy involved him in an approach to the whole created order which was essentially different from that of the Scriptures. Despite his resolute determination to avoid anything in the nature of Gnostic dualism, he remained very much under the influence of the depreciation of the material order, which is so typical of Greek philosophy. The result is that his philosophy is very much akin to the dualism of the Gnostics in spirit, if not in form. There are occasions when he does seem to come quite openly to the conclusion that matter is essentially evil.[2] But his respect for orthodoxy kept him faithful to the symbol of the resurrection of the body. But his compliance here is really only formal. Eugène de Faye says of him :

The divergence in this matter between the author of the *De Principiis* and the general body of Christians is un-

[1] J. M. Denis, *op. cit.*, p. 107.   [2] *Commentary on John*, 20.16.

deniable. The surprising thing is that he himself fails to see it. His sincerity is clear, his unawareness of the divergence is not in doubt. . . . Both as regards final things and as regards the origin, formation and destiny of the cosmos, the accusation might not unfairly be brought against him that he was more of a Platonist than a Christian.[1]

Ultimately, for Origen, the physical cosmos is not at all involved in the redemptive process in a positive way. It is only rational nature that is redeemed, and despite the formal differences between Origen and the Gnostics, this redemption still consists essentially in the deliverance of mental from gross bodily nature. Thus the dualism which he formally repudiates still lies deep in the heart of his thinking. As Cadiou puts it, this physical world is so far from having ultimate value in the eyes of God, that :

L'univers est un vaste purgatoire où Dieu fait peu à peu l'éducation des créatures raisonnables qui ont revêtu la chair et le sang. Si attenüée que soit la faute originelle, le monde present a pour cause un péché.[2]

He refers us also to the words of St. Thomas, who says :

According to this system, all bodily creatures have no other end than to serve as a punishment for sin, and they have not been made in order to participate in the goodness of God.[3]

Thus, as an attempt to translate into philosophic terms the cosmic eschatology towards which the Scriptures pointed, Origen's view of the redemptive process must be regarded as a failure. We have already shown how it is a mistake to interpret the apocalyptic symbol as expressing a purely negative view of the significance of the present physical world. It does assert that the fulfilment of

---

[1] *Origen* (tr. Rothwell), pp. 162–3. [2] *Op. cit.*, p. 60.
[3] *Summa*, I a, Qxlvii.

present world history is not included within that history, but lies beyond it.   But it does not regard present world history as a mere means towards that end, as Origen does. It arises from the prophetic insight into the positive meaning of the present world, in spite of all the evils therein.   It represents the present world as having value for its own sake in the sight of God, even though it be a fallen world.   For Origen, on the other hand, the present world is ultimately a mere means toward the end of restoring fallen rational natures to their original condition.

The fundamental error in the approach of both Clement and Origen to the problem of the imperfections of this world is that, like the Gnostics whom they were combating, they began with the problem of evil and made this their starting-point, instead of beginning with the prophetic insight into the positive meaning of the world, which the Christian Gospel expresses in eschatological terms.   Such an approach could not ever succeed as an interpretation of the doctrine of cosmic redemption which Biblical eschatology implies, for it ignores the fundamental insight on which the whole Biblical position is based.

CHAPTER VIII

THE CONSERVATIVE APPROACH OF THE WEST

IN view of the errors into which the philosophic daring of the Alexandrine school led Origen, it is not surprising that many of the anti-Gnostic Fathers resolutely avoided philosophic discussion and interpretation of the faith. Irenaeus gives us the best and most systematic example of the more conservative attitude of the West to the problem, and it is mostly with him that we shall concern ourselves.

He takes the attitude that Scripture has given us all the knowledge that is necessary for salvation, and any questions that are not fully answered by Scriptures must be left severely alone.[1] Thus, instead of attempting to formulate a real interpretation of Biblical eschatology, he is content to confine his argument against the Gnostics and the cosmic problems which they raised, firstly, to a demonstration of the difficulties and inconsistencies in the heretical solutions which they adopt; and secondly, to a simple reassertion of the Biblical position, without enquiring too closely as to whether it does not involve similar difficulties itself.

This is evident, for instance, in his criticism of the Gnostic conception of the Pleroma. Whatever the vagaries and needless complexities which came to be associated with this aspect of Gnostic teaching, there is a real problem behind it. It is the problem of the existential separation of the world from its divine ground. We have already observed how the problem of evil has two aspects, one moral and the other ontological.[2] The moral problem is

---

[1] *Adversus Haereses*, 2.28.7.   [2] *Supra*, pp. 3 ff.

that of the relation of a world in which there are the positive evils of pain and wickedness, to a God who is all goodness. The ontological problem is that of the relation of a world in which there is the negative and privative evil of finitude, to a God whose perfection implies His infinity. It is the co-existence of these two aspects of the problem of evil which makes it so very complex. For the obvious way in which to absolve God from responsibility for the moral evil and suffering of this world, is to emphasise the independence and separation of the world from God. On the other hand, the ontological problem tends to be answered in the opposite way by asserting the ultimate unity of the world with God, so that its separate finitude is ultimately grounded in His perfect infinity. Thus our answer to one aspect of the problem tends to run counter to our answer to the other.

It is to the credit of most of the great Gnostic teachers that they were in some measure aware of both aspects of the problem ; as indeed it was typical of the whole culture of the second and third centuries A.D. to be conscious of the privations implied in finitude. The Gnostic conception of a creation which is distinct from God the Father, yet which remains within the " fulness " of the Divine Being, provides a partial answer to the ontological problem. But this world in which there is positive moral evil cannot be included within this " fulness " of the Godhead without a slight being cast upon God. Therefore they placed the material world outside the Pleroma, explaining that it was only as a result of the Fall that it had come to be at all.

However unacceptable this account of things might have been to the Christian church, it at least showed a certain awareness of the problems involved. If the attitude to the material universe which this solution implied was not acceptable, then the responsibility of showing the true place of the material universe within the total scheme of things rested on the church.

But from fear of giving rise to further heresy, Irenaeus simply refuses to recognise this responsibility. He is very quick to seize upon the obvious difficulties of the Gnostic teaching. He argues that either the Pleroma, or fulness of God, is infinite, or it is not. If it is infinite, then there is nothing outside it, for anything outside it would be a limitation. Therefore any talk of the creation of a Demi-urge which lies outside the Pleroma implies that God is limited and therefore not God. This is a just enough criticism, provided Irenaeus is willing to apply the same rigorous logic to his own language when he refers to the fallen status of the world in terms of the more Biblical symbol of the Devil. But he does not do so.

This attitude to the problems raised by the Gnostics is typical of the Western Fathers. Thus, while what was ultimately required was a true re-interpretation of the cosmic eschatology of the Bible, this was not forthcoming. Origen, however unsuccessful he may have been, had at least attempted the task. There is a doctrine of cosmic redemption in Irenaeus, in so far as it is involved in the Biblical symbols which he reasserts. But he shows very little interest in the idea for its own sake, and makes very little effort at interpretation.

His conception of the Fall is expressed in terms of the traditional story of the defection of a supra-mundane being who, after his Fall, became the tempter of man. So man was tempted, in his turn, to fall away from obedience to God. Irenaeus prefers to restrict the work of the Devil to that of tempting the heart of man, rather than as being related to the fallen state of the cosmos as a whole.[1] He says of the Devil, as a power influencing the course of the world's events :

The devil, however, since he is an apostate angel, can only go to this length, as he did at the beginning, namely

[1] *Adversus Haereses*, 5.24.

to deceive and lead astray the mind of man into dis-
obeying God, and the hearts of those who would endeavour
to serve him to the forgetting of the true God and the
adoration of himself as God.[1]

This statement seems to deny outright that the Fall of
Satan could have any widespread, cosmic effect, for it
restricts his power to that of a moral tempter.

Irenaeus is very unwilling to make much of the idea of
cosmic Fall because of his distaste for any kind of cosmic
speculation, particularly if it is along lines which might
lead to conclusions like those of the Gnostics. Like
Clement, he would very much like to be able to contend
that the world is all good, and that there is no problem of
evil at all, other than what can be explained in terms of
the moral depravity of man. He does, in fact, attempt to
argue along these lines. He contends that since God is
good, the world as conceived by Him must be good. But
for God to conceive the world ideally is the same as for
God to create it in actuality, since God is omnipotent and
for Him there is no gap between the ideal and its realisation. Therefore the physical universe must be just as God
conceived it, and so good and totally worthy of Him.[2]

This stressing of the absolute sovereignty of God over all
creation is a correct emphasis in relation to Gnostic dualism.
But in terms of the dilemma to which we have already
referred, in emphasising the association of God with the
created world and its events, it makes the problem of what
at least appear to be the imperfections of the world all the
more acute. Thus we are thrown back on one of the main
problems which it was the virtue of the greatest of the
Gnostic thinkers at least to recognise. Irenaeus does not
give all the weight to this problem which it deserves.
(This, of course, is understandable since his main interest
was polemical.) If he could have confined the problem to

---

[1] *Ibid.*, 5.24.3.   [2] *Ibid.*, 2.2–5.

the spiritual realm, then the whole matter would have been much simpler. He could have accounted for the presence of evil in the world simply by reference to the Fall of Satan and his influence as the tempter of men. He does this to a large extent. But he cannot entirely dissociate evil from the ills that are associated with and arise from our physical environment.

While this problem of physical evil does not receive any systematic treatment at the hands of Irenaeus, it is focused by him on the fact of physical death. It is in his treatment of this that we find the key to his attitude to the wider problem. He argues that within the total framework of creation, the material constitution of things is good and worthy of God; but matter, considered in itself, is imperfect and liable to corruption. Therefore it always stands in need of the spiritual. The spiritual is not subject to corruption, and therefore, by being united to matter saves it from the corruption to which it is naturally inclined.

> For what is carnal stands in need of what is spiritual, if indeed it is to be saved, that it may be sanctified and cleared from all impurity, and that what is mortal may be swallowed up by immortality.[1]

If Irenaeus had related this conception of the relation of spiritual and material in the world more systematically to the Jewish Fall story which he accepts, he would have gone far towards formulating a definite doctrine of cosmic Fall. But he says no more of these two aspects of the fallen state of the world than he learns from St. Paul's statement:

> Wherefore, as by one man sin entered into the world, and death by sin; and so death passed upon all men, for that all have sinned.[2]

This is a very suggestive symbol; but it remains only

---

[1] *Ibid.*, 2.19.6.   *Cf.* 1 Corinthians 15/44 and 2 Corinthians 5/4.
[2] Romans 5/12.

symbolic, and Irenaeus makes no attempt at further interpretation. The whole argument can be summarised as follows :

(1) Since the first man sinned, all men became sinners in principle. This sin involved a certain loss of spirituality, so that his nature became predominantly carnal.

(2) Now carnal nature is not in itself a sign of imperfection, but it stands in perpetual need of the spiritual, and as separated from the spiritual it is imperfect. Therefore this loss of spirituality had two results :

(*a*) The flesh, as being in some measure separated from spirit, became a constant source of temptation to actual sin.

(*b*) For the same reason the flesh became subject to corruption and death, and so, by implication, to all the other physical evils of which death is the ultimate consummation.

In all this, I do not think he was adding anything to what Paul had already said. But in reasserting it within the context of the Gnostic controversy, he brought out its full importance as a doctrine of the Fall which takes account, not only of moral evil, but of physical evil as well, yet which does this in such a way that it neither lapses into the dualism of spirit and matter to which most of the Gnostics fell a prey, nor does it saddle the Creator with the responsibility for physical evil.

It does, of course, raise a great many questions. One would like to know just by what process sin results in the loss of spirituality, and what exactly we mean when we say that the material stands in need of the spiritual. One wonders, too, whether the argument does not depend very heavily on a fortunate ambiguity in the word " corruption ", which can mean both moral lack of integrity and physical disintegration as well. The plausibility of the argument which associates death with sin rests to some extent on this ambiguity. But I do not think it is fruitful to press these questions in relation to Irenaeus. It is not so much an argument as a continuation and development of the Fall myth in Genesis III. As such it cannot be fruitfully subjected to logical analysis. But while it is not sufficiently systematic to be treated as constituting, in itself, a doctrine of cosmic Fall, it has very definite significance in relation to such a doctrine, in that in the form of a myth it asserts that there is a definite relationship between the Fall and physical evil.

Irenaeus' Teaching in Relation to the Idea of Cosmic Redemption. In thus relating the corruption of the physical element in human life to the Fall, Irenaeus is very careful not to leave the impression that what is material has become so completely separated from the spiritual as to be entirely given over to corruption. There is still a residual goodness and health throughout the whole life of the physical universe. This is because the eternal Word, through whom in the beginning all things were made, remains immanent in the universe. All the goodness and health and fruitfulness which impinges on man's life in this physical world is directly due to the continued immanence of the Word, who became incarnate in the Christ, and is a kind of foretaste of the full redemption of the flesh which is yet to come, and which is already established in the victory of the Christ in His own person over corruption and death.

This may be illustrated from the following passages :

But it is much more suitable that we, directing our inquiries after this fashion, should exercise ourselves in the investigation of the mystery and administration of the living God and should increase in the love of Him who has done, and still does so great things for us ; but never should fall from the belief by which it is most truly proclaimed that this Being alone is truly God and Father, who both formed this world, fashioned man, and bestowed the faculty of increase on His own creation, and called him upwards from lesser things to those

greater ones which are in His own presence, just as He
brings an infant which has been conceived in the womb
into the light of the sun, and lays up wheat in the barn
after He has given it full strength on the stalk.   But it
is one and the same Creator who both fashioned the
womb and created the sun ; and one and the same Lord
who both reared the stalk of corn, increased and multi-
plied the wheat, and prepared the barn.[1]

It is clearly the main purpose of Irenaeus in this passage
to contradict the typical Gnostic dualism by asserting that
the God who created and rules over this physical world is
one and the same God as the heavenly Father whom we
worship.   But this is not all he says.   There is also the
suggestion that all the material goodness and fruitfulness
which we enjoy in this world is a foretaste of that very
same graciousness in God which calls us " upwards from
lesser things to those greater ones which are in His own
presence ".

This is even more clear in a passage in which he is discussing the sacramental and eschatological significance of
the miracles of the feeding of the multitude and the turning
of water into wine.   He says :

Taking the loaves which the earth had produced, and
giving thanks, and on the other occasion making the
water wine, He satisfied those who were reclining, and
gave drink to those who had been invited to the marriage ;
showing that the God who made the earth, and commanded it to bring forth fruit, who established the
waters, and brought forth fountains, was He who in these
last times bestowed upon mankind, by His Son, the
blessing of food and the favour of drink.[2]

Here again, his main interest is to deny the Gnostic doctrine
of the Demiurge, but again he also makes the suggestion
that the good things of this physical world, regarded in the
light of the faith, are a kind of anticipation of our ultimate

[1] *Adversus Haereses*, 2.28.1.   [2] *Ibid.*, 3.11.5.

salvation. Thus, for Irenaeus, both the doctrine of the Fall and the doctrine of redemption contain some reference to the physical world. Its evils, as epitomised in the ultimate tragedy of death, are accounted for in terms of the separation of spirit and matter which resulted from the Fall of Adam, and its residual goodness is accounted for in terms of the continued in-dwelling of the Creator Word, through whom our ultimate salvation is wrought.

Therefore, when the Word, in the fulness of time, became incarnate in Jesus Christ and entered fully into the realm of matter, He came to His own. In so doing, He re-established the reign of the spiritual in the material order ; for, as He is Lord of the spiritual realm in His eternal being, so when He comes in the flesh, He becomes Lord of the material realm.

> The Word, being made man, summing up all things in Himself ; so that as in the super-celestial, spiritual and invisible things, the Word of God is supreme, so also in things visible and corporeal He might possess the supremacy, and taking to Himself the pre-eminence, as well as constituting Himself Lord of the church, He might draw all things to Himself at the proper time.[1]

But though this saving event is cosmic in its scale and implications, man does not enter into it simply as one incidental factor among all the other aspects of creation. The rest of creation exists only for the sake of man.[2] Therefore it is because of the involvement of man in the material order, that the gift of incorruption is conferred upon that order. It is because it is man's deeds in this material world that determine his eternal destiny, that the whole material order must be involved in the final resurrection, judgment and salvation.

It is this final redemption of the flesh of man and of the whole material order which occupies almost the whole of

---

[1] *Ibid.*, 3.16.6.　　　　　　[2] *Ibid.*, 5.29.1.

his Fifth Book of *Against Heresies*. He realises that this is the point on which the problem of physical evil must finally be met if the dualistic solutions of the Gnostics are to be rejected. If the true God is the author of the physical world, He is responsible for it. If He cannot redeem the flesh, He is either impotent or malignant.[1]

The present continuation of the infirmity and corruptibility of the flesh is, however, in accordance with the purpose of God. It is a continual reminder to us that the material stands in need of the spiritual. But, Irenaeus argues, it is by no means incredible that this situation will be finally brought to an end, and the whole material order will receive the benefits of redemption. If it is credible that God created the material order, then, *a fortiori*, it is credible that He can redeem it. The mystery of the Eucharist shows us that the material is capable of receiving spiritual benefit.[2] Also, the mere fact that the phenomenon of life, which belongs peculiarly to God, is found in this world to be so inextricably bound up with the flesh, precludes us from saying that the flesh has no part in redemption.[3] And there is final proof of the involvement of the material in redemption when we consider the resurrection and ascension of Christ in the body.[4]

Since, however, Irenaeus has no direct interest in cosmic speculation and is very much afraid of the errors to which such speculation can lead, he does not treat the redemption of the material order in any systematic way. His main interest is in the resurrection of the human body. But he cannot finally isolate this special problem from its wider context. Finally, he has to embrace the whole physical universe within his redemptive scheme. In the final chapters of the Fifth Book, he does this quite unequivocally. But he is careful to stick very closely to the traditional picture of this final consummation of all things as it is presented in Jewish and Christian apocalyptic.

[1] *Ibid.*, 2.4.   [2] *Ibid.*, 5.2.   [3] *Loc. cit.*   [4] *Ibid.*, 5.31.

His argument is based on a thorough-going literalism in his interpretation of the apocalyptic images.[1]

The bodies of the dead, he contends, shall lie in their graves until the final judgment. Then all shall be resurrected for the final assize. At this time neither the substance $\left\{ \begin{array}{l} \text{substantia} \\ \upsilon\pi o\sigma\tau\acute{\alpha}\sigma\iota\varsigma \end{array} \right\}$ nor the essence $\left\{ \begin{array}{l} \text{materia} \\ o\dot{\upsilon}\sigma\acute{\iota}\alpha \end{array} \right\}$ of creation will be annihilated, but only the present fashion $\left\{ \begin{array}{l} \text{figura} \\ \sigma\chi\tilde{\eta}\mu\alpha \end{array} \right\}$ of things will pass away. Then

when this fashion of things passes away, and man has been renewed, and flourishes in an incorruptible state, so as to preclude the possibility of becoming old, then there shall be the new heaven and the new earth, in which the new man shall remain, always holding fresh converse with God. And since these things shall ever continue without end, Isaiah declares, " For as the new heavens and the new earth, which I do make, continue in my sight, saith the Lord, so shall your seed and your name remain."[2]

In this, as in the case of so many of the answers which Irenaeus brings to the Gnostic heresies, he is not really adding anything to what is already contained in this aspect of the Biblical tradition. But, as in the case of his re-assertion of the Pauline treatment of the myth of the Fall, the important thing is, that in emphasising this aspect of the Biblical tradition in relation to the problems raised by the Gnostics, he showed something of its significance for speculative thought, even though he did not embark on the work of interpreting it.

The Symbol of the New Heaven and the New Earth in Early Western Christianity. This kind of expectation of a literal restoration of the conditions of paradise in the physical world at the end of the times was almost universally held in Western Christianity during the first three centuries, though as is well known, the more philosophical

---

[1] *Ibid.*, 5.35.   [2] *Ibid.*, 5.36. *Cf.* Isaiah 66/22.

temperament of the East was inclined to reject it or allegorise it. In the West, it was conceived either as an eternal paradise in the material world which would be inhabited by the righteous for ever, or else, more commonly, as a temporary kingdom, lasting for a thousand years. I do not think there is any very deep significance in this difference of opinion as to the duration of the Messianic kingdom. It is simply a reflection of the differences already referred to[1] in the various apocalypses themselves.

Justin does recognise that there are those who are called Christians who do not hold this belief. But he insists that, because of its relation to the doctrine of the resurrection of the body, it is an essential part of the faith.[2] Harnack comments with surprise on this wide acceptance of a doctrine which carries with it so many intellectual difficulties, especially when it is held by men of such intellectual sophistication as Justin, Irenaeus, Hippolytus and Tertullian. He is rather obviously at a loss to explain this. In his article on the "Millenium" in the *Encyclopedia Britannica*, he says :

> The Western Fathers, Irenaeus, Hippolytus and Tertullian believe in Chiliasm simply because it is part of the tradition of the Church, and because Marcion and the Gnostics would have nothing to do with it.[3]

But he contradicts this in a very forthright manner in his *History of Dogma*, where he says :

> But it would be a great mistake to assume that Irenaeus merely repeated the hopes of an earthly kingdom just because he still found them in tradition, and because they were completely rejected by the Gnostics and guaranteed by the *regula* and the New Testament. The truth is rather that he as well as Mileto, Hippolytus,

[1] *Supra*, p. 84.   [2] *Dialogue with Trypho*, Chapter 80.
[3] *Ad. loc.*

Tertullian, Lactantius, Commodian, and Victorinus lived in these hopes no less than did Papias, the Asia Minor Presbyters and Justin.[1]

Whether Harnack is to be condemned for inconsistency or praised for the modesty of his self-criticism in this, I do not know. But of the two statements, the latter comes much nearer to the truth. The conception of Christ as victor in a cosmic conflict, and of the renewal of the whole material universe at the end of the times, is not a mere anachronistic survival in the work of the Western Fathers, but occupies a key position in their whole theological system.

As has already been seen from our analysis of Irenaeus' argument against the dualistic outcome of the cosmic speculations of the Gnostics, the literal interpretation of apocalyptic symbols played a central part. Just as his answer to the dualism of mind and body, which entered into the Gnostic treatment of salvation at a personal level, was to assert the resurrection of the body ; so in his answer to the dualism of their cosmic speculations, he had to assert the cosmic aspect of the apocalyptic hope and proclaim the final renewal of the whole earth at the end of the times. His only alternative would have been to produce a re-interpretation of this aspect of the Biblical faith in the form of a philosophic doctrine of cosmic redemption. But he was unwilling to face the risks which this task undoubtedly involved.

The Western Fathers, as a whole, are associated with him in this conservative caution. It is this which explains the persistence of this rather unsatisfactory expression of the cosmic significance of the work of Christ in the forefront of the church's teaching. The reason why it did not so persist in the East was simply that in the more Greek and philosophic atmosphere which prevailed there, there

[1] Vol. II, pp. 295 f.

was a willingness to produce an alternative and more intellectually satisfying account of the cosmic significance of the work of Christ. Origen, for example, could afford to dispense with the literal interpretation of these apocalyptic symbols because he was willing to meet the Gnostics on their own speculative ground and work out a more systematic doctrine of cosmic redemption—whatever his success or failure in that attempt.

It must be emphasised, however, that the conservatism of the Western Fathers in this matter is not quite so stupid as might at first appear. I have already argued that the literal interpretation of a religious symbol does not necessarily destroy its value as such.[1] Whether it is treated as literally true or is consciously recognised as a myth, it can continue to express the same religious attitude on the part of the believer. I showed how this can be true of the myth of the beginning of the world and that therefore there is no reason why it should not be true of the myth of the end of the world. On these grounds it is possible to find some justification for the attitude of Irenaeus and the Western Fathers on this question of the literal fulfilment of the promises of apocalyptic literature.

When Irenaeus argues that such passages in the Bible must not be allegorised so as to make them refer only to super-celestial blessings, he is not advocating literalism simply for its own sake. He is not arguing so much against the interpretation of these apocalyptic symbols, as against their misinterpretation. It is one thing to interpret apocalyptic, as I have done, as a religious symbol, analogous to the creation myth, which expresses certain aspects of the ultimate meaning of history and of the world. It is another thing to allegorise it in such a way that it has no longer any reference to this material world at all, but refers only to a super-celestial, spiritual realm. It is against this latter interpretation that Irenaeus was arguing. The issue

[1] *Supra*, pp. 15 f.

of the former interpretation simply did not arise. Just as it was one aspect of Gnostic dualism to allegorise the creation myth in such a way as to dissociate the true God from the material world, so also it was another aspect of that same dualism to allegorise the promises associated with the final consummation of God's redeeming act, so that they, too, contained no reference to the material world. In so far as the issue was one between this kind of allegorising on the one hand and sheer literalism on the other, Irenaeus was right in taking the stand he did.

We have pointed out that the literal interpretation of what is essentially symbolic does not necessarily destroy its value as religious symbolism. But we must add this important qualification. If such a symbol continues to be interpreted literally at a time when that interpretation can no longer be integrated with the dominant beliefs and presuppositions in the culture of those who entertain it, then, for obvious reasons, its effectiveness as a symbol is considerably impaired. We have seen this happen in times that are almost within living memory in the case of the creation myth. While for many centuries its effectiveness as a symbol was quite independent of the conscious recognition of it as myth, a situation has now arisen in our culture which makes such conscious recognition a necessity.

In the case of the apocalyptic symbol, this situation arose much earlier in the church's life. Much more than the creation story, it was characteristically Jewish, whatever distant roots it may have had in the cultures of Persia, Greece and Babylon. I have already given recognition to the fact that the hope that a new world-age was about to be born had been entertained in a number of the cultures that were beginning to merge with one another around the Mediterranean basin in the young Roman Empire just before the Christian Era.[1] But none of these were quite the same as Jewish apocalyptic, which, despite its many

[1] *Supra*, pp. 43 ff.

and varied excursions into the realm of exuberant fancy, kept the covenant principle at its heart. Thus, from the very beginning, the Gentile world was never quite at home with this peculiarly Jewish thing. This difficulty became more and more acute as the popular spread of Stoicism gave an increasingly philosophical emphasis to the culture of the Roman Empire.

Thus, although Irenaeus and the other Fathers of the West were right in rejecting the kind of allegorising with which they had to contend in the Gnostic heretics, the extreme conservatism which induced them, in spite of their cultural environment, to insist on the literal acceptance of the Biblical symbols and studiously to avoid any attempt at re-interpretation, destroyed all possibility of the doctrine of cosmic redemption reaching the maturity of expression which it came so near to achieving in this period. In this form it could never become integrated with the rest of their religious thinking. Harnack's comment on the situation is :

> The union of a precise Christological Gnosis, such as we find in Irenaeus and Tertullian, with the retention in their integrity of the imaginative series of thoughts about Antichrist, Christ as the warrior hero, the double resurrection, and the kingdom of Glory in Jersualem, is really a historical novelty.[1]

But even Harnack, who has at no time shown himself very sympathetic in his appreciation of the apocalyptic symbol is forced to add :

> There is, however, no doubt that the strength of the old Catholic theology in opposition to the Gnostics lies in the accomplishment of this union, which, on the basis of the New Testament, appeared to the Fathers possible and necessary.[2]

But when the menace of Gnosticism had gone—or at

---

[1] *Op. cit.*, Vol. II, p. 297.   [2] *Loc. cit*, Book XX.

least had been driven to assume a less obviously heretical form within the church—the cosmic symbolism of apocalyptic became more and more a meaningless and unwelcome adjunct to the otherwise tidy system of the faith. This degenerate Chiliasm was rightly declared heretical in the middle of the fourth century. When Augustine identified the earthly kingdom of Christ with the present reign of the church and the saints on earth, the doctrine entered on a new phase which was to last right through the Mediaeval period. But the idea of cosmic redemption has never again featured in the forefront of the church's thinking as it did in those early centuries.

Conclusion. The criticisms which I offered of Aulen's treatment of what he calls " the classic idea of the Atonement " will now be more clear. The criticism was, in brief, that while he was right in asserting that in this early period the atoning work was conceived primarily in terms of the victory of Christ over the forces of evil—a victory won on a cosmic battlefield, and cosmic in its implications— he was wrong in treating this view of the Atonement as though it were one single, definite type of theory comparable to the more modern Anselmic and *Liberal* types of Atonement theory. In apocalyptic proper, where this *Christus Victor* conception has its main roots, one single and fairly definite conception runs through all the wide variety of symbol and disagreement in detail. Gentile Christianity inherited the idea from this source. It never quite knew what to make of it, however, so there was never really one agreed interpretation of it. This aspect of Atonement doctrine emerges in not one, but three main lines of thought.

(1) The Gnostics misinterpreted it entirely by so allegorising it that it had a purely spiritual reference, and dualistic implications. This challenged the church to re-interpret its cosmic implications. But on the one hand

(2) the Father of the Alexandrine school, whose interests

I

were sufficiently philosophical for them to attempt a real re-interpretation, were themselves so preoccupied with the Greek depreciation of matter, that they obscured the typically Jewish, physical reference of the symbol into insignificance. Though Origen's system formally asserts the regeneration of the whole physical cosmos, the real intention of his doctrine comes perilously near to the Gnostic dualism which he was combating.

(3) On the other hand, the Fathers of the West, typified for us by Irenaeus, were sufficiently conservative in their outlook to retain the Jewish, physical reference of the symbol, but this conservatism was so extreme that they scarcely attempted any re-interpretation at all, but simply reasserted the Biblical symbols with a literalism which was no longer possible in their cultural environment.

So between these various schools of thought, the doctrine of cosmic redemption, towards which Scripture seemed to point, fell, as it were, between three stools.

It will be obvious that while all of the foregoing is historical in form, it is not simply historical in intention. I have brought to light no new facts, nor have I tried to give an account of all the known facts relating to the development of these ideas. My interest throughout is systematic rather than historical. That is to say, my interest has not been in the many contingent factors which may have impinged in this way or that upon the development of the doctrine, but in the logical and systematic reasons for its development. In my first Part I tried to show that it was not by chance, but of practical and logical necessity that Biblical theology developed towards a doctrine of cosmic redemption. In this second Part I have tried to show that the same principle holds good in the period of patristic theology, even though they failed to arrive at an adequate formulation of the doctrine.

The idea of cosmic redemption never again figured so prominently in Christian theology. But the problem which first drove the early church to entertain such an idea persisted—the problem of the relation of the Redeeming Work to man's physical environment and its ills. In the next section we shall see how this problem persists, in very different forms, into modern times, and continues to drive us, as it drove the early church, to try to find some satisfactory interpretation of the cosmic significance of the work of Christ.

PART III

TRANSITION TO A NEW PHASE

CHAPTER IX

THE MIDDLE AGES

ALTHOUGH the notion of cosmic redemption can no longer be said to occupy the central position in the field of theological controversy which it did in the first centuries of the Christian era, the fundamental problems which it helped to answer still remain and are as live as ever. The form of the problem has changed very considerably, and we shall find that it is more in the field of secular philosophy than in that of theology that it has been raised. Also the form in which it has been raised by secular philosophy has not always been such as to make its theological importance immediately obvious. At the root of the problem, in its theological formulation, there lie the two questions :

(1) What is the relation of our physical environment, with all its apparent imperfections, to the ultimate values of goodness and holiness which we find in God ?

(2) What is the relation of God's redeeming act to this environment ?

Summary of the Argument of Parts I and II. We have seen how primitive Judaism, in the face of the various difficulties and hardships which the Jewish people encountered in their environment, was forced to choose between two alternative interpretations of the redemptive aspect of the Covenant. Either they could regard it as providing simply a release from their environment, thereby excluding that environment from the realm of those values which it is the purpose of God to realise in His creation. Or else they could relate the redemptive aspect of the Covenant in some positive way to their environment, so that the evil which appeared to be in it was somehow to be overcome. It was the latter alternative which they adopted. We illustrated this from the eschatological significance which they gave to the various events in their search for and conquest of the promised land.

This conception of the Covenant principle was widened in its reference and deepened in its spiritual meaning by the prophets. Its reference continued to widen with the ever-expanding horizon of the Jewish people until it finally acquired the all-inclusive reference of the cosmic symbolism of apocalyptic literature. It was against this background that the work of Jesus as the Christ was interpreted in the Synoptic Gospels and in Christian apocalyptic. This is the basis of the cosmic eschatology of Christianity.

Right at the very start of her life, however, the church encountered two serious difficulties in this doctrine. Firstly, the expected literal fulfilment of these apocalyptic promises was delayed. Secondly, there was the problem of interpreting them to the Gentile world.

As soon as these difficulties began to obscure the meaning of eschatology in its relation to physical environment, the old problem of the evil in that environment arose again with a new acuteness. This evil was symbolised by the demonic forces thought to be operative in the world, particularly those associated with the planets. In the face of these questionings, St. Paul attempted to re-formulate the cosmic eschatology of Christianity in such a way as to make its relevance to these problems more apparent. St. John followed him in this, giving Paul's re-formulation a more systematic expression. The difficulty, however, was not entirely overcome, and in the second and third centuries we find that the church at large was convinced that in some sense or other the Christ had won a cosmic victory, but rather bewildered as to what might be the exact significance of this victory.

The Gnostics, who were particularly concerned with the

problem of evil, raised the question in a more definite way than ever before. This challenge forced the church to make some statement of the place of the physical world in the redemptive scheme of things. An attempt at such a statement was made ; but, as we have seen, the Fathers of the Alexandrine school, who had the philosophic interest to attempt a real re-interpretation of the cosmic eschatology of the Bible, were themselves too much under the influence of the Greek depreciation of matter and thus compromised too far with the dualism which they were opposing. The Fathers of the West, on the other hand, were so extremely conservative that while they preserved the thoroughly physical reference of the apocalyptic symbolism, they merely reasserted it and did not provide the required re-interpretation.

The Mediaeval Dualism. This brief outline of the argument of the foregoing chapters shows how the problem of the relation of man's outward environment to the goodness and redeeming love of God runs through all the various phases in the development of cosmic eschatology which we have considered. During the Middle Ages, the problem did not arise with the same acuteness. This was due to the very clever casuistry[1] developed by the Mediaeval church, which, while it did not ultimately solve the problem, at least served as a working hypothesis. The Middle Ages managed to set the problem aside, first of all by defining evil in purely privative terms, and secondly by regarding the church as the repository of the *donum superadditum* in which the privations of the natural state are overcome. I do not intend to analyse this solution in any detail, but it is necessary to mention it, firstly in the interest of continuity, secondly as explaining the comparative insignificance of the ideas of cosmic Fall and redemption during this period, and thirdly as providing something of the background of the modern problem.

[1] I use this word without any pejorative connotation.

The treatment which St. Thomas Aquinas gives to the problem of evil shows how the necessity of the doctrine of cosmic Fall as a solution to the problems of theodicy was obviated.[1] Evil is mere deficiency, the absence of good. As deficiency, it has no positive existence, but only negative existence. Nor has it any formal cause. It has only an accidental cause. The reason why there must be deficiency is that while the perfection of God is single, the perfection of the creature has to be manifold. Therefore, in order that the perfection of God might be reflected in His creation, it is necessary that all degrees of goodness be manifest. Therefore some creatures must be less perfect than others. But God does not will this imperfection or deficiency for its own sake, but only for the sake of the perfection of the whole. Therefore its cause is only accidental. And so, while evil cannot be said to have any cause other than God, He cannot be blamed or held responsible for what has only an accidental cause.

So long as this view is maintained, there is clearly neither any need, nor any place for a doctrine of cosmic Fall, other than the Fall which occurred through Adam in the human race. There are, says Aquinas, two senses in which a thing can be perfect.[2] There is, first of all, the perfection of the form of the whole. Then there is the final perfection which is the end of the whole. Now the first perfection, which is that proper to nature, has never been lost, in that the various privations in nature merely represent different degrees of goodness, so that the whole represents the fulness of the goodness of God. What was lost at the Fall was the second perfection—the perfection which is the end of the whole. For the final perfection, which is the end of the whole universe, is the perfect beatitude of the saints.[3] But this properly does not belong

---

[1] *Summa Theologica*, P.I, QQ XLVIII and XLIX.
[2] P.I, Q LXXIII A1.   [3] *Loc. cit.*

to nature, but is a special, added unmerited favour which God bestows upon man.

In his state of innocence in Paradise before the Fall, man enjoyed this *donum indebitum*—this grace—in part, though not in full.[1] This was what man lost at the Fall (though he did regain something of it through penitence). But since grace does not belong to nature, but is held in sharp contrast with it, nothing from nature was lost at the Fall, but only this added extra. So nature retained the first perfection—the perfection of the formal completeness of the whole—which is the perfection proper to it as nature. What was lost was the second perfection—the perfection of the end. But this is a matter of grace rather than of nature.[2] Therefore, nature as such remained unimpaired.

As in the case of the Fall, so it was also in the case of redemption. The work of Christ was not an inward renewing of nature, but a restoring in fuller measure than ever before of the additional gift of grace.[3] The perfection of nature and the perfection of grace remain distinct throughout, each with its distinct cause. Aquinas says of the final consummation of the world that it

> existed previously in its causes, as to nature, at the first founding of the world, as to grace in the Incarnation of Christ.[4]

Nature does indeed participate in the final end of all things. It does this fully in so far as there is a union of nature and grace in man. The bodies of the saints enjoy immortality along with their souls and are transformed and transported into an empyrean heaven. But nature as a whole does not participate in this transfiguration. The transfiguration of man's body as he is taken up into heaven does not imply a transfiguration of nature as such, but rather the complete

[1] *Ibid.*, P.I, QQ XCIV—XCVII.
[2] *Ibid.*, P.I, Q LXXIII, A1, Reply Obj. 1.
[3] *Ibid.*, P.III, QQ VII—VIII.
[4] *Ibid.*, P.I, Q LXXIII, A1, Reply Obj. 1.

removal of man out of the realm of nature altogether.

In so far as nature as a whole participates in the final end, it does not do so as receiving any direct benefit from the work of Christ, but only in virtue of that natural goodness with which it was created[1]—a goodness independent of the additional gift of grace, and therefore unaffected by the Fall, in which grace was lost, and equally unaffected by the work of redemption, in which grace was restored.

Aquinas, of course, is not the whole theology of the Middle Ages. But his attitude to nature and the sharp contrast in which he holds the concepts of grace and nature is largely typical of the whole world-outlook of the church in this great period of her life. Formally this contrast between nature and grace cannot be said to represent a dualism in that both have their origin in the goodness of the one Creator. But despite this formal monism, it does represent a covert dualism. It is true that there is only one Creator, but there are two distinct creations which exist, as it were, side by side, and have very little organic relationship with one another. There is the realm of grace to which the angels and man, in his unfallen state or in his redeemed state, belong. In sharp contrast with this there is the realm of nature to which this physical world in the main belongs. In comparison, this is a very poor affair, not because it has become involved in man's fallen situation, but simply because it was made so by God. By the casuistry of describing the evils of the realm of nature in purely privative terms, the implied dualism was obscured so that it became more of a duality than a dualism. But the practical outcome was the same. The evils of present environment—be they described in positive or negative terms—were regarded as essential to it, and therefore redemption was ultimately to be conceived in terms of escape from that environment and as in no way involving its restoration or transfiguration.

[1] *Ibid.*, P.II, Q I, A8.

It has, of course, always been an essential part of the Christian Gospel, and of the apocalyptic tradition in which it first expressed itself, to contrast " this world " with " the world to come ". Such a contrast is essential to any eschatological view of the world. Christianity does despair of this world as such. But I have already tried to show how this despair is not such as to exclude this world from the reference of the final hope in which that despair is transcended, and which is expressed in the symbol of the world to come.[1] On the other hand, the Mediaeval contrast between nature and grace is exclusive. Nature has an inferior goodness of its own which is appropriate to it. The realm of grace has a superior and sanctified goodness and from this realm nature as a whole is permanently excluded. The difference between the early " classic " view of the work of Christ as the restorer of all nature, and the Mediaeval view of Christ as the bringer of the extra, supranatural gift of grace may be illustrated by a comparison of the attitude to nature which we find in Irenaeus, and that of Augustine, who was, more than any other, the founder of the covert dualism of the Middle Ages.

Augustine is perfectly prepared to admit the goodness of nature. Indeed, he describes it with unrestrained enthusiasm.[2] But he hastens to add :

Yet all these are but solaces of man's miseries, in no way pertinent to his glories.[3]

That is to say, even the goodness of this world has no significance whatever when we speak in terms of the benefits bestowed in Christ. The hope which we have in Christ bears no relation to this world whatsoever.

In Irenaeus, on the other hand, there are not two orders of goodness, but only one. All goodness, whether it belongs to this world or to the final consummation, is a

[1] *Supra*, pp. 13 ff.   [2] *De Civitate Dei*, 22.23.   [3] *Ibid.*, 23.

manifestation of the grace of God.   It is the same grace of
God which sustains nature even in its fallen state and
which confers salvation in Jesus Christ.   The residual
goodness in nature can even be regarded as an anticipation
or foretaste of that salvation.[1] The same difference
appears also in Irenaeus' attitude to the sacraments as
compared with that of the church of the Middle Ages.
For Irenaeus, the union of spiritual and material benefit in
the Eucharist symbolises the ultimate unity of nature and
grace implied in Christian salvation.[2] But for Aquinas,
the fact that the sacraments are administered in a material
element is merely God's gracious concession to man's
regrettably sensuous nature.[3] For Irenaeus, the Incarnation and saving work of Jesus Christ meant that the promise
of grace was held out to the whole of nature, and that
henceforth nothing could be called common or unclean.
For the church of the Middle Ages, on the other hand,
nature was essentially common, and, if not positively
unclean, at least seriously deficient in the shining whiteness
of the saints in the empyrean heaven, and essentially
incapable of sharing in such glory.

This covert dualism of nature and grace determined the
whole world-view of the Mediaeval church, and expressed
itself practically in the dualism of church and world, of
spiritual and temporal.   The church, with the incarnate
Christ as her head, was the only point in which nature and
grace impinged on one another.   The whole church, both
in heaven and on earth, was the realm of grace and the
repository of the *donum supernaturale*, which it dispensed
through the sacraments.   To this extent, the visible church
did represent a real union of nature and grace.   Such union
as there was came about only by way of special miracle,
not by way of any transfiguration of nature as such.
Every celebration of the sacrament was a new and special
miracle.   The rood screen, whatever its historical origin,

[1] *Supra*, pp. 105 ff.   [2] *Supra*, p. 106 f.   [3] *Op. cit.*, P.III, Q LXI, A1.

became the symbol of the division of secular and temporal, clergy and laity, the realm of grace and the realm of nature.

This is not simply a recurrence of the acute dualism which we considered in Gnosticism. It is quite a different thing and has a character of its own. It is not a blatant and obvious dualism. Formally considered, it is a monistic view of the world in that it does not trace grace and nature to two different gods, but to a double act of creation in the one true God. But of this double creation one part was essentially inferior to the other. And even though that inferiority is described in terms of privation rather than in terms of positive evil, its practical outcome in relation to the doctrine of cosmic redemption was the same as that of the Gnostic dualism. It meant that the hardships and evils in and associated with man's physical environment could be accounted for as inevitably arising from an essential defectiveness in nature without in any way blaming or holding the true God responsible for that defectiveness. Therefore His ways were already justified in nature, and the question of cosmic redemption did not arise.

The wide acceptance of this world-view kept the problem at bay for a full thousand years, and it was only with the dissolution of this covert dualism in the cultural Renaissance and the Protestant Reformation that the modern problem began to take shape. On the one hand, the growing respect for nature as such, which the whole Renaissance movement expressed, especially in its later phase,[1] denied the privative conception of the natural order on which the Mediaeval dualism rested. On the other hand, the attack of the Protestant Reformers on Roman Catholic sacramentalism and their assertion of the priesthood of all believers was a denial of the other side of this dualism—the conception of the church as the repository of the *donum superadditum*.

[1] *Cf.* Basil Willey, *The Seventeenth-Century Background*, pp. 24–40.

If it was only the dualistic structure of Mediaeval theology which prevented the problem of cosmic redemption from arising as a central issue, it might be expected that as soon as this dualism had been broken down, the whole issue of the relation of the evils in and associated with our physical environment to the goodness of God and His redeeming Act would arise again with the same acuteness and centrality as it had in the early centuries of the church before the Mediaeval dualism was established. But this did not in fact occur. The idea of cosmic redemption did not immediately arise as a central theological issue. But this is easily understandable when we consider the main emphasis and enthusiasm of the Protestant Reformation. The rediscovery of the principle of justification by faith and the emphasis upon it, over against the principle of salvation through the objective efficacy of the sacraments, left the whole Protestant movement very much preoccupied with problems of inner personal experience. This emphasis has tended to persist in Protestantism right down to the present. Therefore, in strictly theological circles, while the idea of cosmic redemption has received occasional lip-service, it has never become the central issue which it was before the Mediaeval dualism arose.

CHAPTER X

THE EFFECT OF THE RENAISSANCE

THE Renaissance changed the face of the whole problem to such an extent that it is at first difficult to realise that it is still the same problem that we are dealing with. The corpus of scientific knowledge, which began to develop in the Italian Renaissance, and is only now beginning to show the fulness of its growth, was a new thing. In the experimental method which it developed, it was not like anything that had gone before. It established the distinction between scientific knowledge and other kinds of knowledge with a clarity and emphasis which had never before been recognised. Scientific knowledge was experimentally verifiable and therefore "certain". It was thus sharply distinguished from any element in human knowledge which was not open to such experimental verification.

The action of the church in attempting to suppress the results of these earliest attempts to apply the experimental method systematically to the realm of nature has often been criticised, and rightly so. But it is often criticised for the wrong reasons. It is suggested that this was simply a case of the church meddling in affairs that did not concern her. The presupposition which lies behind this criticism is that the scientist is in no way concerned with the articles of religion. His function is to describe the facts and to show their relations to one another. The faith of the church is not concerned with the same facts, or if it is concerned with them, is not concerned with them in the same way. This may well be true, and it is a position which is certainly widely adopted today. But it is only

after one has known modern science and the kind of knowledge which it offers and accepted it for what it is, that
this conception of the relation between religious and
scientific knowledge becomes acceptable. Until one has
accepted modern scientific knowledge for what it is, it is
not at all so obvious that the rise of such a science had no
direct bearing on the church's faith.

The ground for the church's concern at these new
developments was not simply that the findings of men like
Copernicus and Galileo contradicted the cosmology, both
of the Bible and of Aristotle. A much more fundamental
issue was involved. At any moment of consciousness, a
person's awareness of his physical environment is made up
not only of the simple awareness of sense data, but also of
a vast number of vaguely formulated judgments. Of these,
some simply describe and relate objective facts, such as
" This is red ". Then there are others of which it is
difficult to say whether they simply describe given fact or
subjective reaction. These are judgments which ascribe to
the situation such qualities as beautiful, ugly, noble, sub-
lime, horrible, mysterious, and so on.[1] In normal experience, all these different kinds of judgment flash quickly
through our minds without being very clearly differentiated
one from another. For instance, if I stand on the shore
and look out to sea, I am at once aware of the sea as blue-
green, as flaked with white, as exhibiting the properties of
water, as beautiful, as mysterious, as vast and frightening.
I may in this or that moment direct my attention to this
or that group of judgments which pass through my mind,
but the sum of them go to make up the unity of experience.
However, when I begin to apply the experimental method

[1] The terms " objective fact " and " subjective reaction " are, of course,
question-begging expressions. But it is only *after* one has offered a solution
to the epistemological problems here involved that one can be precise
about such a distinction. Therefore we must make do with such vague
expressions as this for the time being. While recognising that they are
not ultimately legitimate expressions, one is aware of the kind of distinction
to which they refer. Thus they will serve our purpose until the occasion
for more accurate treatment presents itself. (*Infra*, pp. 159 ff.)

of investigation systematically to the world, then I isolate certain judgments which record simple observations of fact from all the other types of judgment which normally form the background to those observations. In so doing, I create what we may call a " laboratory situation ", where certain aspects of experience are isolated from their context in experience as a whole. For if I am to apply the experimental method systematically, I must confine myself to those judgments which will submit to experimental verification.

However useful this may have been as a technique of investigation, it did mean, among other things, that all religious reference was deliberately excluded from serious systematic investigation of the physical universe. The pioneers of modern science were not concerned to deny that certain theological and philosophical propositions might be true. But their strict use of experimental method, involving as it did the exclusion of any reference to such propositions, meant that, for purposes of science, they treated the world as though it had no transcendental significance such as might be ascribed to it in theological propositions.

This did raise an issue which genuinely concerned the church. It meant that a very important aspect of human culture, namely the study of nature, was being formed into a closed system from which all reference to God was deliberately excluded. This was a new and significant development in the history of man, and the church was aware of its dangers. Regarded in this light, one can see the deeper significance of the injunction of Pope Urban VIII that Galileo could publish his *Dialogue on the Two Chief Systems of the World* (which was concerned chiefly with a discussion of the tides) only on condition that he conclude with the argument :

God is all-powerful. All things are possible to Him. Therefore the tides cannot be adduced as necessary proof of the double motion of the earth without limiting His Omnipotence.[1]

Fundamentally this is simply a protest against the formation of an autonomous compartment of knowledge in which theological propositions and other propositions of a similar kind are deliberately treated as irrelevant.

However, the advantages of the new and rapidly developing scientific method were too great to be foregone so lightly. The objectivity and apparent certainty of knowledge proved by experimental verification justified its claim to stand apart as a separate system from opinions which did not lend themselves so easily to the same kind of objective verification. The division of European culture into a number of more or less autonomous compartments after the Renaissance has been too frequently remarked upon to require any discussion here. But this distinction between experimentally verifiable propositions and those whose truth must be otherwise established had an important effect on men's attitude to the physical world, and it is of this particular point that we must here take note.

Propositions which ascribe any kind of religious significance to the world are all of the kind which do not lend themselves to simple experimental verification in the sense in which the propositions of science can be verified. It may be difficult to say how, in fact, they are verified. But at least this negative statement about their verification may be easily assented to. Empirical evidence—the evidence of experience—is certainly important in their verification. But all genuinely religious judgments (as distinct from theological propositions, which may or may not involve religious judgment) involve a reference, either explicit or implicit, to God or to some transcendent quality, such as " the Holy ". Now God, or " the Holy " or any of the transcendent factors which we appear to encounter

---

[1] *Cf.* Charles Singer, *Science, Religion and Reality*, p. 135.

in religious experience cannot be treated as the simple objects of scientific investigation. The employment of such a method presupposes a denial of their transcendence.

This affects not only those judgments which are of an explicitly religious character, but even those more primary judgments which, while not being obviously religious in themselves, often lead us to ascribe religious significance to the world. To this class belong judgments, such as : " The sea is vast and mysterious " or " There is a noble sublimity in these hills ". Whatever is the correct method of verifying such propositions, it is certainly not scientific experiment—or if it is, then they are essentially meaningless and unverifiable. Therefore all our judgments of this kind are excluded from the corpus of scientific knowledge.

Within the total *Gestalt* of any given moment of experience, judgments of the kind in which we record simple sense-data are held together with judgments in which we record the moral, aesthetic and religious factors in the situation. They are held together within the unity of consciousness. But through the influence of post-Renaissance science, the system of knowledge in which we interpret such a moment of experience, or any other moment of experience, has come to be divided into at least two main groups of propositions, the one group bearing very little systematic relation to the other. They simply co-exist. On the one hand, there is the class of propositions which state the objectively verifiable facts, and on the other hand, a class— or several classes— of propositions referring to other factors in the situation which do not lend themselves to this kind of treatment.

The result of this dichotomy is seen writ large in the development of European culture in the seventeenth century and afterwards. That aspect of experience which lends itself to experimental treatment, divorced from the original unity of experience, expressed itself in a growing positivism. The remaining aspects of experience, equally divorced from the original unity, expressed themselves in an unrealistic romanticism. One could describe the world in terms of one type of proposition or the other, but both could not be held together in any kind of systematic unity.

Thus the world of objectively observable phenomena became separated from any significance which it might have in terms of ultimate religious values. At root, this was an epistemological and logical difficulty, but it soon began to reflect itself in metaphysical theory. In Descartes, the first great philosopher of the new science, the only point of direct contact between the physical world and the realm of religious values was the pineal gland which he mistakenly believed to be peculiar to man and therefore the seat of the soul. In this tiny organ alone all the mystery of creation was concentrated. All the rest was a mere mechanical system and nothing more. The division of knowledge into two main sections thus tended to reflect itself in a dual view of the universe. On the one hand, the world was pure system and an appropriate object of scientific investigation ; yet on the other hand, there appeared to be a very important element in reality which was the object of moral and religious judgment. But there seemed to be no positive relationship between them whatsoever.

In the face of this situation, any reference to " cosmic redemption " becomes a meaningless confusion of two entirely alien languages. It would appear, on the face of it at least, that the doctrine of cosmic redemption belongs with the demons, astrology, the geocentric universe and all the other rejected errors of an outmoded culture. At any rate, the Church, both Protestant and Catholic, being preoccupied with other more immediate and pressing problems, was content to regard it as such or else to pay only lip-service to the doctrine, letting the matter rest until the last trump should settle the question once and for all.

But if the theological doctrine fell thus into abeyance, the problems which it had once helped to solve could not be so easily dismissed. We have seen how it was only the covert dualism of Mediaeval theology which kept these problems at bay. With the dissolution of Mediaeval Christian culture they reappeared in an acute form and in a new guise. In their theological formulation these problems had centred on the question of the relation of our physical environment, with all its apparent imperfections, to the ultimate values of goodness and holiness implied in the idea of God. But it was not within the theological thinking of the church that these problems reasserted themselves. It was in the field of secular philosophy that they aroused real vexation and perplexity. Or rather one should say it was the philosophical problem which immediately underlies these specifically theological questions.

We have already recognised that the problem of evil has two aspects : the ontological, which is concerned with the existential separation of the self and the world from God ; and the moral, which is concerned with moral and physical evil in relation to the goodness of God. In the secular, philosophical context in which these problems arose after the Renaissance, the problem of the existential separation of the world from God became that of the relation of the phenomenal world to Reality. The problem of the existential separation of the individual from God became that of the relation of the conscious self to the Reality which he seeks to know. The moral problem became that of the relation of the phenomenal world to the absolute values with which the inner personal life is concerned.

The form of the questions is greatly changed. They had once been framed in terms of a demon-possessed universe. Now they are framed in terms of epistemology and metaphysics. It is a far cry from one to the other. But the inner meaning of the questions is essentially the same. The church had once tried to solve these problems in terms of a doctrine of cosmic redemption. It is an interesting coincidence that German Idealism, working independently on this entirely new formulation of the problem, culminated in Hegel with what is, if not a doctrine of cosmic redemption, at least the only great attempt in modern times to interpret the whole cosmic process in terms of the person and work of the Christ.

Any attempt at a serious interpretation of the doctrine of cosmic redemption cannot afford to ignore this modern, philosophical phase of the problems underlying it. For it is only by relating the primitive doctrine to these modern formulations of the problem that we can hope to reach a statement of it in terms which are significant within the context of the entirely new cultural situation which has developed since the Renaissance.

Competent treatment of this phase of the problem involves a fair amount of purely philosophical analysis. Moreover, the complete change, not only in the language, but in the very concepts in which the problem is couched, gives the impression that we have departed entirely from our original argument. This is tiresome, but must be borne with if we are to reach the heart of the problem. When this is done, perhaps the ultimate unity of the problem in all its phases will be more evident.

CHAPTER XI

THE KANTIAN SOLUTION

THE scientific Renaissance emphasised the contrast between man's outward environment and his inner spiritual nature. It emphasised the incongruity of the determinate laws governing physical environment with the religious and moral aspirations of personal life. What had once been conceived as the enmity of the demons in nature to personal life was now recognised simply as the sheer moral indifference of the natural order.

The basis for this sharp dichotomy between experimentally verifiable propositions and those whose truth appeared to rest on other considerations was the peculiar kind of objectivity and " certainty " which seemed to pertain to the former. This raised two fundamental problems for philosophy :

(1) What is the epistemological basis for this objectivity and " certainty " in scientific propositions ?

(2) If there is a real epistemological basis for this distinction, how are the two types of proposition related to one another within the total system of knowledge ?

These problems became the major interest of post-Renaissance philosophy. Three main types of solution emerged : that of the Rationalists on the Continent, that of the Empiricist school in Britain, and finally the solution of Kantian Idealism, which was, in a sense, a synthesis of the other two approaches, and yet at the same time a distinctive and independent development.

The choice of Kant as the philosopher in whom we can illustrate the relevance of these formal problems to our special theological interest is a random one in that the

point could be illustrated from either the Rationalists or
the Empiricists. But Kant commends himself for this
purpose in that the issue is clearer in him, and his treatment
of it is more directly related to the Hegelian attempt to
refer the ultimate solution of these problems to the work
of Christ.

The Kantian solution is one which at once confirms and
discredits the distinctively scientific type of knowledge.
He confirms it by contending that the fixity and consistency in the structure of experience, which is a condition
of the successful employment of the experimental method
as a source of reliable knowledge, is not to be considered as
a contingent factor among the other " given ", contingent
factors in experience. Rather than belonging to the
contingent " given ", this structure is the structure of the
understanding itself. It is guaranteed in the categories
of the understanding and in space and time as the outward
and inward form of experience. Wherever there is empirical awareness it must come through the understanding, and
therefore in these categories and forms. Therefore this
structure in experience is necessarily constant.

This necessary fixity of structure in experience was held
by Kant to provide an epistemological justification for the
certainty ascribed to experimentally verified propositions.
Scientific propositions were thus confirmed as providing
reliable knowledge. But they were at the same time dis-
credited in that it was a condition of their certainty that
they be regarded as describing reality only as it appears to
the understanding, and not as it is in itself— as descriptions
of *phenomena* and not of *noumena*. The guarantee of the
necessary truth of the propositions of science, namely the
necessity for the understanding to apprehend all experience
in terms of its own subjective structure, was also the
condemnation of such propositions as descriptions of mere
appearance.

But moral knowledge appeared to Kant to be in quite a

different situation. The unconditional, categorical nature of the moral imperative implies its independence of empirical considerations. It is in practical reason, the principle of the moral Will, that we have knowledge of this imperative. Thus moral knowledge, as being independent of the categories of the understanding, is real knowledge of the noumenal world. The Will, as being free, transcends the category of causality and all the other categories of the understanding, and belongs to the noumenal world. Therefore immediate knowledge of noumenal reality in the rational principles of the moral Will is possible. So, too, the judgments of religious faith (in so far as Kant's conception of faith can be said to involve anything that can be called knowledge) are referred to the noumenal world and remain unaffected by and unrelated to our judgments about the empirical world.[1]

Now what Kant did in adopting this position was to accept what was already a *de facto* dichotomy in European culture and, by making a critique of reason, to uncover what he took to be the epistemological basis for such a dichotomy. In emphasising the dichotomy as he did, he not only succeeded in suggesting a possible basis for the objective certainty of scientific truths, but managed to do this in such a way as not to prejudice the validity of moral judgment or the judgments of faith. But this was done at the cost of sacrificing the unity of knowledge and by adopting a metaphysic which reflected the dichotomy of knowledge in the sharp division between phenomenal appearance and noumenal reality. The world of ultimate moral and religious values was held strictly apart from the ordinary world of outward experience.

The Religious Significance of the Kantian Solution. This strict separation of the sphere of phenomenal experience from the sphere of ultimate moral and religious value meant

[1] These few paragraphs cannot be regarded as a full statement of Kant's position. Such a statement would inevitably be fairly lengthy. But the above is a sufficient statement for our present purpose.

that any statement about our empirical environment could not as such have any ultimate moral or religious significance, and any properly moral or religious statements could not directly imply any judgments about the empirical world. Judgments about our immediate environment were inevitably judgments of the empirical understanding, whereas moral and religious judgments must be judgments of practical reason, without any empirical reference. A philosophy of morals which permits any mingling of these two kinds of judgment is not worthy of the name " since by this confusion it even spoils the purity of morals themselves, and contradicts its own end ".[1]

Whatever be the element of truth contained in this position, it not merely negates the idea of cosmic redemption in the sense of the inclusion of human environment within the reference of the redemptive work of Christ, but it even makes the meaningful formulation of any such doctrine impossible. If propositions about our immediate environment can bear no systematic relation to propositions about the moral and religious values implied in the idea of redemption, then it is impossible to speak meaningfully about the redemption of immediate environment. Thus the only moral judgment which Kant can make about the phenomenal world as a whole, is one which asserts its moral indifference.[2]

This sharp duality of the moral and the natural has some serious implications of which Kant was well aware. It means that man, though an essentially moral being, is always living in an environment which is essentially amoral and entirely cut off from the realm of moral values. It is this situation which gives rise to what Kant calls " the antinomy of practical reason ". He describes it in these terms :

The practical connection of causes and effects in the

---

[1] *Kant's Ethics* (tr. Abbott), p. 5.   [2] *Ibid.*, pp. 209 f. and p. 221.

world, as a result of the determination of the will, does not depend upon the moral disposition of the will, but on the knowledge of the laws of nature and the physical power to use them for one's purposes ; consequently we cannot expect in the world by the most punctilious observance of the moral laws any necessary connection of happiness with virtue adequate to the *summum bonum*.[1]

Now this is simply a recurrence of the very same problem as that which we have found continually appearing as a determining factor in the development of the doctrine of cosmic redemption—the problem of the relation of physical environment to the moral and religious values which it is the end of man's life to realise.   In its theological formulation, we have found that this problem continually presents us with the alternative of accepting either a dualistic view of the world or else some doctrine of cosmic redemption which resolves the dilemma.   It was this problem which was solved for primitive Judaism in terms of the idea of the promised land.   It was essentially the same problem which vexed the prophets and which, in turn, was solved for them by a wider application and a deeper understanding of the Covenant promises.   It was essentially the same problem that was answered by a further extension of these principles in the cosmic imagery of apocalyptic eschatology. On the other hand, when the apocalyptic symbol was no longer understood and was thus no longer effective as an answer to the problem, it was this same problem—the problem of the evil or moral indifference of man's physical environment—which drove the Gnostics to adopt the alternative conclusion in a dualistic view of the world. And it was the same problem which determined the nature of the church's answer to that heretical dualism in a reassertion of the relevance of the saving work of Christ to the whole of creation.   Again, it was only by a covert

[1] *Ibid.*, p. 209.

dualism that the same problem was kept at bay during the Middle Ages. And now in Kant, in a secular context, it appears again in the antinomy of practical reason. So in spite of appearances, we have not really moved so far away from our central problem.

Kant's solution was indeed a theological one. But it is a solution which leaves the immediate duality of nature and morality unresolved and asserts it to be essentially unresolvable. He was aware of the relevance of Christian eschatology to the problem. Commenting on the lack of moral justice in nature, he says :

> Now Christian morality supplies this defect (of the second indispensable element of the *summum bonum*)[1] by representing the world in which rational beings devote themselves with all their souls to the moral law, as a *kingdom of God*, in which nature and morality are brought into a harmony foreign each to itself, by a holy Author who makes the derived *summum bonum* possible. *Holiness* of life is prescribed to them as a rule even in this life, while the welfare proportioned to it, namely, *bliss*, is represented as attainable only in eternity ; because the *former* must always be the pattern of their conduct in every state, and progress towards it is already possible and necessary in this life ; while the *latter*, under the name of happiness, cannot be attained at all in this world (so far as our own power is concerned), and therefore is made simply an object of hope.[2]

Kant is, of course, perfectly right in maintaining that the final fulfilment of the kingdom of God " is represented as attainable only in eternity ". There is no question that this is a correct interpretation of New Testament teaching. But as we have already pointed out at some length, it is quite wrong to take this as implying a purely negative attitude to the world of nature as it exists in time. Kant does, it is true, treat the kingdom of God as immanent in

---

[1] Namely a just apportionment of happiness to virtue.
[2] *Op. cit.*, pp. 225–226.

this world in the moral determination of the Will. But this is simply because the act of moral decision in its pure form belongs to the transcendental, noumenal world, and not to the phenomenal world.

Any suggestion of the immanence of the kingdom of God in the phenomenal world is for Kant a sheer impossibility and a contradiction in terms. Thus, while the kingdom of God may be immanent in the inner moral life, it has no significance for the outward physical world at all. The hope of an eventual harmony between morality and nature is thus directed entirely away from the present towards a transcendental world which is intelligible rather than sensible, and of which we can say nothing in our present condition other than that in it there is a just apportionment of happiness to virtue. This is the only sense in which nature is brought into harmony with morality.

Thus the duality of the moral realm and the realm of phenomenal experience remains unbroken. The resultant position is one which, despite the wide divergence in the concepts employed, has essentially the same theological implications as the Gnostic dualism which the early church had to counter by reasserting the cosmic significance of the work of Christ. This, of course, is the kind of parallel which we can draw only in the most guarded terms and with extreme caution. The suggestion is not that Kant and certain of the Gnostic schools were really saying the same thing. On the contrary, as regards the actual content of their thought, they are so far removed from one another that even comparison is difficult. The typical Gnostic speculations about the nature of the Pleroma and the relations of the spiritual beings therein are just the kind of speculations that Kant would disallow as involving the transcendental employment of the categories of the understanding, or else would simply dismiss as " fantastical theosophical dreams ".[1]

[1] *Ibid.*, p. 219.

It is not so much a similarity between the content of Kantian philosophy and the content of the Gnostic speculations that I am suggesting.   The only real similarity is in the practical religious outcome—that is, in the way it affects our religious attitude to our immediate situation in this physical world, the world in which we act.   It is in this respect (but only in this respect) that we may justifiably compare the noumenal world of Kant with the Pleroma of the Gnostics.

For Kant, it was in our experience of the noumenal world that the holiness of God is known and His existence implied, and it is in this realm that the kingdom of God is realised. Correspondingly, the Gnostic Pleroma is the realm of the true God, and the realm of the true religious values which the revealed *gnosis* brings to light.   The Kantian noumenal world is conceived as being of an intelligible nature as contrasted with immediate environment, which is sensible. The Gnostic Pleroma is conceived as being spiritual and invisible as contrasted with this world, which is material and visible.   The visible phenomenal world in Kant is, by its essential nature as mere appearance, excluded from any participation in the moral and religious values realised in the noumenal world.   In Gnostic dualism the visible material world is excluded, by its essential nature as matter, from any participation in the values realised in the Pleroma.

It is true that, for Kant, this simply meant that the phenomenal world as such has no moral significance whatever, while for the Gnostics it meant that physical environment was positively evil.   But in the long run, the practical effect is the same ; for in relation to the idea of the *summum bonum*, the sheer amorality of the phenomenal world becomes itself an evil.

This means that, for Kant, as for the Gnostics, the final aim of the religious life was to escape from immediate environment into a realm of spiritual values.   To this process our immediate phenomenal experience remains ultimately irrelevant. The real determining factor with regard to our eternal destiny is simply the moral determination of the Will in accordance with the principles of practical reason. This belongs, not to the phenomenal world, but to the noumenal world. This duality in Kant's analysis of experience has often been criticised on the grounds that it is only by action in the phenomenal world that duty can be fulfilled and only on the basis of the phenomenal evidence of such action that a man can be judged to have acted rightly. Even his motive must be judged by phenomenal evidence.[1] Surely, therefore, it is argued, there must be some more positive relation between the phenomenal world and the realm of moral values.

In inviting this criticism, the Kantian system is again similar in its practical outcome to the Gnostic dualism, at which Irenaeus levels the parallel criticism that, since it is in the body that acts that are deemed righteous are performed, the righteousness or the reward thereof cannot be entirely dissociated from the body.[2]

Finally, we can compare the astrological background to Gnosticism with the astronomical background to Kant. Nowadays we do not think of astrology as a science, and the surviving manifestations of it are rightly treated as mere superstition. But in its own day it did represent a real scientific advance and was associated with a considerable amount of careful observation of the movements of the stars—observations which, in themselves, were on a thoroughly scientific basis, whatever other beliefs may have come to be associated with them. Astrology was founded on the Ptolemaic astronomy, and the transition from the more primitive world-view to that spherical and systematic conception of the universe was just as great a cultural

[1] Kant, of course, was well aware of this difficulty in his position and seemed prepared to accept its consequences in that he recognised that it is impossible for us, if we accept his system, to be perfectly sure whether any act is really moral and whether, at any time, there ever was such a thing as a truly moral act. *Cf.* Abbott, *op. cit.*, p. 23 f.

[2] *Adversus Haereses*, 2.29.

L

upheaval as the transition from the Ptolemaic to the Copernican and Newtonian conceptions in more recent times. Then, as in the time of Newton, there was a real conflict between science and religion.

Robert Eisler, to whom Burkitt refers[1] as giving the best account of the growth and development of this tension in primitive cultures, distinguishes between the mystical or religious cosmologies which represent the world as being in some sense the " dwelling-place " of man—as a great tent, or house, or temple—and an entirely different line of development in cosmological theory which describes the universe primarily in terms of system.[2] To this latter line of development, the Ptolemaic world-view belongs. The spread of the Ptolemaic theory and the *Weltanschauung* which it implied created a crisis for culture at the beginning of the Christian era, just as the Copernican astronomy and its complement in the Newtonian physics created a new crisis in more recent times. The transition from the conception of the world as the house or dwelling-place of man to that of the universe as a system of concentric spheres seemed to carry with it certain implications. In the words of F. C. Burkitt :

This view immensely enhanced the importance of each planet. It was no longer a tiny point of light mys-

---

[1] F. C. Burkitt, *The Church and Gnosis*, p. 30.

[2] " Die lange noch gleichnisweise fortlebende Kosmologie der ältesten griechischen Philosophen, des Pherekydes, der die Welt als siebenwinkelige Höhle wie das Heiligtum der Mithraisten den sichtbaren Himmel als Zeltbau, wie das babylonische ' Hirtenzelt der Welt ' auffasst, des Anaximines und Heraklit, die die Sonne nachts hinter dem Nordberg verschwinden lassen, des Parmenides, der von der Himmelsmauer, und der Orphiker, die von der viersäuligen μέγαρον der Welt sprechen, des Anaximander, der wie die Perser, Inder und die nachexilischen Juden von Kosmischen Sternenrädern spricht und zu oberst die Sonne, darunter den Mond, zu unterst die Sterne kreisen lässt, gehört einer ganz andern Entwicklungsreihe an als die stolze Folge von Systemen die in einer verhältnismässig kurtzen Spanne Zeit, von den primitivsten Gleichnissen der alten Mystik, vom Ei, von der Nuss oder dem Apfel herauffuhrt biszum System des Ptolemäus einerseits, zu den unvergänglichen gedanken eines Aristarch von Samos anderseits." Robert Eisler, *Weltenmantel und Himmelszelt*, p. 630 f.

teriously wandering among the other heavenly bodies. To the believer in the Ptolemaic astronomy it was the Lord of a Sphere which encased the Earth itself. If it was high or low above the ground, nearer or further from other heavenly bodies, it seemed reasonable to suppose that it exerted a special influence on the Earth and its inhabitants. And along with this belief there was another, intimately bound up with the scientific character of the Ptolemaic system. " Planets " might indeed be " wandering stars ", and the rules of their courses were very imperfectly known even to the most learned astronomers, but the very observations that had led to the excogitation of the system had taught the compara-tive regularity and inevitableness with which the heavenly bodies, planets included, do move. If then the planets (or their spheres) had an influence on men, that influence came inevitably and inexorably. Astrology as a doctrine is a doctrine of Fate, of inevitable and inexorable Fate.[1]

The implication seemed to be that the world was not simply the dwelling-place of man, but rather a mighty system of inexorable forces within which man was im-potently enmeshed. Thus, this whole enmeshing planetary system came to represent to the people of that era all the evils in and associated with physical environment. There-fore the problems raised by this scientific view of the world and its astrological associations became a central concern for the Gnostics in their treatment of the problem of evil. How could man be saved from this impersonal, uncontrol-able, machine-like situation ? How could he enter into that fullness and freedom of life for which he longed ? The obvious answer was that he could only do so by escaping from this whole, vast, enmeshing, material system into a realm more suited to the development of personal life.

This was the kind of answer that was typical of the Gnostic schools. But it led them into a dualistic philo-sophy which denied the union of the divine with true

[1] *Op. cit.*, pp. 32–33.

human flesh in Christ.   Therefore the church had to reject
it and provide an alternative answer to the problem of evil
as it was represented by this whole enmeshing system of
the inexorable movements of the stars.   This answer, as
we have seen, lay in a reassertion of the cosmic significance
of the work of Christ, so that He became Lord of the
powers in the stars themselves, as well as Lord of human life.

Now the parallel between this situation and the situation
which arose within the secular context of German Idealism
is very close.   During the Middle Ages men had grown
accustomed to the Ptolemaic universe and had lost their
fear of this vast, impersonal system.   This sense of security
was largely mediated through the church and the promises
associated with the sacraments.   Then two things happened.   For a number of reasons the whole religious
structure of Mediaeval life began to break down, and at the
same time there came a new and even more frightening
revolution in astronomy.   When the findings of Copernican
astronomy began to establish themselves in the popular
mind, an entirely new threat appeared.   Man was no
longer simply " shut in " by the universe.   Rather, he was
lost amid its boundless space and ceaseless motion, and had
no place of his own at all.   Then as a development of this
theme, there came the Newtonian physics which seemed
to imply the universal reign of the laws of motion.   Thus,
instead of being enclosed within an impersonal system
which menaced his personal life, man appeared to be in
danger of discovering that he was simply part of the
system and that personal life was an illusion in any case.
What had been the menace of Fate at the beginning of the
Christian era under the Ptolemaic astronomy, now, under
Newtonian physics, became the menace of sheer determinism.   This was related to the development of the
whole new experimental technique in science.

The result was that the world-view which was engendered
by the new science came to represent certain aspects of the

problem of evil in a manner very different from, but quite parallel to that in which the Ptolemaic world-view and its associations at one time represented the problem of evil for the Gnostics. This new problem was not taken up in the theological realm with the same concern as it had been in its older form in the **primitive** church. But we have seen how the problem did arise in a secular formulation in philosophy and how the Kantian treatment of it runs parallel to the Gnostic treatment of it in its earlier form. We may summarise the points of similarity as follows :

(1) The Ptolemaic astronomy and its astrological associations in the popular mind set the problem of evil in the particular form in which the Gnostics had to deal with it. In the case of Kant, it was the scientific developments from Copernicus to Newton that set the problem in the form in which he had to deal with it.

(2) For the Gnostics, it was the problem of knowing the relation of the world of gross matter to God. For Kant, it was the problem of knowing the relation of the scientifically observable world of nature to the *summum bonum*.

(3) The Gnostics attempted to answer the problem in terms of a sharp dualism between the heavenly realm of light—the Pleroma—and the world of gross matter. Kant attempted to find a solution in terms of a sharp duality between the noumenal realm, which we know directly only in moral decision, and the phenomenal realm of empirical knowledge.

(4) Salvation for the Gnostics meant escape from the system of physical nature and the influence of the stars. For Kant, the final fulfilment of the moral life in the realisation of the *summum bonum* could be looked for only in the hope of the soul's escaping from the phenomenal realm and its amoral causal determinism—a determinism which, in this age too, was witnessed to primarily by the movements of the heavenly bodies.

If, in the light of the foregoing statements, we make a

comparison of the following two passages, the true parallel, both in the initial problem and in the final outcome, between these two otherwise incomparably different systems becomes apparent.   The first is a passage from the *Excerpta ex Theodoto* as edited and translated by R. P. Casey.   It is a collection of notes on and quotations from the work of a Valentinian Gnostic.   The notes may have been taken by Clement of Alexandria himself.   The following is, in some sense, a key passage to the thought of the whole work :

> Fate is a union of many opposing forces and they are invisible and unseen, guiding the course of the stars and governing through them.   For as each of them arrived, borne round by the movement of the world, it obtained power over those who were born at that very moment, as though they were its own.
>
> Therefore, through the fixed stars and the planets, the invisible powers holding sway over them, direct and watch over births.   But the stars themselves do nothing but display the activity of the dominant powers, just as the flight of the birds (for omens) indicates something but effects nothing. . . .   From this situation and battle of the powers the Lord rescues us and supplies peace from the array of powers and angels, in which some are arrayed for us and others against us.[1]

The second passage is from Kant's *Critique of Practical Reason*—one in which he lays aside some of his usual philosophic reserve and goes a little beyond the bare formal implications of his argument in making a more personal, religious statement of the conclusion to which it leads :

> Two things fill the mind with ever new and increasing admiration and awe, the oftener and more steadily we reflect on them : *the starry heavens above and the moral law within*.   I have not to search for them and conjecture them as though they were veiled in darkness or were in the transcendental region beyond my horizon ; I see them before me and connect them directly with the consciousness of my existence.   The former begins from

[1] P. 91.

the place I occupy in the external world of sense, and enlarges my connexion therein to an unbounded extent with worlds upon worlds and systems of systems, and moreover into limitless times of their periodic motion, its beginning and continuance. The second begins from my invisible self, my personality, and exhibits me in a world which has true infinity, but which is traceable only by the understanding, and with which I discern that I am not in a merely contingent but in a universal and necessary connexion, as I am also thereby with all those visible worlds. The former view of a countless multitude of worlds annihilates, as it were, my importance as an *animal creature*, which after it has been for a short time provided with vital power, one knows not how, must again give back the matter of which it was formed to the planet it inhabits (a mere speck in the universe). The second, on the contrary, infinitely elevates my worth as an *intelligence* by my personality, in which the moral law reveals to me a life independent on animality and even on the whole sensible world—at least so far as may be inferred from the destination assigned to my existence by this law, a destination not restricted to conditions and limits of this life, but reaching into the infinite.[1]

In these two passages we see at once the vast difference between the two systems of thought, each belonging, as it does, to its own age. Yet at the same time, they illustrate the parallel. Each, in terms of its own cultural and scientific background expresses fear, awe and a feeling of insignificance in the face of the vast, uncontrollable, impersonal forces of nature. Each expresses this in a different way, but to both such a universe appears to be ultimately incompatible with the final fulfilment of personal life. Therefore both accept a dualism which ultimately divorces physical nature entirely from the realm of moral and religious value.

The Problem Raised for German Idealism by Kant's Dual Conception of the World. In presenting Kant in this light, I have stated his dualism in its most extreme form. This is

---

[1] *Kant's Ethics*, p. 260.

justifiable in that Kant himself often does present the distinction between *phenomena* and *noumena* in just this form. But it must also be recognised that he did not maintain this extreme position too consistently and that, particularly in his later revision of his work, he appears anxious to modify it so far as this can be done without altering his main position. However, since it is not Immanuel Kant as such that primarily concerns us here, but the dual conception of the world which he represents, I have confined myself to discussing this duality in its most extreme form, and to showing the parallel between it and the cultural situation out of which it arose and the development of Gnostic dualism in the second and third centuries.

As we have seen, the church, in its efforts to combat the dualism of the Gnostics, was ultimately forced back upon a reassertion of the cosmic significance of the work of Christ. It is interesting and, I think, significant that the parallel is here continued, in that when the German Idealists tried to solve the problems raised by this sharp duality in Kant, their work culminated in the philosophy of Hegel who, just as the early church had done, sought his solution in the cosmic significance of the work of Christ (however unorthodox he may have been in his conception of that saving work). However, since we are now dealing with the problem as it was raised within secular philosophy, sheer respect for Biblical and credal orthodoxy is no longer a motive for criticising such a dual conception of the world. Such considerations are irrelevant to the philosophic context. But there were other reasons for dissatisfaction with the Kantain position.

It would be unprofitable to digress on a detailed analysis of these reasons. We shall refer to them only in general terms.

(1) There is a fundamental unity of all the elements of experience—a unity of which Kant himself gives a profound treatment under the heading of *The Transcendental*

Unity of Apperception. The fact of such a unity is a *prima facie* reason for looking for a more positive relationship between moral experience and the kind of experience which we describe in terms of empirical science.

(2) There is a unity in Reason itself which will not permit it to have two standards of ultimate truth. There may well be a number of more or less arbitrary norms for different types of proposition, but philosophers as a whole are inclined to believe that such norms must be related to one ultimate norm—if for no other reason, simply as an act of faith. (Though, of course, there are exceptions to this, ranging from Heracleitus to the modern Logical Positivists.) Where this belief in the unity of truth is held, it implies a more systematic relationship between value propositions and the propositions of science than the Kantian system allows.

(3) This concept of the unity of truth is correlative with the metaphysical concept of the unity of Reality. Appearance as appearance is real. Therefore there must be some ultimate principle of unity between the phenomenal and the noumenal world of Kant.

Difficulties of this kind pressed the German Idealists to look for a more positive relationship between the phenomenal world and the realm of moral values. Both Fichte and Schelling made their attempts to find the underlying principle of unity—Fichte by treating the phenomenal world as dependent for its existence on the creative moral Will, and Schelling by treating it as ultimately dependent on aesthetic creativity.[1] The whole movement culminated in Hegel, whom we now proceed to consider.

[1] Of these men, the thought of Schelling in particular could be profitably analysed in relation to the idea of cosmic redemption. There is a unity of development from Kant through them to Hegel. But since Hegel himself raises all the major issues which need concern us, we need not follow this development right through. For a treatment of the development from Kant through Fichte and Schelling to Hegel from this point of view, I would refer the reader to Dr. Richard Kroner's difficult but rewarding book, *Von Kant bis Hegel.*

CHAPTER XII

THE HEGELIAN SOLUTION

HEGEL is notoriously a difficult philosopher to interpret, firstly because of his genuine profundity, but secondly because of his very vague habits, not only of thought, but of speech as well. Therefore one is continually forced to ask of any Hegelian argument, not only whether it is valid, but also what it means, and sometimes even whether it means anything at all. This, of course, is apt to raise the whole question of the meaning of any kind of metaphysical proposition—an issue which it would clearly be unprofitable to open here. I propose, therefore, first of all simply to state the outline of the Hegelian argument in so far as it is relevant to the idea of cosmic redemption. In this outline I shall use the Hegelian terminology quite freely and uncritically. After this has been done, we shall then proceed to the questions whether, and in what sense, it can be regarded as a significant argument.

The sharp duality between nature and value in Kant arose fundamentally from an epistemological problem, and was an expression of the already existing dichotomy in culture, brought into being by the rise of the new science. We saw how this tended to divide propositions into two classes—those which had the certainty deriving from experimental verification, and those which did not lend themselves to this kind of treatment. The problem arises fundamentally from the absence of any systematic relation between these two types of proposition. The Kantian system tends towards dualism simply because, at the outset, it accepts this dichotomy as ultimate, and develops an epistemological and metaphysical basis for it. Hegel was aware of this. Therefore it is with an investigation of the epistemological basis of the objective judgments of science that he begins his *Phenomenology of Mind*. It is chiefly on his argument as stated in that work that I shall rely.

When we first introduced the epistemological problems which were brought into prominence by the experimental technique of modern science, we referred to the typical object of scientific judgments in terms of the naïve and uncritical conception of " objective fact ". Occasion now arises to give some analysis of what is involved in this conception, for it is with this that Hegel begins.

At this preliminary, naïve level, the concept of objective fact implies :

(*a*) an observed datum or complex of data, and

(*b*) an observing self who is distinct from the datum.

In the simple sense-datum this ideal appears to be realised. On the basis of such simple observations of sense-data the whole structure of the distinctively scientific type of knowledge is built up. Hegel therefore begins by subjecting this idea of the simple sense-datum to closer examination. He begins with what he calls simple sense-certainty. That is, the certainty of my being aware of a simple sensation now, in this moment. Such a situation must be regarded as breaking up into two pure " this's "—one " this " as " I " and the other as the object. Yet when this has been recognised, it becomes impossible to describe the relation between the " I " and the object. As soon as we try to express the distinction, it disappears and leaves us with bare identity. The sensation and my awareness of the sensation are one and the same thing.

Awareness is a function of mind, and as such, Hegel argues, must involve some element of conceptual thought. Even at its simplest level it must involve certain basic conceptions, such as " this ", " here ", " now ". But conceptions are universals or *meanings*, and not particular objects. This means that regarded from this point of view, the sense-datum, which appeared to be as particular and concrete as anything could be, turns out to be not a particular object at all, but is ultimately a universal. Thus :

> If we compare the relation in which knowledge and the object first stood with the relation they have come to assume in this result, it is found to be just the reverse of what first appeared. The object, which professed to be the essential reality, is now the non-essential element of sense-certainty ; for the universal which the object has come to be, is no longer such as the object was to be for sense-certainty. The certainty is now found to lie in the opposite element, namely in knowledge, which formerly was the non-essential factor. Its truth lies in the object as my (*meinem*) object, or lies in the " meaning " (*Meinen*), in what I " mean " ; it *is* because *I* know it. Sense-certainty is thus indeed banished from the object, but it is not yet thereby done away with ; it is merely forced back into the I.[1]

But although it proves impossible to describe even this, the simplest kind of knowledge, in terms of a simple relationship between subject and object, it is equally impossible to describe it in terms of the knowing subject alone. On the one hand, when we try to describe the particularity of the concrete object of knowledge *qua* object, it turns out to be a universal, a " meaning " that we are dealing with. On the other hand, when we try to describe knowledge from the standpoint of perception, that is, from the standpoint of the knowing " I ", which is from the start recognised as involving a subjective conceptual element, a universal, a " meaning ", we find that simply because this universal is not a bare universal, but is referred as a meaning to a particular object, we cannot describe the knowledge by reference to the knowing subject alone.

We are thrown back again on the necessity of describing

[1] *Phenomenology of Mind*, p. 153.

the object as this particular concrete object. But again when we ask what is the "this" which constitutes the particular concreteness of the object, we find that it does not belong to the object at all. What constitutes the "this" is *my knowing* now, in this particular moment. A moment later I turn round and perceive a different object. Yet it is still "this" object. It is "this" because it is still I who perceive it. What constitutes the "this", therefore, is simply the bare unity of the "I". But, says Hegel, a bare, undifferentiated unity is a pure universal and not a particular at all. Thus we are again forced to deny the particularity of the object and assert simply the bare unity of the subject.

But again, this pure universal, the bare unity of the "I" is nothing at all except as characterised by this or that particular perception in this or that particular moment. Hegel uses the simile that the bare unity of consciousness, undifferentiated by particular perceptions, is like a seeing eye in the midst of pure light in which there is nothing to be seen. All is seeing, yet there is no seeing, for there is nothing to be seen. Therefore, despite the fact that the particularity of the object of perception, when subjected to this kind of analysis, continually "dissolves" into the bare abstract unity of consciousness, we must nonetheless continue to assert the particularity of the object, because without it the abstract unity of consciousness is nothing at all.

Yet if we begin by asserting the particularity of the object as essential, the "I", the unity of consciousness, becomes simply the insubstantial "also" connecting one perception with another. So if we take the object as primary, we deny what we have said about the subject. Yet if we take the subject as primary, we deny what was said about the object. Each exists *for* the other ; yet in asserting the one we negate the other. Thus the naïve conception of "objective fact" with which we began turns out to be self-contradictory and untenable.

Hegel attempts to find a way out of this impasse by resorting to the idea of force or movement. Thought, he contends, must be described in terms of a moving force. It must be described as a dual movement of self. Since in perception (*capio*—I take)[1] it is the " I " which *takes* cognisance of the object, the movement must be regarded as that of self towards bare identity with self—a denial of the concrete particularity of the object. But since perception involves a reference to a concrete particular, which is not-self, it must be regarded as a movement away from self towards the concrete particularity of the object. Thus in knowledge the self is continually suffering diremption into self and not-self.

The Relation of this Problem to the Problem of Evil. Hegel was more acutely conscious of the relation of this epistemological problem to the problem of personal unhappiness than was Kant. For Kant, as we saw, the epistemological problem of describing the status of scientific propositions finally led him to the problem of describing the relation of the phenomenal world, as the object of the understanding, to the noumenal world, as the realm of personal and moral decision. In this relationship, the sheer moral indifference of the phenomenal world in relation to the *summum bonum* came to represent for him one of the ultimate questions in the problem of evil. But we have already recognised that the problem of evil, in the context in which we have been considering it, has two main aspects. From the theological standpoint these are :

(*a*) the metaphysical problem of evil, which is the problem of the existential separation of the self from God, and

(*b*) the moral problem, which is that of the relation of the imperfections of this world to the holiness of God.

We have also recognised that, in the secular context, these become :

----

[1] *Ibid.*, p. 166.

(*a*) the problem of the separation of the knowing self from the reality known, and

(*b*) the problem of the relation of the natural world to our standards of ultimate value.

It is only of the second of these two aspects of the problem that Kant is fully conscious in the antinomy of practical reason. Hegel, on the other hand, is fully conscious of both aspects of the problem, and, for him, it is the former aspect which tends to become primary and the latter to be subsumed under it.

The double movement of knowledge which Hegel calls the diremption of self into self and not-self creates a continual tension within the self which is the source of " unhappy consciousness ".[1] This is the form in which the existential separation of the self presents itself to him. The self continually longs to be complete and to be completely at one with itself—to be the bare identity of self with self. But, as such, the self would be a bare abstraction. It is only in the concrete particularity of this or that moment of experience that the self has actuality. But such concrete particularity always involves the relation of self to an object. Thus the longing of the self for complete self-existence and complete self-identity must be continually frustrated. Our enjoyment of our own consciousness is shattered and becomes " unhappy consciousness ". It is unhappy because it can realise its own unity only by regarding all that impinges on consciousness and gives it a determinate content as belonging to consciousness and as being part of it ; yet at the same time, it can realise its own actuality in the determinateness of that content only by regarding the content as object, as not-self, as separate.

Kant, too, in his own way, was aware of the difficulty that the world as object of the understanding does not finally accommodate itself to the ideal of knowledge. This was expressed for him in the antinomies of pure reason.

[1] *Ibid.*, pp. 251 ff.

But he is not particularly conscious of this as a source of unhappiness. It is simply a limitation of the understanding, which he is prepared to recognise and to compensate for in his more optimistic analysis of practical reason as operative in the moral Will. But because Hegel had come to describe rational consciousness, not in formal logical terms, but in terms of dynamic movement, he was able to regard this double movement of consciousness as being quite literally a frustrated longing or desire, and therefore a source of real personal unhappiness. The problem becomes not simply that knowledge, as a system, must remain somewhat incomplete, but that the whole desire and longing and labour of consciousness to be at one with itself must be continually frustrated by the double and contradictory nature of this movement which arises in the separation of self and not-self. It is the fundamental movement of the human spirit that is frustrated.

Because Hegel conceives knowledge in these dynamic terms, he is able to identify its process with the whole movement of living consciousness, which he calls Spirit. The activity of pure reason in knowledge as well as the activity of practical reason in the Will, is of a conative nature. Thus the dialectical process, which was at first introduced as a description of knowledge, becomes a description of the whole movement of human life. Both the Will and the Understanding are different manifestations of the effort of Reason to realise itself in the double movement described above, and to find a synthesis of these two opposing forces in which it can rest. Just as in the Understanding there is a continual diremption of self into self and not-self, so also in the action of the Will there is a similar double motion.

Corresponding to the movement in knowledge which asserts the universality and abstract unity of the self and negates the concrete particularity of the object, there is the effort of the Will towards sheer domination of the not-self. This is the impulse towards lordship. Corresponding to the movement in knowledge which asserts the concrete particularity of the object and negates the universality and unity of the self, there is the phenomenon of the subjection of the Will to the Will of another and the effort to accommodate oneself to one's environment. This is the impulse towards bondage.[1] On the one hand, we must seek our happiness by accommodating environment to self. On the other hand, we must seek our happiness in the discipline of accommodating self to environment.

This is simply another example of the double movement of consciousness which we found in the process of knowledge. Thus Hegel finds that he is able to describe the whole of human life and the whole of history in terms of what was originally the analysis of a purely epistemological problem. The formal epistemological problem expands into the whole problem of the relation of self to environment and of the unhappiness which arises out of that relationship.

Now this is precisely the problem which we have found to be the dominant factor in determining the development of the idea of cosmic redemption. It is a problem which, we have found, presents us with a choice between either some form of dualism or else a doctrine of cosmic redemption. Kant, formulating the problem in his own way, found his solution in a dualism of phenomenal and noumenal—a solution which we found to be in many respects parallel to the dualism of the early Christian Gnostics. The Christian church answered the Gnostics in terms of a doctrine of the cosmic significance of the work of Christ. And so we find the parallel again continued in that Hegel too, in rejecting the dualism of Kant, refers us to his own peculiar interpretation of the cosmic significance of the work of Christ.

For Hegel, the unhappy diremption of self into self and

[1] *Ibid.*, pp. 234 ff.

M

not-self is to be overcome, not in the acceptance of a
dualism of mind and object, of spirit and world, but in the
ultimate unity of the two.   He contends that when consciousness is described in terms of the dynamic conceptions
which he employs, both self and object are recognised as
different movements of the one self in knowledge.   Therefore the possibility of a final synthesis is implied.   This is
the difference between simple consciousness and self-
consciousness proper.   At the level of simple consciousness
there is no resolution of the contradiction between the two
opposite movements of consciousness.   But the fact that
in self-consciousness we are able to recognise both movements at once, implies the beginning of a synthesis.   The
self is recognised at once as being simply observer—pure
undifferentiated unity ;   yet at the same time, as having its
actuality only in the concrete particularity of the object.
These two movements of self are thus held together in
some kind of makeshift unity.

The completion of this movement—now a triple movement of thesis, antithesis and synthesis—takes place in
what Hegel calls the Notion (*Begriff*), which is the active
form of pure rational consciousness.   As being the form of
pure rational consciousness the Notion is pure subjectivity.
But as having a determinate content and reference, it has
a subjectivity different from the subjectivity of self in
immediate consciousness, which remains within itself and
in complete contradiction with the object.   The Notion is
referred away from itself to the object, and so exists concretely in the object.   Thus both self and not-self are held
together within the unity of the Notion.   But there remains
a tension within this unity until the complete identity of
self and not-self is fully realised.   In the Notion, rational
consciousness, or Spirit recognises itself in the object.   But
it is self as estranged from self that it recognises.   It
recognises what Hegel calls objective Spirit in tension with
itself as subjective Spirit.   Until the complete identity of

these two is realised, the development of the Notion is not fulfilled.

The whole movement of history is interpreted as the effort of Reason to reach its final fulfilment in the self-development of the Notion. For example, the progress from the two extremes of tyranny on the one hand and anarchy on the other to the democratic ideals, finding expression in the liberal politics of the early nineteenth century, is interpreted by him as a manifestation of the self-development of the Notion in history. It is a development from the two extremes of slavish subjection of self and assertion of self towards the identity of self and not-self in the state. The same principle runs through all aesthetic development. For example, Greek sculpture is interpreted as an attempt to realise the form of the self in the not-self. In this way all growth and development is interpreted by Hegel in terms of his epistemological analysis of the Notion. Religion is the ultimate manifestation of this development. In seeking communion with a not-self which is Absolute Spirit, the self is seeking the final identity of self and not-self.

As religious, the self is aware of God as Absolute Spirit, and is aware of its communion with, and participation in the Absolute Spirit. But this union with Absolute Spirit cannot be complete while Absolute Spirit remains purely abstract and universal, and the self is estranged from itself in particular concrete objectivity.

The principle of the Incarnation can alone solve this dilemma ; for it is only when we recognise Absolute Spirit as becoming concrete Spirit and manifesting itself in an objective self, belonging to objective nature, that we finally perceive the unity of subjective and objective Spirit. Only then do we recognise the self in the not-self. We recognise it not merely as particular, individual self ; but as the unity of individual, concrete self and Infinite Self or Absolute Spirit. This means :

(*a*) that we become aware of the unity of subjective and objective Spirit within ourselves, and

(*b*) that we become aware of the unity of our total self with Absolute Spirit.

The internal logic of this revelation, which the Christian faith pictorially portrays, corresponds to the various moments of the Notion in self-conscious experience. In the Notion we may distinguish three moments. There is

(1) the abstract universal idea which suffers diremption

(2) into its other in the concrete particular, the external object, and then

(3) returns to identity with the universal in the individual.

This is the movement of Reason and it is revealed in Christianity to be also the movement of Absolute Reason, which is to be identified with Absolute Spirit. These three moments may be made to correspond with the three persons of the Godhead, conceived in a kind of economic Trinity.

First of all, there is the kingdom of the Father, who is pure Absolute Spirit, abstract and universal. As such, God the Father corresponds to the abstract idea, and has no reality until He becomes estranged from Himself and enters the concrete world of objectivity. This going forth from Himself on the part of God takes place in the person of the Word, the Logos, the Son. It occurs first of all in what Christianity figuratively represents as an act of creation. Creation is an act of *kenosis* on the part of God in which He goes forth in His Word into existence. This, of course, is not a temporal process. It is only the figurative idea of creation that presents it as such. The various moments of the Notion are not successive phases, but elements which depend upon one another at any time.

There thus arises an opposition between these two moments in the Divine, corresponding to the contradiction between self and not-self, or between idea and concrete particular in human self-consciousness. From the point of view of the simple thought of Spirit (i.e. from the point of view of the thought of God as abstract and universal) the abstract universal is essential, and natural existence and the self are unessential and " are to be cancelled ".   From the point of view of the thought of the " other "—Spirit as concrete and self-existent—this self-existence passes for what is essential, and the simple Divine is regarded as unessential.

But we have not said enough when we describe the world simply as the objective " other " of the Divine Spirit.   For since Spirit is essentially self, the world, as objectively existent Spirit, is individual self, and distinguishes itself as world, as " other ", from itself.   It is in and through man that the world has this consciousness of itself as at once self, and also what is estranged from self.   But because, at first, man is not aware of himself as Spirit, the two moments are not reconciled in him.   This state is not itself evil, but rather an innocent, unwitting separation from God.   But because it is self-contradictory, it contains the seeds of discord—and therefore of evil—within it.

In this respect, the Christian myth is correct in placing the origin of the Fall in a pre-cosmic setting.   It lies in the very root of Reason itself.   Evil manifests itself in the contradictory self-assertion of the " other ", the world, against the Divine Spirit, while within the Divine Spirit this evil has its counterpart in the wrath of God against the world.   This wrath of God must itself be regarded as simply the other side of evil.   This is a thing which traditional theology cannot understand, because, being purely figurative in its thought, it lacks the Notion and therefore cannot perceive the necessity of the opposition between the two moments of Absolute Spirit.

The final dissolution of this opposition is not to be achieved by the assertion of one element against the other. The condition of the unity of the moments is that each must dissolve itself.   This is achieved in and by Christ, the Son, in whom simple Divine Spirit abandons its abstract universality and enters into the world of the concrete particular, emptying itself and giving itself unto death. Yet also, through this very death, the concrete returns to universality and Absolute Spirit is reconciled with itself.

This is the final form of the kingdom of the Son, and this reconciliation, as mediated through the collective consciousness of the believing community is the kingdom of the Holy Spirit. In the believing community Spirit finally knows itself as Spirit. The self and the not-self are finally reconciled when we see the reality, which we are aware of as over against us in consciousness, manifesting itself as individual self—yet not merely as individual self. If Christ had not died, He would have been merely individual self. He would have remained a particular object within the natural world. But as dead and risen, He returns in His individuality to the universal, and is known not as an object of perception, but in universal thought. It is as in communion with this resurrected Christ that the community of the Holy Spirit exists.

The Christian faith (not as an abstract system of dogmas, but as a historical actuality in the mind of the believing community) contains the moments of the Notion of Spirit. This means that it not only expresses the content of Spirit, but also that it *is* actual Spirit. As the religious consciousness thus beholds the Absolute, the distinction between itself and the reality which it beholds is done away with. The self is no longer alienated from its own universality. The duality has been overcome.

But the religious communion is not fulfilled so long as we are conscious of it only in terms of the figurative symbols of Christianity (i.e. so long as we are aware of it only in terms of *Vorstellung* and not of *Begriff*). So long as we express it, for example, in the language of the natural human relation of Father and Son, the return of Reason to itself is not complete. This fulfilment takes place only when Spirit becomes conscious of itself in terms of the Notion—i.e. in terms of Hegelian philosophy.

Thus the inner conflicts which are the ground and source of man's unhappiness are seen to be but the small reflection of a vast cosmic process which is the expression of the mind of God Himself. This process is itself redemptive, the tension of contending opposites being finally resolved in the full development of rational self-consciousness in man.

Conclusion. In the whole course of Christian theology there have been only two really great attempts to reconstruct the doctrine of cosmic redemption in terms of a systematic philosophy. Origen's was the first and Hegel's was the second. There is a striking similarity in their thought ; but not as regards precise content. The concepts which each employed were so widely different as to defy any comparison of this kind. It is a similarity of the same kind as that which we have already observed between Kant and the Gnostics—a parallel in the pattern of their thought rather than the content.

Origen was faced with a Gnostic dualism of spirit and matter. He attempted to restore the unity of matter and spirit by deriving matter from spirit. Hegel was faced with the Kantian dualism of phenomenal and noumenal. His solution runs parallel to that of Origen in that :

(1) He too, tries to restore the unity of spirit and matter by deriving matter from spirit. (For both, spirit is identified with Reason.)

(2) Both identified the process which produces material existence out of pure rational consciousness with the event which is mythically portrayed in Scripture as the Fall.

(3) Both traced the origin of all suffering and evil to this event, which produced the material world as a thing alien to the inner life of Reason.

(4) Both regard the whole of cosmic history as a continuous process of redemption to which Christ is the key

and of which His Incarnation, Crucifixion and Resurrection constitute the central event.

(5) For both, the aim and final outcome of this process is that Reason, alienated from itself in matter, is finally restored to itself again.

This is only a rough and ready parallel. One would have to stretch things overmuch to make it any more precise. For example, Hegel's concern with the mind-matter problem was quite different from Origen's. Origen, like others of his day, was repelled by the sheer grossness of matter. Hegel, on the other hand, like others of his age was obsessed with the problem of the relation between subject and object, and it was as an aspect of this that the mind-matter problem arose for him. If one were to try to overlay the two systems, their differences would be more apparent than their similarity. But these differences are what one would expect. It is the similarity that is striking.

Both ended in error and, in a sense, it was the same error. Origen failed because he attempted to identify Christianity with an improved and refined form of Stoicism. Hegel failed because he attempted to identify Christianity with an improved and refined form of German Idealism. One is left wondering whether his account of the work of Christ justifies us in using such Biblical terms as " redemption " and " salvation " at all ; and whether, if the retention of such concepts is justified, this can still be called Christian redemption.

But quite apart from any questions about Hegel's orthodoxy there is a prior question as to the validity of his argument and indeed as to whether it means anything at all. The outline which we have given of Hegel's position has been quite uncritical. We have accepted the Hegelian idiom of thought and language without making any serious attempt at precise interpretation.

When subjected to logical analysis, Hegel's argument is not merely shown to be mistaken in the sense that it involves a logical miscalculation, but it is exposed as sheer nonsense in the strict sense of the word. It does not make sense. But in spite of this there is real value in the new insights which he affords into the fundamental problem underlying the doctrine of cosmic redemption. It is these positive insights which chiefly concern us. So I have relegated the negative criticism of Hegel's argument to an appendix. In the next chapter I seek to show how Hegel's " nonsense " is of profound significance.

CHAPTER XIII

THE REAL SIGNIFICANCE AND VALUE OF HEGEL'S THOUGHT

IF I may put my next point in a personal way, I can never refer to Hegel's work as being mere nonsense without feeling some sense of my own irreverence. When I read Hegel, I am certainly aware of the difficulty of his thought and the extreme obscurity of his language. But I am by no means aware of it as mere nonsense. I am aware of being challenged to struggle with his meaning, and one does not struggle with sheer nonsense, because there is no meaning in nonsense to struggle with. Yet the only outcome of such a struggle, if clear analysis is insisted upon all the way, is finally to expose the sheer absurdity of the whole argument.

One is therefore forced to invoke a distinction which has been quite frequently employed in recent times—the distinction between significant and insignificant nonsense. There are innumerable ways in which nonsense can be significant. It is significant, for instance, in poetry, and then, in an entirely different way, nonsense becomes significant in psycho-analysis, and so on. There are two senses in which the absurdities of the Hegelian argument become significant in relation to the problems with which we are concerned. The first is from the formal standpoint of logic. It becomes significant in this sense in relation to the formal problem with which Hegel begins. If the pursuance of the analysis of the rules of logic leads us to formulate propositions which themselves cannot be made conformable to the rules of that logic, then these propositions are condemned, by the rules of the logic being investigated, as being nonsense propositions. But the resultant nonsense may be significant in that it shows forth the impossibility of reaching a final analysis of the rules of any given system of logic in terms of that same logic. This, indeed, is the only method by which such an impossibility can be shown. In this sense Hegel's nonsense about thesis, antithesis and synthesis becomes important and significant.

When Hegel tries to analyse the relationship of subject and object in knowledge in terms of the same language as that which we use to express our knowledge of the world as object, he is driven to make contradictory statements. On the one hand, he must say that even in immediate consciousness the object is known only in so far as it belongs to his consciousness and is therefore part of himself. On the other hand, the object, *qua* object, does not belong to his consciousness, but is held in contrast with it as that of which he is conscious. Hegel is faced at the outset with these two contradictory statements. We need not go again into the manner in which he relates this problem to the relation of universal and particular. The important point is that Hegel can solve this problem only by telling a little story about it, in which the two contradictory propositions are the chief characters. The thesis is the movement of self towards unity with self; the antithesis is the movement of self away from self towards the object; and the happy ending to this little drama comes about with the appearance of the fairy god-mother in the form of the synthesis which unites the two movements.

This is nonsense; but it is significant nonsense in that it demonstrates the impossibility of describing the relation of knowing self to the object known in terms of the same language as that which we use to express the knowledge itself. That is to say, the language which expresses knowledge cannot express the ultimate analysis of the process of knowledge itself.

Even this is ultimately as nonsensical as Hegel's statement, for it raises a question which can have only a nonsensical answer ; and such a question is itself non-sensical. But one cannot state this point in any other way. One can only show it forth by arriving again and again at the same kind of nonsense from several different approaches. In this formal aspect, the relation of knowing subject to object known is the same as that of a proposition to what it denotes. The same conclusion can therefore be stated by saying that a proposition can never describe itself but must always describe something other than itself. Or again, in the language of idealist philosophy, a pro-position, *qua* proposition, is an ideal content and not a fact. *Qua* fact it may describe itself as marks on paper, or as a sonic or psychological event. But it is a proposition only in so far as it has meaning, and as such it is an ideal content to be held in contrast with the fact which it describes.

It is a far cry from Hegel to the Logical Positivists, and it is more usual to contrast rather than compare them. But in this point the Logical Positivists reach essentially the same dilemma as Hegel. Hegel shows us that you cannot give an account of the logical relation of the knowing subject to the object known without making contradictory statements. The Logical Positivists have succeeded in isolating this purely formal problem from irrelevant psychological considerations, and have stated the difficulty by showing that it is impossible for any language to give an account of its own logical syntax.

Carnap, in *The Logical Syntax of Language*, attempts to overcome this difficulty by using two sets of symbols. He uses Arabic letters as symbols in which to set out his logic, and then uses Gothic letters as symbols in which to describe the syntax of this logic. But the result is only to show with great clarity and infinite complexity that the difficulty cannot be overcome. One requires yet another set of symbols to describe the second system and its relation to the first, and so on *ad infinitum*.

Professor Wittgenstein, in his *Tractetus Logico-philoso-phicus*, tackles the same problem.   In company with a great many who have struggled with Wittgenstein's rather oracular style of writing, I must confess that there is much in this book which I simply do not understand.   But the main difficulty with which Wittgenstein has to contend is just this fact that a proposition cannot give an account of itself and of its own relation to what it signifies.   This is a thing which can only be " shown forth ".   It cannot be said.   Wittgenstein says :

No proposition can say anything about itself, because the propositional sign cannot be contained in itself. . . .

A function cannot be its own argument, because the functional sign already contains the prototype of its own argument and it cannot contain itself.

If, for example, we suppose that the function $F(fx)$ could be its own argument, then there would be a pro-position " $F(F(fx))$ " and in this the outer function F and the inner function F must have different meanings ; for the inner has the form $\phi(fx)$ the outer the form $\psi(\phi(fx))$. Common to both functions is only the letter " F ", which by itself signifies nothing.[1]

This fact, that a proposition cannot give an account of its own relation to what it signifies, or that a language cannot give an account of its own syntax, is simply a more strictly formal statement of the same difficulty as has come to light in our criticism of Hegel, namely that the knowing subject cannot give an account of its own relationship to the object known in the language in which it expresses its knowledge of the object.

This is not what Hegel made of his own insight into the contradictions into which we are led when we attempt to give such an account of our knowledge of an object.   Hegel, in imagining that his " myth " about the movements of thesis, antithesis and synthesis was a literal description of

[1] Propositions 3.332–3.333.

the formal relations of subject and object in thought, and in confusing a formal with a material problem, thought that he had overcome the contradiction. This is a source of very serious confusion in his thought. But it does not destroy the value of the critical insights which enabled him to draw attention to the problem which these contradictions represent.

All this has no obvious connection with any idea that would normally be associated with that of cosmic redemption. But it is by no means a needless digression. It is the necessary starting-point for any modern reconstruction of the cosmic implications of the Christian faith. It will be remembered that the starting-point from which the Kantian dualism was evolved was the epistemological problem raised by modern science. It was not for its own sake that we described this Kantian dualism, but we investigated it as giving expression to a dichotomy running through the whole of post-Renaissance European culture—a dichotomy between the world as it is known as the object of science and the world as it is known as a realm of moral and religious values. This dichotomy is seen in its widest manifestation in the split between Positivism and Romanticism. We saw how this split derived from the acceptance of science as an autonomous system of knowledge. It was because he accepted, and sought to find a justification for this position that Kant reached the dualistic conclusion which he did.

However, it is a condition of the autonomy of any department of knowledge that it be able to give an account of its own norms of truth and to provide from within itself a guarantee of the validity of those norms. If this cannot be done, then our acceptance of these norms must rest on a decision arrived at on the basis of considerations outside and independent of the system. Thus it is ultimately not autonomous, but dependent on that which is outside itself.

This is precisely the point which arises out of the foregoing epistemological considerations. The system of knowledge which is objective in the way peculiar to empirical science cannot give a final analysis of the relation of knower to known, of knowledge to the object of knowledge. The attempt results only in nonsense. This makes it impossible for us to ascribe any final autonomy to the propositions of empirical science on the grounds of their peculiar objectivity. It may be a useful epistemological device to treat them as though they were autonomous. Indeed, it is essential to take this standpoint if we are going to create what I have called the " laboratory situation " on which experimental investigation depends. But this autonomy cannot be absolute unless this system of knowledge can contain an account of its own epistemological basis. And this, we have seen, is impossible. When this absolute autonomy is denied, the source of the Kantian dualism is removed. If the system of objective knowledge of this kind is not autonomous, then the circle is not closed, and the sharp distinction on which the Kantian dualism is based is removed.

But all this is quite negative. It denies that the distinction between the world as the object of scientific investigation and the world as a realm of moral and religious values is essentially irreducible. But it tells us nothing about their positive relationship to one another or about the ground of their ultimate unity. This is inevitably so at the level of formal inquiry, for the nonsense at which we arrive repeatedly when we try to establish the autonomy of objective knowledge can have only negative significance from the formal standpoint. It can only show the impossibility of formally establishing the autonomy of objective empiricism. Beyond that it is mere nonsense.

But we must now consider a second and more material sense in which propositions which are nonsense from the standpoint of objective thinking are nonetheless significant.

The fact that we cannot describe the relation of the knowledge of an object to the object known in terms of the language in which the simple knowledge of the object is expressed, is, in itself, a purely formal problem.   As I have tried to show, it is the same problem as is raised by the fact that a proposition cannot describe itself but must always describe something other than itself.   But when we turn to the material problem of describing the situation of our own self-consciousness in existence—that is, of describing the relation of our own self-consciousness to the world—the same logical difficulty frustrates all our efforts.   Thus, what was a purely formal problem becomes a material problem related to human concern, and the kind of nonsense at which we arrive when we attempt the purely logical analysis becomes itself an expression of our situation in existence.

This is the real ground of Hegel's facile transition from the purely formal problem of the analysis of objectivity to the material problem of what he quite aptly calls " unhappy consciousness ".   His great error was in failing to realise that a real transition was involved—in failing to recognise that there is no direct line of reasoning from the formal to the material problem. Thus Hegel's argument remains dominated by the fact that he still thought he was dealing with what was primarily a logical question—the self-development of the Idea, as he calls it—when, in fact, he had moved to an altogether distinct, even if closely related, problem.

The fact that the systematic, objective thought in which we know the world as object cannot describe its own relation to the object becomes a material problem when it is considered in relation to our concern to feel secure in our own existence.   This phrase, " to feel secure in our own existence " is frankly symbolic.   It is impossible either to raise or to answer questions relating to the situation of the self *qua* self in existence without using figurative language of this kind. If it were possible to describe what has nowadays come to be described as the existential situation of the self in terms of systematic, objective thought, the formal problem of describing the relation of the subject to the object known would be overcome. Or, to state this in another way, any complete description of the situation of the self in existence in terms of the language of objective thought would involve a proposition which described its own relation to the object of its reference. This is impossible. Therefore we must abandon the type of precision which is the great virtue of objective thought and use figurative language. There is no shame in the use of such language in an academic work provided we are aware that we are using it and understand why we must use it.

But this immediately raises the questions : If thought is not systematic and precise, is it thought at all ? If language does not define its terms as it goes along, can those terms have any meaning ? To answer these questions by describing such thought as " intuitive " is simply to add another metaphor, and perhaps not a very helpful one at that. The same is true when we describe the kind of meaning which this kind of language carries as being " figurative ".

One can best describe the type of meaning which these " figurative " statements can bear as follows. Objective thought is systematic, and the meaning of any of its propositions, if the language is strictly used, is entirely determined by the definitions and rules of the system. Its meaning is therefore entirely independent of the psychological act of thinking it. This is what constitutes its objectivity. But in existential thinking—that is to say, in thinking in which we do not take the subject-object relationship for granted, but seriously attempt to give an account of the situation of our own self-consciousness in existence—the meaning of our propositions is not independent of our personal act of attempting to think them

N

and understand them. The propositions at which we
arrive cannot be given meaning simply in terms of the rules
of the language and its definitions. For the propositions
are contradictory and condemned by the rules of the
system as being nonsense. It is in the psychological act of
attempting to think this nonsense clearly and systematically, and in the frustration of the attempt, that our
attention is drawn to our own awareness of our situation
in existence—a situation of which we are aware, but which
we cannot describe in the same way as we describe the
world as the object of our knowledge.

It is as related to the deep-seated anxieties associated
with our own consciousness of the insecurity of our situation
as self in existence, that the formal problem of describing
the relation of subject and object in knowledge becomes a
material problem. The anxiety is one which belongs to
our conscious life, but which we cannot describe systematically. The contradictions into which we are led when we
attempt to describe the situation of self-consciousness in
existence are our only way of expressing it.

This deep-rooted, indeterminate anxiety which is associated with the conditions of finite self-consciousness has
received a great deal of attention from that ill-defined and
rather hysterical group of thinkers on the Continent who
have come to be known as the Existentialists. It is
unfortunate that such a hysterical atmosphere should have
prevailed among those who have focused attention on this
aspect of experience, for it tends to discredit all their work.
Yet there is in our private experience an element which
corresponds to this concept of existential anxiety. The
difficulties of describing the situation of self-consciousness
in existence make it difficult to give an account of this
fundamental anxiety. On the one hand, if we give over
the controls of the systematic language of objective description, we tend to become involved in the same kind of
hysterical utterance as is only too common among the

existential thinkers. On the other hand, if we confine ourselves strictly to what I have described as objective thinking, we can say nothing at all about the question.

The anxiety with which we are here concerned is not simply the sum of the particular anxieties of everyday life as to whether we can pay our income-tax or satisfy the examiners in an examination. It is the indeterminate anxiety which lies behind these particular anxieties. It is the anxiety which we feel in association with the thought of death, though it is not exhausted in this either, for it persists even when the thought of death is not in our minds. It is the sense that our existence as self is somehow insecure, and in this sense is the ground and source of all our particular anxieties. It is in relation to this underlying sense of the insecurity of our existence as self, that the contradictions into which we are forced when we try to give an account of our own existence as self in the world become a matter of material concern to us. In this sense, Hegel's account of " unhappy consciousness " as the diremption of self into self and not-self has significance.[1]

Our assurance of our own actuality in existence as self— our assurance that we occupy a particular concrete place in the world which we see existing around us—is grounded in the particular determinations of our consciousness in any given moment. It consists for me in my sitting in this chair now, thinking this particular thought now, and looking at this particular tree now. This is my assurance that I exist in this particular moment. And yet it is only part of that assurance, for it does not assure me that I

[1] The association between our experience of anxiety and the problem of describing the situation of the self in existence is witnessed to by the fact that it has always been in situations of general insecurity that the type of philosophy now known as existential thinking has been most widely indulged in. The social unrest in Europe which produced the French Revolution also produced Schelling, who was the first to use the term *Existentzphilosophie*, and Kierkegaard. Then in the insecure conditions of the Weimar Republic, " Existentialism " came into its own in Jaspers and Heidegger. And now again in the conditions of post-war Europe this kind of problem is again receiving wide-spread attention.

exist as self. It assures me that this or that thought or this or that particular perception occurs now. But it cannot be said to be the whole of my assurance that *I* exist. The unity which constitutes my existence as self does not consist in this or that particular determination of my consciousness in a particular moment, but simply in my continuing consciousness of myself as subject. From this standpoint I must regard those particular determinations of my consciousness which at first assured me of my existence as being essentially not-self—as that of which I am conscious and therefore held in contrast with the self as object over against subject. And yet again when considered merely as subject, apart from any particular determination of my consciousness, the self is merely an abstraction which I can separate in thought from its particular determinations in experience, but which I never know in actual experience as a separate existent. The self thus becomes what Hegel calls " the mere insubstantial 'also ' ", connecting one experience with another.

In a sense this is merely another expression of the difficulties of the Cartesian intuition— *cogito ergo sum*—as it relates to our existential anxiety. It shows the intuition falling into two parts. On the one hand, there is not a *cogito*, but only a *cogitatur*—a thinking or perception which is going on. On the other hand, there is the intuition *ego sum*. The problem, however, is not merely that it is difficult to find any necessary connection between these two parts of the intuition. It is rather that when we try to relate the two we become involved in self-contradiction. Regarded from the standpoint of objective thought these contradictions remain mere nonsense and arise from an essentially unaskable question. But from the standpoint of our concern to be secure in our own existence, they become an expression of our existential anxiety.

This is the diremption of self into self and not-self which constitutes what Hegel calls " unhappy consciousness ".

There is a genuinely profound insight into the universal ground of human anxiety here, if one disentangles it from Hegel's error in thinking that he was still dealing with a purely logical problem.

It will be understood, of course, that when it is said that the foregoing considerations express a universal ground of human anxiety, this does not mean that as plain John Smith sits by his fireside, he is perpetually worried by the thought that he cannot ultimately describe his situation in existence without contradicting himself. He will no doubt find happier and more profitable ways of occupying his time. But though he will not be concerned with the intellectual analysis of the situation, the fact of his being in the kind of situation which these contradictions symbolise will continue to constitute the ground of his personal anxiety.

It is the situation which the schoolmen of the Middle Ages attempted to describe as lack of *aseity*. Here the human situation is described by contrast with that of God. God alone has the property of *aseity*—of being by Himself. His being is entirely within Himself and He remains entirely at one with Himself. Man, on the other hand, has not the property of *aseity*. It is only in relation to an environment—a not-self—that he has actuality as self. He is thus never completely at one with himself. It is only as being in the situation of " having this experience here and now " that he has actuality.[1] Yet he can assert the unity of his selfhood only by denying that his true being consists in the particularity of any given moment of experience.

It is not these contradictions in themselves, but the situation to which they witness that is a matter of concern to us and the ground of our anxiety. It is the ground of our anxiety because it is the situation which creates the very possibility of our experience of anxiety. It is the root of our sense of insecurity in relation to our environment.

[1] What Heidegger describes as *dasein*—being in a particular place.

In this sense Hegel's treatment of " unhappy consciousness " is a profound insight.   It has no direct connection whatsoever with the purely formal problem from which he sets out—except in so far as the contradictions to which the formal problem leads us become an expression of our situation in existence, in the manner which I have described.   Hegel thought he had overcome the perplexity of " unhappy consciousness " in its diremption into self and not-self by showing how, in the self-fulfilment of the Notion, there is a final synthesis of thesis and antithesis— of the subjective and the objective.   But this, of course, is founded on the double error of thinking, first of all, that the formal and the material problems were one and the same— and therefore that the material problem could be solved in terms of the formal—and secondly, of thinking that his dynamic metaphors were a solution and not merely a statement of the problem.   Therefore, it is not so much Hegel's solution to the problem of " unhappy consciousness " as his analysis of it that has permanent value.

It must be understood, however, that while, in the interest of clarity, I have insisted on the distinction between the formal problem of the relation of subject and object in knowledge, and the material problem of the relation of consciousness to environment, the relation between these two problems is not one of mere analogy. " Consciousness " is an epistemological concept.   Therefore the contradictions into which the formal problem leads us present the formal aspect of the very same contradictions as those into which I am led when I try to describe my own situation as a self-conscious being in existence.

I have tried, as best I can, to show how these contradictions, which must remain nonsense from the standpoint of systematic, objective thought, can none the less be a significant expression of our existential situation.   They show forth what cannot be said in systematic language. I close this section with the words of Ludwig Wittgenstein,

who, having struggled with the same problem in its purely
formal aspect, concludes his book with the words :

> My propositions are elucidatory in this way : he who
> understands me finally recognises them as senseless,
> when he has climbed out through them, on them, over
> them. (He must so to speak throw away the ladder,
> after he has climbed up on it.)[1]

[1] *Op. cit.*, Proposition 6.54.

CHAPTER XIV

THE NEW SETTING OF THE PROBLEM

THERE are four aspects in which Hegel's thought, thus critically appreciated, has an important bearing on the problems associated with the idea of cosmic redemption.

(1) The first is that it cuts at the root of the Kantian dualism. As has been pointed out, this dualism is important to us not merely because of the place it holds in the Kantian system itself, but also as being a systematic expression of a dichotomy running through the whole of European culture since the rise of modern science in the Renaissance. We showed how the experimental technique of modern science, and the autonomous system of objective knowledge which it produced, led to a divorce between this aspect of experience and the moral, religious and other aspects which did not lend themselves to such treatment.

Kant's problem was, first of all, to find the epistemological basis for this peculiarly scientific type of knowledge and secondly, to explain the absence of any systematic relation between such knowledge and our moral and religious judgments. The former question he answered in terms of his theory of the categories of the understanding as determining the structure of phenomenal experience. The latter he answered by reference to the absolute separation of the phenomenal sphere and the noumenal sphere to which moral decision belongs. This sharp division, however, raised its own problems, which were expressed, for Kant, in the antinomy of practical reason. The absence of any relation between the phenomenal and the noumenal spheres made the realisation of the *summum bonum*—the conjunction of virtue and happiness—impossible; for such a conjunction would depend on the accommodation of the natural, phenomenal order to the moral, noumenal order. Kant, however, maintained his dualism and held out hope of the realisation of the *summum bonum* only in a life after death.

We pointed out how this position was closely parallel to that of the Gnostics of the second and third centuries—a position which the church then answered by asserting the cosmic significance of the work of Christ, and which, in the Kantian formulation, was answered by Hegel in an attempted re-interpretation of the cosmic significance of the work of Christ. Quite apart from any question as to the orthodoxy of Hegel's interpretation of the work of Christ, however, it was recognised that his whole argument was based on a confusion of thought, and could not be accepted as it stands. But a critical appreciation of Hegel's work reveals the fundamental weakness in Kant's dualism.

The sharp division between the phenomenal and the noumenal, the empirical and the moral, can be maintained only if we assume the complete autonomy of empirical science. It is only if scientific judgments do form a completely closed system that the absolute dichotomy between empirical and moral judgments can be maintained. Now as has already been pointed out, it is a condition of the autonomy of any department of knowledge that it should be able to give an account of its own epistemological basis. And Hegel's analysis of the difficulties of giving an account of the relation of subject and object in knowledge in terms of the language of objective description shows that the judgments typical of empirical science do not, in fact, possess this essential autonomy. This takes away the whole basis of the absolute dualism of the empirical and the moral as it arises in Kant.

It may well be a convenient epistemological device for science to create what we have previously called a " laboratory situation " by assuming its own autonomy. It assumes that the position of the self in any experiment may be described simply as that of an observer set over against that which is observed. But the contradictions into which we are forced when we try to give an analysis of this situation show that this can only be an epistemological device and not the final truth about man's relation to the world of his experience. The critical analysis shows that man's relation to the world cannot be described simply as that of a subject to an object. This realisation forces us out of the " laboratory situation " which science creates and throws us back on the original unity of experience.

Let us return again to the illustration which I have already used. I can stand on the shore and look at the sea and see it as being at once blue-green, flaked with white, having the properties of water, as vast, mysterious, awe-inspiring, beautiful, etc. Now empirical science, in assuming that the situation of self-consciousness in the world can be described simply as that of a subject observing an object, thereby creates the type of " laboratory situation " in which the experimentally observable qualities of colour, shape, texture, chemical composition, etc., are those which constitute the objective world. The other qualities do not belong to this " laboratory situation ". They may represent merely our subjective reaction to the facts or they may belong to an entirely different order of facts. Science makes no judgment on this point. But it certainly excludes them from the world which it investigates.

But when it is shown that the situation of self-consciousness in existence cannot ultimately be described simply as that of a subject standing in relation to an object and that the autonomy of objective, empirical knowledge is therefore not absolute, we are thrown back on a situation in which the original unity of the total *Gestalt* of any given moment of experience is restored. The ground of the sharp division between objectively observable phenomena and the moral, religious and aesthetic factors in the situation is thus removed. This does not in itself give a guarantee that there is any systematic integration of our moral and religious experience with the natural, non-value elements in our experience. But it at least opens up the possibility of finding some positive relationship between those aspects of experience and so is an important qualification of the pessimism of the Kantian dualism. It opens up the possibility that the phenomenal world may have a religious significance related to or correlative with our more inward experience of the moral demand and the saving grace of God.

Quite apart from the criticisms which Hegel has suggested to us here, the same kind of criticism is latent in Kant's own system. He is able to avoid the difficulties involved in describing the situation of self-consciousness in existence only because of his rather naïve acceptance of the distinction between inward and outward experience, with time as the form of inward experience and space as the form of outward experience. If one simply accepts such a division of experience into two disjunctive sections, it is then an easy matter to give an account of the situation of self in the world as being simply that of a subject observing an object. But such a division of experience into what is inward and what is outward is open to the very same kind of objection as the simple analysis of experience in terms of subject and object.

The real situation is far less simple. Experience which is under the form of space is also under the form of time. All experience, whether merely temporal or spatio-temporal, is the experience of a conscious subject and therefore in some sense within the unity of that consciousness. Yet at the same time, all experience, whether temporal or spatio-temporal, as being that of which the subject is conscious, is distinguished from the unity of the self.

This difficulty becomes apparent in Kant's treatment of

what he calls the *Transcendental Unity of Apperception*. We find that at one time he has to speak of this as constituting the unity of the subject as self in the manifold series in time. Yet at the same time, he has to speak of it as the unity of the manifold of the phenomenal world. It is essential to his argument that it provide the unity of both. This points to the very same difficulty in giving an account of the relation of subject and object in knowledge as that which Hegel brought to light. On the one hand, the unity of all experience is the self, for it is this which constitutes the existence of self. On the other hand, the unity of experience is the unity of the world, for it is that which the self experiences and is held in contrast with the self. The challenge of these contradictions renders the naïve acceptance of the distinction between outward and inward experience impossible, and so lays bare the difficulties in maintaining the absolute autonomy of the empirical judgments of science. Thus the whole basis of the Kantian dualism is called in question.

(2) The second important point which emerges from our criticism of Hegel is the distinction between two senses in which we use the term " world ". One cannot discuss the idea of cosmic redemption without at some point raising the question : In what sense do we use the word " cosmos " or " world " ? Up to the moment we have been forced to proceed without such a definition. Now, however, the ground is prepared for the drawing of the necessary distinction.

From the standpoint of objective thought and the language of objective description, the world is purely and simply object. " The world is the totality of facts "[1]—the facts being whatever can be described in the language of objective description. In this sense, the term " world " is used as though it referred to an object in the same way as the term " this chair " refers to an object. It is dis-

[1] Wittgenstein, *Tractatus Logico-philosophicus*, Proposition 1.1.

tinguished from other terms referring to particular existents
only in that it refers to the totality of existents.   The
relation of any particular existent to the world in this
sense is simply that of part to whole.

The use of the term " world " in this sense involves no
implicit reference to conscious selfhood.   This is a convenient use of the term, but when any question is raised
which involves us in a serious attempt to describe the
situation of self-consciousness in existence, it is no longer
permissible.   The contradictions into which such an
attempt lead us show that the relation of self and world
cannot be described in terms of either simple disjunction
or simple conjunction.   The relation of self and world
cannot ultimately be described simply as that of part to
remainder or part to whole.   The particular determinations
of consciousness which constitute experience belong to the
unity of self ; yet they also constitute the given, the not-
self, the world which is held in contrast with self.   In this
context " self " and " world " are correlative terms.   One
cannot speak of " self " except as a self having a world.
One cannot speak of " world " except as the world of a self.

This distinction between the two senses of the term
" world " is not clearly stated.   It cannot be clearly stated,
because the situation of self in existence cannot be clearly
described.   As we have already shown, it is only as the
contradictions into which we are led express for us, and
refer us to, our own actual experience of our situation in
existence that the distinction between those two senses of
the word " world " can be understood.   Henceforth I shall
refer to the former sense as " the world as object ", and to
the latter sense as " the world as correlative with self in
experience ".

This distinction is important for any discussion of the
religious significance of the world.   For any religious proposition (as distinct from a merely theological proposition)
contains a reference, either implicit or explicit, to God or to

some transcendent attribute, such as " the Holy ". Now
God is never known simply as object. God does not exist
in the same way as an object exists. If God existed in
this way, He would be an object among other objects, and
this contradicts what we mean by God. Whatever else is
implied in the idea of transcendence, it at least has this
negative connotation that it cannot be known simply as
object. An object may have transcendental significance
for us, but *qua* object it is not transcendent.

Now if the world is described from the standpoint of the
autonomy of objective knowledge, i.e. if it is regarded
simply as object, there will be no reference to any factor
which cannot be described simply as object. There will,
therefore, be no reference to any element of encounter with
the transcendent which may, in fact, enter into our experience of the physical world. But when it is shown that
the autonomy of the system of objective knowledge is not
ultimate, and that the world cannot be completely described simply as object, we are thrown back on this other
sense of the term " world " which does not exclude *a
priori* any reference to that which cannot be treated simply
as object. We are thrown back on the conception of the
world as " that which is correlative with self in experience "—this being understood in terms of the foregoing
analysis of the situation of the self in existence. This,
then, is the primary sense in which we shall expect to use
the term when we try to describe how the world enters
into our experience of redemption.

(3) The third point which arises from our criticism of
Hegel is a new formulation of what we have found to be
the central problem determining the development of the
idea of cosmic redemption, namely the evils in and associated with our environment. For primitive Judaism, it
was first of all the hardships of life in the desert, then the
difficulties of occupying the promised land, and after the
occupation the perils of the life of a small nation surrounded

by expanding empires, and finally all the woes of the present
world as expressed in both Jewish and Christian apocalyptic. Then in Gnosticism with its background of
Ptolemaic astronomy, we found another expression of the
fear that the life and aspirations of man would be overwhelmed by a morally indifferent environment. In the
Middle Ages, something of the same fear was expressed in
the opposition of the realm of nature and the realm of
grace. Then against the background of the beginnings of
modern astronomy and physics we found a further expression of the fact that man's aspiration to beatitude and to
the fulfilment of his personal life is continually frustrated
by his environment. This was formulated by Kant in the
antinomy of practical reason.

But in all these cases, this fear is expressed with reference
to a particular cultural and historical situation. Our critical treatment of Hegel leads us to a more general statement of the same problem which is not dependent on this
or that particular scientific view of the universe, but which
reveals that element in the human situation which must
always leave man open to this kind of anxiety.

The insight into the situation of self-consciousness in
existence, which we have derived from a critical treatment
of Hegel, shows that this type of anxiety is inevitably
associated with the conditions of finite self-consciousness.
We have seen that this situation cannot be systematically
described in the same clear way as we describe the world
as object. It is only as our attention is directed to our
own experience of our situation in existence that we can
understand what is meant by " our situation in existence ".
But in the personal act of trying to understand this situation, we become aware of the very ground and possibility
of our anxiety.

It is not simply that the life of man and his destiny as a
personal self is menaced from without by capricious,
impersonal forces in nature, such as the droughts of the

desert or the great mass movements of history, or by the universe viewed as this or that particular type of mechanical system. The fact that man's existence as self in relation to a world cannot be ultimately described in terms of simple disjunction expresses the fact that environment impinges on the self, not only in an external way, but also as being in one sense within the self. In the ultimate analysis, it is man's experience which constitutes his world ; yet at the same time, it is equally true to say that it is man's experience which constitutes his self. Therefore, so long as the *given* in experience which constitutes the world is primarily presented as a sub-personal or impersonal content, whether it be mechanical or indeterminate in its structure, it must set up a tension within the life of the self. This gives us a profounder understanding of those problems of man's relation to his environment which we have found to be determining factors in the development of the idea of cosmic redemption.

(4) The broad lines of the solution to the problem as formulated in this way are also suggested to us by Hegel, even though we cannot accept the kind of argument by which he arrives at his solution or the terms in which he states it. Hegel's way of dealing with this material problem as though it were completely identical with the formal problem with which he begins, is based on a confusion of thought. This invalidates the whole argument by which he claims to overcome the diremption of self into self and not-self in the self-development of the Notion and in the unity of the three moments of thought in Absolute Spirit. As the answer to a logical problem, this must be regarded as nonsense. But here, as in his description of the situation of self-consciousness in existence, we can distinguish a genuine insight in the midst of his confused treatment of the systematic aspect of the problem.

The insight here is that it is only in so far as all man's experience becomes in some sense an encounter with God that there can be fulfilment of the personal life of self and that the problem of " unhappy consciousness " can be overcome.   The formal argument by which he reaches this conclusion may be invalid, but over and above the argument, there is a genuine insight into the ultimate problems and the longing of personal life.

In this sense it is a problem of religious mysticism rather than of systematic philosophy with which Hegel is contending.   So much is this so, that there are considerable sections of Hegel's work that can be read with much less intellectual struggle, and with much more enjoyment, if we approach his statements in the same way as we would those of a mystic like Jacob Boehme.[1]   If, for instance, we compare Hegel's account of the three-fold movement of Absolute Spirit[2] with Boehme's account of the seven-fold movement in God,[3] the presence of this mystical idiom of thought in the midst of what purports to be a systematic argument becomes evident.   Regarded in this light, Hegel's contention that the self can find fulfilment and rest only in finding God in the not-self answers to an element in our religious experience.

The problem of the evils in and associated with man's environment is ultimately that, in one way or another, man is continually frustrated in his longing for the blessedness to which he aspires as the fulfilment of his personal life.   That blessedness has been traditionally associated with the vision of God and communion with God.   The problem behind the Gnostic dualism was not merely or even primarily that of physical pain and privation, but rather that involvement in the system of the present world obscured that blessed communion with God.   So it was, too, in the covert dualism which we found to be typical of Mediaeval Christianity.   The poverty of the realm of

---

[1] Boehme did, in fact, have a considerable influence on the thought of Hegel.
[2] *Phenomenology of Mind*, pp. 757 ff.
[3] *The Incarnation of Jesus Christ*, pp. 151 ff.

O

nature lay primarily in its unheavenly character—its lack of the immediate presence of God. The miracle of the Mass, which translated natural bread and wine from the realm of nature into the realm of grace, was the real presence (the presence *in re*) of God in these consecrated elements. And again, even in the more secular, Kantian type of dualism, the hope of blessedness is referred away from the impersonal, phenomenal world to heaven, which is the traditional Christian symbol for life in the eternal and glorious presence of God.

This would seem to indicate that if these dualistic solutions are to be avoided in the alternative of a doctrine of cosmic redemption, then a central problem in our discussion of that doctrine must be to show how the redemptive act of God makes possible the fulfilment of personal life in an impersonal environment in such a way that all experience becomes an encounter with God. This need is symbolised in the longing of the ancient Hebrews, which was not merely for the promised land as a pleasant change from the nomadic life in the desert, but as a place where God would dwell with them. It is symbolised, too, in the name Immanuel (God with us) and in the significance which later came to be attributed to it both in Jewish and Christian circles.

All this, however, leads right away from the kind of problem with which we have been dealing in this section, and will be the main burden of the next. Meantime, the function of this section has been :

(*a*) To show, primarily by reference to the philosophy of Immanuel Kant, how essentially the same kind of problem as forced the early Christian church to re-assert the cosmic significance of the work of Christ is still a significant element in modern European thought.

(*b*) To show how Hegel also tried to solve the problem by reference to a re-interpretation of the cosmic significance of the work of Christ.

(*c*) To show that, while Hegel's attempt must be regarded as a failure, none the less, as critically appreciated, his work is of importance in relation to our subject, firstly, in attacking the Kantian type of dualism at its source, and secondly, in suggesting to us the foregoing insights into the problem and its solution.

PART IV

TOWARDS A MODERN FORMULATION

CHAPTER XV

REDEMPTION AND SUFFERING

WE have now two related, but very different, formulations of the problem which lies behind the doctrine of cosmic redemption. The first, which we dealt with chiefly in Parts I and II, stated the problem of man's relation to his environment in terms of the demonic forces operative in nature, and sought a solution in the proclamation of the victory of Christ over these forces. The second, which was reached after the transition period of the Middle Ages, stated the problem of man's relation to his environment, first of all in Kant, in terms of the antinomy of practical reason, and then in Hegel, in terms of the unhappy diremption of the self into self and not-self.

In the early period the problem was pointed most sharply by the Gnostics, and the anti-Gnostic Fathers sought a solution in the work of Christ. In its more modern phase, the problem was pointed most sharply by Immanuel Kant. Hegel, in his own peculiar way, sought a solution in the work of Christ. Despite the vast differences between these two phases of the problem, we were able to show the very close parallel that there is between the problem as formulated by the Gnostics and the problem as formulated by Kant. Therefore, although immediate appearances reveal no relationship whatsoever between these two phases of the problem, there is a fundamental, underlying unity.

We must now proceed to relate these two formulations of the problem to contemporary religious experience and thought ; and, by further analysis, to discover more clearly what this underlying, unitary problem is.

The Idea of Redemption in Our Own Experience. Any discussion of what we mean by redemption is bound to be fruitless unless it is related to our actual religious experience ; for it is ultimately only in terms of our own religious experience that we can give meaning to such a term. I do not intend to imply here that redemption is primarily a subjective experience. If the Atonement is an objective event, it is still only in our experience in the face of that event that we can know it as objective and efficacious. It is only in the enjoyment of redemption that we can know what redemption is. John McLeod Campbell, in his reaction against some excessively formal types of Calvinist theology, makes this point rather aptly in saying that it is only as seen " by its own light " that the Atonement can be rightly understood.[1]

Redemption, as known in this way, is an essentially personal experience. Without committing ourselves to this or that particular view of how the work of Christ is efficacious for our salvation, we can say that redemption is familiarly known throughout the Christian church primarily as a special personal encounter with God, arising out of the life and work of the Christ. It is an encounter in which we are aware at once of the awful holiness of God and of His inexhaustible forgiveness mediated to us in Christ.[2] It is the putting right of our relationship as persons with God by an act of God, and a renewal of life which proceeds from this reconciliation.

But this reconciliation cannot be exhaustively described simply in terms of the relationship of the individual and God. The renewal of life which proceeds therefrom finds expression in the recognition of a new relationship between man and man. The reconciliation with God is to be expressed in our lives in a reconciliation with fellow man.

---

[1] *The Nature of the Atonement*, pp. 98–110.

[2] There are, of course, those who dissociate the Atonement from the idea of forgiveness, notably Hastings Rashdall in *The Idea of the Atonement* ; but this is in no way a typical expression of Christian experience.

The forgiveness which we encounter in God is to be reflected in a forgiveness of " those who trespass against us " ; the inexhaustible love towards us which we encounter in God is to be reflected in love of neighbour.

All this is rather homiletical and does not say anything that is not common knowledge in Christendom, whatever be the differences in its practical interpretation. It is purposely vague, so as to avoid involvement in controversies which would not, at this stage, be profitable. But one point emerges quite clearly from it. The characteristic features of our experience of redemption are essentially personal. At its core it involves the personal relationships of forgiveness and love. If the meaning which we give to the term " redemption " is to be understood in the light of our experience and enjoyment of it, it must retain this essentially personal character.

The Idea of Cosmic Redemption. It is a common fallacy to imagine that if two words, which are each in themselves meaningful, are put together in a manner which is grammatically correct, they will produce a meaningful combination. And the phrase " cosmic redemption " has, at first sight, all the appearances of a fallacy of just this kind. The Greek word κόσμος has been adopted in the English language to serve in a number of capacities, some more clearly defined than others. But, in the main, it is associated with the ordered system of physical nature. The very fact that physical nature appears as a cosmos in this sense—an ordered, mathematically calculable system—sets it in contrast with the personal relationships with which we are concerned when we speak of redemption. What, then, can " cosmic redemption " mean ? How can a word which refers us primarily to an impersonal system be meaningfully associated with a word which is essentially personal in its significance ?

In New Testament times the situation was quite different. If one believes that the whole order of physical nature is inhabited by and directed by personal or semi-personal beings, then one can speak meaningfully about cosmic redemption. But such a conception of the order of physical nature belongs to another age and another culture. The modern European mind can only toy with such an idea. It cannot take it seriously. Nor is there any weight of evidence that would induce us seriously to reconsider this world-view. And so the question of interpretation, which had become a serious problem for the church as early as the second century, becomes much more difficult when we are speaking in terms of the twentieth century.

Yet while there is this difficulty on the one hand, it is equally difficult, on the other, to dissociate the idea of redemption entirely from any reference to the realm of physical nature. Man's life as a person is so intimately bound up with his life as a physical creature in a physical environment that anything that involves man as a person also involves him as a physical creature. We have already seen, in the work of Immanuel Kant, a very serious attempt to establish an absolute separation between man's life as a part of the physical cosmos and his life as a moral, personal being. We found not only that this position was closely parallel to an aspect of Gnosticism which the church condemned as heretical, but also that it did not ultimately represent a true account of the situation of self in the world.

It is only when man is under analysis and we are separating in thought what is united in actuality that this kind of sharp division appears. In the actual experience of the psycho-somatic unity which constitutes a living human person, the integration of the psychical and the physical is such that bodily considerations are introduced right at the very outset. It is true that Christian love, when we consider it in its essential nature for purposes of moral and theological analysis, may be described in purely psychical terms. But actual love is always love for a person in an actual situation. If that actual situation is physical, as the human situation universally is, then it involves concern for the physical well-being of the person loved. A love which is not so concerned is mere sentimentality.

Thus the perfect love of God which we encounter in our experience of redemption in Jesus Christ is known as being concerned with our physical life. And so the whole problem of the relation of the evils in and associated with our physical environment and our physical nature is raised, not in an impersonal way, but within the context of the personal encounter with God in redemption. Unless one is prepared to accept the type of dualism which condemns the whole physical order as being not of God and interprets redemption simply as release from the physical order, then one is forced to raise the question of cosmic redemption not in contrast with, but as an implicate of the idea of personal redemption. Physical nature cannot be treated as an indifferent factor—as the mere stage and setting of the drama of personal redemption. It must either be condemned as in itself evil or else it must be brought within the scope of the redemptive act.

In the light of this consideration, the words " cosmic redemption " can bear at least a formal significance. Assuming that we reject the dualistic solution as being in fundamental contradiction with the whole Christian faith, then cosmic redemption will mean that aspect of the redemptive work of Christ which manifests the love of God in relation to the physical situation of persons. This is only a formal statement. We can give little or no positive content to the idea until we have formed some definite conception of how the essentially personal event of our redemption could make any difference to the impersonal aspects of the human situation. This conception can only be reached, if at all, at the end of our enquiry. Meantime, in terms of the problem with which we are faced when we reject the dualistic interpretation of redemption, it has at least this formal meaning.

The Problem of Physical Evil and Privation. One's immediate reaction to this account of the significance of the idea of cosmic redemption is to conclude that if there ever were such an aspect of the work of Christ it would simply mean the removal of all pain and suffering. This clearly has not taken place.

But questions of this kind, as to whether God should have created a universe in which there was no pain, or whether He should have removed all pain and suffering in the work of redemption performed in Jesus Christ, have the trick of looking like straightforward moral issues when, in fact, they are not. The idea of a painless Utopia is quite meaningful to us and a delightful source of entertainment to the imagination as, for instance, in some of the charming, though somewhat fantastic, novels of C. S. Lewis. But whether it can be the subject of a serious moral judgment is another issue. This is a source of confusion which continually besets all discussion of the problem of suffering.

All suffering must, in one sense, be unequivocally condemned as evil—as a bad thing, as the opposite of blessedness. Otherwise it would not be suffering. But it does not follow that we can proceed from this to make moral judgments as to whether there ought or ought not to be such a thing as suffering in the universe of a good God. There is already in existence a vast body of literature which raises, and attempts to solve, this bewildering question. I do not propose to enter into it. My point is rather that it is a fruitless discussion which arises out of a fundamentally meaningless question. The question as to whether God should have removed all pain and suffering in His redemptive act of love is a moral question and as such can only be answered by reference to our own moral consciousness. But our moral experience is such that some element of suffering always enters in, and it is not merely as an incidental factor, but as an element essential to the whole structure of our moral experience. It is essential to moral

experience as we know it that there be some element of
resistance to the will—some desire which must be left
unsatisfied, some unpleasantness which must be accepted—
and it is this which gives reality to the moral struggle.   It
is only in terms of such a situation that we can make moral
judgments at all.   Therefore, even though we may be
capable of constructing in imagination a universe in which
there is no pain, we cannot meaningfully make moral
decisions about such a state of affairs.

What I am saying here must be distinguished from the
argument which says that since the possibility of suffering
is a condition of the moral struggle, therefore it is a
morally good thing that there should be suffering in the
universe.   The point is rather that since it is only in
situations where suffering in one form or other is a factor
to be reckoned with that we can make moral decisions at
all, any question as to whether suffering as such is morally
good or bad is ultimately meaningless.   The fact of suffering must be accepted as part of the " given " constitution
of experience, just as we accept the fact that our spatial
experience is three-dimensional, or any of the other " given "
elements in the constitution of experience which it is not
profitable to question.   I can ask significantly why God
should allow me to suffer in this particular way in this
particular moment.   But I cannot ask significantly whether
there should be suffering at all, when I am discussing the
life of moral persons ; for suffering enters constitutively
into the only thing that we know as moral personal life.
I cannot conceive of serious moral decision without there
being some element of " cost " to be reckoned with in the
making of that decision.   Nor can I dissociate the idea of
a *person* from such moral decision.

Therefore when we say, as it is our first impulse to do,
that since God's love for us will involve a concern for our
physical situation, the redemptive act of that love in Jesus
Christ is to be expected to remove all suffering and priva-

tion, we are making a statement which at first sight seems obvious, but which comes to mean less and less the more we think about it.

The problem is not simply that of suffering and privation as a whole, for some such element belongs essentially to the structure of personal moral life. The real problem is the vast amount of suffering which does not appear to belong to the moral structure of personal life at all. There is a vast difference, for instance, between the pains of martyrdom and the pains of a virulent and fatal cancer. Both may lead to the last extremity of physical pain. But in the case of martyrdom, the pain fits significantly into a pattern of personal decision. The martyr can say " I suffer this *for the sake of* . . . ". The pain is no less painful, but it holds a significant place within the context of personal life and moral decision. It is the extreme instance of pain manifesting itself as the hard core of resistance to the moral will which makes the moral struggle real. But the pain of a cancer is different. It may be no more painful, but it does not hold the same significant place within the personal life of moral decision. It is an impersonal and meaningless obtrusion upon personal life. Such suffering may, of course, provide the occasion for the manifestation of magnificent qualities of personal courage, but this is only incidental. It does not in itself provide grounds for accepting the pain and being content to bear it.

To come to an instance which, though less dramatic, is more in line with our everyday experience, suppose I have been over-working and have reached that miserable condition of both mental depression and physical weariness of which we all have our taste at one time or another. If this is prolonged it is an intensely unpleasant experience. But in the face of it, I may well find reason to continue working even in defiance of medical advice. This particular suffering is an integral part of a certain pattern of personal life and I can accept it as such. But when I compare this with the suffering associated with a gastric ailment which beset me for over two years, my attitude in this case is entirely different. It was not an acutely painful disease, but it left me permanently in the same condition of physical exhaustion and mental depression as can result from a prolonged period of over-work. Thus the actual discomfort suffered in both cases is much the same. But while the one is suffering of a kind which is an integral part of my life as a moral person, the other is just a sheer meaningless obtrusion on that personal life—a thing to which I cannot take up any positive attitude at all. In the one I realise myself as a person. The other is sheer frustration of my personal life.

This is a point which is brought out very clearly by Dr. H. H. Farmer in *The World and God*.[1] He begins by pointing out the futility of any questions in this connection about a painless universe. Some element of suffering is essential to the structure of moral personal life as we know it. He then goes on to say :

> How then do pain and frustration become a problem for the religious mind, and indeed for the mind of man generally ? They become a problem precisely at the point where they seem no longer to serve the high ends of zestful endeavour and strong personal life, but rather to run counter to them ; that is to say at the point where they seem to negate human personality rather than to minister to it.[2]

Dr. Farmer then enumerates three main ways in which " the frustrations of life take on this dysteleological quality ". Firstly, there are natural calamities of all kinds, such as earthquakes, typhoons, famines, etc. This impression of ruthless indifference is only reinforced by the " picture of nature as a blind concatenation of mechanical cause and effect relationships ". Secondly, there is the

---

[1] Pp. 93 ff.   [2] *Op. cit.*, p. 94 f.

fact that man always seems doomed to frustration. " Always man's reach seems to exceed his grasp ; he solves one problem and another rises in its place ; from the midst of one satisfaction another dissatisfaction is born ; like Moses on Mount Nebo he views the promised land and then inevitably hears the chilling words : ' I have caused thee to see it with thine eyes, but thou shalt not go over thither.' " Thirdly, there is the fact of death—the apparent end of self.

Of these three ways in which suffering appears as a mere impersonal obtrusion on the personal life of self, only the first is our primary concern here since our immediate problem is that arising out of the relation of environment to self. The physical constitution of the world is an important factor in both the other two aspects of suffering, but it does not enter into them in ways which could not be subsumed under a wide interpretation of the first point— namely the impersonal nature of environment and its indifference to personal values. It is this which constitutes the real problem of suffering.

The Tension Between the Personal and the Impersonal as Constituting the Underlying Problem Which Gives Unity to all our Previous Formulations of the Problem of Man's Relationship to his Environment. We have looked at the problem of man's relationship to his environment from the point of view of Judaism and Jewish apocalyptic, of primitive Christianity, of Gnosticism, of the anti-Gnostic Fathers, of Mediaeval Thomism, and of the scientific Renaissance and German Idealism. We have now approached the problem from the standpoint of our own moral experience considered in relation to physical environment. Our analysis of the problem of physical evil and privation has led us to a new formulation of the moral problem of man's relationship to his environment. We found that the problem is not simply that of the existence of suffering and privation The real problem is that of the impersonal nature of environment and its indifference to personal moral values.

In all the various phases through which we have traced the fortunes of the idea of cosmic redemption, we have consistently found that the determining factor was the attitude to the problem of suffering and privation and the solution offered thereto. We found this problem formulated in many different ways, ranging from the conceptions of primitive Judaism to our interpretation of the Hegelian conception of unhappy consciousness. We must now find one formulation of the problem under which all these different formulations can be subsumed. We shall then know clearly where the essence of the problem lies. I believe that we have found such a formulation when we describe the problem of suffering as resolving itself ultimately into the problem of the relation of the personal and the impersonal in the world. This is not immediately obvious but requires some demonstration, to which we now proceed.

One can easily see how certain aspects of the problem of suffering, as it has appeared in our previous chapters, can be subsumed under this one head. The longing and the prayer of man has not appeared simply as being for a world with all the harmless properties of a padded cell. The sufferings from which man has sought redemption have always been those arising from impersonal events and qualities in the world which obtrude upon and frustrate his life as a personal being—the great mass movements of expanding empires which had ceased to be the expression of a personal society and had become an impersonal force taking no account of the moral dedication of the small nation of Israel to a holy God ; the unaccountable caprice of the elements of nature ; the visitation of disease and of death, the greatest enemy of personal life ; the fateful and inexorable movements of the heavenly bodies as witnessing to the impersonal determinism of the forces to which man's

P

life was subject; the mechanical determinism of the
universe of Newton. Kant's formulation of the problem
in the antinomy of practical reason refers us in more
general terms to the same aspect of our environment—the
impersonal structure of the world and the indifference of
its laws to personal moral values.

In the last analysis, Hegel's problem of " unhappy
consciousness ", as we have interpreted it, refers us in a
subtler way to the same factors in our experience. This
can be seen from the following considerations.

So long as we think of the impersonal forces which
obtrude upon man's personal life only as external factors
which frustrate the realisation of his purposes in the world,
we have not felt the full weight of this problem. The kind
of solution which we found in the Gnostics and in Kant
tries to restrict the problem within these limits. It may
be pessimistic in that it despairs entirely of this universe
as a suitable place for the full realisation of man's life as
person ; yet at the same time it does offer hope of salvation
of a kind. The sharp distinction between " the starry
heavens without " and " the moral law within " may be
the source of Kant's despair as it is expressed in the antinomy of practical reason ; but at the same time the very
sharpness of the distinction endows the inward life of self
with a kind of isolated, unassailable security. If only one
can be assured that the moral law and the centre of personal
life which it implies is unassailably shut up " within ", and
the menacingly impersonal structure of the world and the
heavenly bodies is entirely " without ", so that though it
may in some degree frustrate the purposes of self it can
never seriously menace the essentially inward life of self,
there is real comfort in this assurance. This is the source
of its religious appeal and of the widespread acceptance of
this kind of world-view in some forms of pietistic Christianity.

But this happy assurance of the inward security of self,

whatever may be the frustrations that come from without, must always be qualified by the knowledge that it is in this world and in some sense as part of it that we exist. This forces upon us the realisation that the impersonal structure of the world not merely frustrates the personal life of self from without, but even negates the inner integrity of free, personal selfhood. At its simplest level, this consists in the recognition that physically man is only a minute particle in this vast, impersonal system. The inward threat which this fact offers to the life of self is expressed in the fear which it engenders that perhaps our life of personal decision is somehow only an illusion.

At the level of philosophic inquiry there are many cogent arguments with which to allay such a fear. But the moment of despair in which this fear is an actual, lived experience remains real and frightening and is by no means confined to the philosophers, though others may not be so articulate in their verbal expression of it. One may, for instance, in a moment of bereavement look upon the " last remains "—all that has been left by the relentless progress of natural forces as they cut right across a personal life—so obviously a dead thing and not a person any more—and experience the despairing fear that perhaps all the inwardness of personal life is merely a brief illusion which finally fades again into the impersonal structure of the universe. Or again, the awe which Immanuel Kant admitted he felt when he contemplated the " starry heavens without " was not merely the outcome of his philosophic inquiry. Despite the extreme austerity of his emotional life, he here expresses something of that sense of personal insecurity which we all sometimes feel in the face of so terrifying a vista.

This brings us to a point where we can see more clearly the relevance of the anlaysis of the difficulties of giving an account of the situation of the self in existence, which arose out of what may at the time have appeared as a tedious and unnecessary criticism of Hegel. If only one could give an account of the relation of self and world in terms of simple disjunction or conjunction, the menace which the impersonal structure of the world offers to the personal life of self would not be so serious. If the relation of self and world could be described in the same way as we describe the relation of one object in existence to the totality of objects, then the inner nature of self could be regarded as unaffected by the impersonal nature of the world. Self and world could be regarded as two distinct natures co-existing and only externally related to one another. The outward realisation of the purposes of self might be frustrated by the impersonal nature of the world, but its inner nature would remain secure. But when it is realised—as in our previous chapter we tried to show—that the relation of self and world cannot ultimately be thus described and that ultimately self and world are correlative terms, two consequences follow. On the one hand, the source of the Kantian type of dualism is taken away so that at least the possibility of integrating man's experience of the natural world with his inner moral life remains open. But on the other hand, it also opens up the possibility that man's inner life as person, as well as his outward expression of that life in purposeful activity, may be overwhelmed by the impersonal structure of the world.

The ground of personal anxiety in the situation of the self in existence, as we tried to describe it, turns out to be just this conflict between the personal and the impersonal in the correlation of self and world. It is the totality of " given " experience which constitutes my awareness of the world as over against me ; yet it is also that same totality which I recognise as constituting my concrete existence as self. All experience is both inward and outward at the same time. Ultimately the outward structure of experience as my world is correlative with its inward structure as myself. Therefore the inward structure of self does not remain unaffected by the impersonal structure of its world.   This is the problem of the " diremption of self into self and not-self " which became so hopelessly confused with a purely logical problem about the relations of universal and particular in Hegel's treatment of it.   In reality it is simply this problem of the conflict of the personal and the impersonal in the correlation of self and world.

This at least shows that the tension between the personal and the impersonal is a constant factor appearing in all the different formulations of the problem with which we have been dealing.   It runs like a single uniting thread through all the wide variety of ideas with which we have been concerned.   But this, in itself, is not sufficient to establish the ultimate unity of the problem.   We are still faced with the fact that the problem has appeared in two main phases which are very widely different from one another.   There is the early phase, covering the Biblical and patristic periods, which forms a recognisable unity.   Then there is the modern philosophic phase which forms another recognisable unity.   We have already recognised certain parallels between these two.   This appeared most clearly in the parallel between the Kantian and the Gnostic treatment of the problem.   The recognition that the problem of the tension between the personal and the impersonal is the central factor which is common to both enables us to state this parallel in more general terms.   But unless we can relate the concepts employed in the early phase in a more positive way to the concepts employed in the modern, philosophic phase, then we are still dealing with two largely unrelated problems.

In the early period the problem was conceived primarily in terms of the demonic possession of nature.   In the modern phase the problem is conceived primarily in terms of the relationship of personal beings to an impersonal universe.   How are these very different concepts related to one another ?   This is the question we must now try to answer. But before we can hope to do so we must carry out further analysis of what these concepts mean in this context and further investigation of the ways in which they enter into our experience.

CHAPTER XVI

THE MEANINGLESS AND THE DEMONIC

IF man's world were entirely impersonal and incapable of entering in an integral way into his life, man could not be a person at all. He would be a creature responsive to an environment, but not a person in a world. If there is no element of personal *meaning* in the not-self which is correlative with the personal structure of self, then there could be no such inner personal structure. The nature of self is such that it can exist only in correlation with a world which has significance for it.

When we say that there is an element of personal meaning in man's world, we must distinguish between mere conventional meaning and real meaning—or in the terminology of Dr. H. H. Farmer, between extrinsic and intrinsic symbols. The symbols " 1, 2, 3 " have meaning for me, but it is an artificial, man-made meaning. This artificiality is manifest in the fact that ultimately they can have any meaning I care to give them—though normally it is advisable for me to use the same convention as my banker in interpreting them. On the other hand, real or intrinsic meaning does not depend upon any convention, but simply waits for us to perceive it for what it is.

An intrinsic symbol is any object or situation which evokes a personal response from us. Mere environmental stimuli evoke biological response, but this in itself is subpersonal, for it does not involve the intentionality of self. By intentionality I mean all that involves personal decision or the deliberate adoption of a particular attitude. H. H. Farmer points to the bodily acts of persons as the most

obvious example of intrinsic symbols.[1] Words, in the
main, have their meaning only by convention and are
extrinsic rather than intrinsic symbols. But in the bodily
acts of persons there are attitudes and gestures which speak
directly to us as persons and evoke decision and modifica-
tion of attitude on our part. They do so because they
bespeak the unseen inward attitude of another person. It
is not simply that we *infer* the other person's attitude from
his bodily gestures. When I am introduced to a man who
smiles or frowns when he shakes my hand, I do not make a
rapid mental calculation about his inner attitude. I react
immediately to the situation. Indeed, any such calculation on my part would be regarded as an offence, because
I would be regarding him as a calculable factor rather than
encountering him as a person. In the meeting of persons,
bodily gesture has intrinsic meaning in its own right and
evokes personal response.

This factor in the world which evokes our response as
persons, while it may best be illustrated from our relations
with other human beings, is by no means limited to this
field of experience. For instance, in a different way, but
still in a way which involves us as persons, all serious works
of art have intrinsic meaning for us. Aesthetics is one of
the most neglected and badly handled topics in the whole
realm of philosophy. I do not propose to right this wrong
here, but merely wish to draw attention to certain factors
in our artistic experience which are important to our
understanding of the relationship of persons to a world of
things.

There is an intimate relationship between the beautiful
and that which has intrinsic meaning in relation to the
intentionality of persons. Art is certainly concerned with
the production of the beautiful. But beauty is a subtle
lady who will not be wooed unless we have a gift to bring
her. That is to say, it is not enough that the artist should

[1] Farmer: *The World and God*, p. 75.

set out with the sincere intention of producing something beautiful. He must have something worth saying before he can say it in a beautiful form. The work of art cannot be beautiful unless it has some kind of meaning—though not necessarily a meaning which can be otherwise expressed. If a poet sets out with the dominant intention of simply producing a beautiful poem, the result can be at best pretty, but not beautiful. So it is, too, with the painter whose dominant intention is simply that of producing a beautiful painting. But while the work of art must say something—must have a meaning—it cannot rely too heavily on conventional, artificial, extrinsic symbols for the expression of this meaning. Extrinsic meaning is as much out of place in the field of art as intrinsic meaning is essential to it. One becomes aware of this in certain types of programme music where the use of conventional sonic representations of certain actions or events tends to detract from, rather than add to the artisitc value of the piece. One finds the same thing, too, when extrinsic, conventional symbols are introduced into a painting as representations of certain objects or thoughts. Or again, the inherent weakness of all truly didactic poetry is that it must rely so heavily on the use of purely extrinsic symbols.

This confirms that the kind of meaning with which art is concerned is not extrinsic but intrinsic meaning. That is to say, the true work of art has meaning for us because it claims our response as persons. It not merely receives our attention, but claims it and holds it. It is not at our service, ready to be used for whatever may be our purpose, the way other things are—not until we have deliberately refused to recognise it as a work of art. We do not merely experience it as a work of art. We meet it as we meet persons.

When we try to describe what the work of art means to us as persons, we find ourselves saying the same kind of thing as we say of our encounter with other persons.

Martin Buber, in his *I and Thou,* is mainly concerned with this whole problem of the relation of persons to an impersonal world—a problem which he describes in terms of the contrast between the " I-it " relationship and the " I-Thou " relationship. Of the work of art he says :

> This (the I-Thou relationship) is the eternal source of art : a man is faced with a form which desires to be made through him into a work. This form is no offspring of his soul, but is an appearance which steps up to it and demands of it effective power. . . .[1]
> I can neither experience nor describe the form which meets me, but can only body it forth. . . . In bodying forth I disclose. I lead the form across into the world of " it ". The work produced is a thing among things, able to be experienced and described as the sum of its qualities. But from time to time it can face the receptive beholder in its whole embodied form.
> —What then, do we experience of Thou ?
> —Just nothing. For we do not experience it.
> —What then, do we know of Thou ?
> —Just everything. For we know nothing isolated about it any more.[2]

Buber's thoughts are his own and must be understood within the context of his own work. But he is clearly referring here to the same element in our artistic experience as I have in mind. We encounter a work of art in the same way as we encounter a " Thou " because the kind of meaning which it bears cannot be understood in terms of any mere convention of language, but only in the response which it evokes from us as persons. It is not itself a person. It belongs to the world of " it " ; but as correlative with our intentionality as persons it transcends the world of " it " and enters in an integral way into the structure of personal life.

This takes us one stage further in our appreciation of

[1] P. 9.   The words in brackets are mine.   [2] Pp. 10–11.

the manner in which the world as correlative with self enters into the structure of personal life instead of standing simply in impersonal conflict with it. The first example was in the direct personal response which the physical gestures and actions of other persons evoke from us. This is the first point at which we would expect to find an integration of the physical world with the personal life of self. In finding that we can make the same type of response to a work of art, however, we discover a wider sense in which elements in the physical world can stand in an essentially personal relationship to us. It is true that the personal activity of the artist lies behind the work of art, but in the work of art we find an element of personal meaning which is one stage further removed from the realm of the immediately personal. It shows the sense in which a purely inanimate object can enter into relations with us as persons.

From this it is only one further step to the sense in which the natural order can have significance for us in terms of what is essentially personal in our nature. The whole natural order can have intrinsic meaning for us in so far as it evokes a response from us as persons. It can evoke from us the same kind of response as we make to the bodily presence of another person or to a work of art. Though the quality of the response may be very different in each case, it may still retain the same essentially personal character. Just as the response we make to a work of art can be recognised as belonging to the same genus as that which we make to persons, in that it is *as persons* that we respond in both cases, so again in the face of nature we can discern in ourselves another different manifestation of this same kind of response.

The idea that at least some objects, events, situations or elements in the natural order can have intrinsic significance for us is by no means new. Indeed, it represents what is perhaps the oldest form of religious experience. At the

level of primitive polytheism it is expressed in the belief
that all things are full of little gods. The same element
persists in experience even when these primitive expressions of it have long since been discarded from our culture.
The wide popularity of Otto's book, *The Holy*, and his
analysis of our experience of what he calls the *mysterium
tremendum et fascinans* in nature has drawn general attention to the persistence of this element in experience and its
continued importance in our religious life. As Otto makes
clear at the outset, it cannot be understood except by those
who can recognise such an element in their own experience.
But this includes most, if not all men. It is in their
intellectual analysis and interpretation of the experience
that they differ. I have looked upon a great rock and in
that moment understood why men could fall down and
worship a stone. Most people can recall a number of such
occasions on which they have become aware of this sense
of the numinous in nature. Even the awe which Immanuel
Kant felt when he surveyed the " starry heavens without "
has something of this quality in it.

I do not propose to reiterate Otto's analysis of the
emotional elements involved in this experience. It is well
known, and there is no point at which I would differ fundamentally from him so far as the description of the characteristic emotions involved in this experience is concerned.
But when this has been accepted, there are two related
points of criticism which are very relevant to our problem.
The second will become relevant shortly. The first must
be treated now.

What we are looking for at this stage in our argument is
an element in the natural order which has intrinsic meaning
for us as persons in that it claims a personal response from
us and is not merely an impersonal obtrusion upon personal
life. Some such element does seem to be associated with
this experience of the *mysterium tremendum et fascinans* as
an encounter with the Holy in nature. But if we are to

regard this experience as entirely irrational and as pure feeling response, as Otto tends to do, then what we are dealing with is not an essentially personal response but rather a mere animal reaction.   John Oman, in his critical review of Otto's book, brings out this point very clearly. There is one paragraph in this article which is sufficiently instructive and amusing to be worth quoting here in full.

The first question concerns what he calls the Numinous. In identifying it with religion and maintaining it, in spite of all he says about the rational, to be the essential in religion throughout, is he not making the very mistake he condemns, of treating as mere evolution what really is transmutation ?   The sense of the numinous, which etymologically is " what nods ", may stir and pass over into the sense that the ultimate reality is personal, but is it the same ?   The higher animals have it, possibly in a higher degree than man.   Prof. Otto tells a story of his horse, but I have one of mine much more relevant. When a boy of fourteen or thereabouts, I was riding through the Standing Stones of Stenness on a winter afternoon when dusk was settling into darkness.   They stand on the top of a lone narrow neck of land between two lochs.   The close-cropped heather crackled under my horse's feet, the loch on the right was still shining under the glow of sunset and the loch on the left was dark almost to blackness, and across a bay the grave-stones in the churchyard stood white and clear over it. The circle of stones had a look of ancient giants against the grey sky, and the gaping mounds which had been opened stood shadowy and apart.   A more numinous scene, at a more numinous hour, could not be found on earth.   And the feeling which suddenly struck me is not inaptly described as the *mysterium tremendum et fascinans*. But at the same moment, it struck my old horse at least as vehemently as myself.   He threw up his head, snorted, set his feet, trembled, and finally bolted at a rate I should have thought impossible for his old bones. Now there is little doubt that Prof. Otto is right in finding the reason why the early Briton erected this circle of stones on that particular spot in the peculiar eerie feeling it created rather than in merely intellectual ideas ; but, as the feeling had probably not yet arrived at being religious for my horse and had ceased to be religious for me, it would be necessary to ask, what was the peculiarity which, without disrespect to his intelligence, I may assume my horse not to have attained and which, without excessive pride in my state of civilisation, I may assume I had passed beyond, which made it for primitive man religious ?   In spite of the mechanical ideas imposed upon me by a scientific age, I persist in thinking that the feelings aroused by nature which gave rise to animism have more to say for themselves than the people whose acquaintance with nature is chiefly in laboratories and tourist resorts admit ; and it is easier to have a religious sense of a living world than of a dead one.   But are these feelings in themselves religious ?   They may stir and pass over into the holy, to use Prof. Otto's own correct description, but are we not then in a new order ? And is not the essence of it that it is an order of absolute value which, when it escapes from its material form, is just the ethical sacred, the sense of the requirements of a Spirit in the world which is absolute and of a spirit in ourselves in its image which has its worth in accepting as its own these absolute requirements and refusing to bring them down to the level of our temporal convenience ?   It may only appear in an irrational material taboo, but, if man has said, " This is sacred, and I would rather die than disregard it ", he is not only religious, but, by his religion, he has won a footing amid the sands of changing impulse and association.   My horse, we may assume, had not reached this valuation, and I was at least learning to make it by less material ways.[1]

Oman's criticism here is perhaps too severe in that when Otto speaks of feeling response and of the irrational in experience he does not mean anything quite so irrational and sub-personal as Oman does.   This becomes clear in Otto's treatment of what he calls the aesthetic element in religious experience in his *Philosophy of Religion*.   In Chapter X of this work he deals with the element of feeling

[1] *The Journal of Theological Studies,* Vol. XXV, April, 1924 ; "The Idea of the Holy," pp. 282–283.

response in religious experience. He recognises these feelings as involving an element of judgment. He claims that they are irrational in the sense that they do not involve what he would call *logical* judgment.[1] It may be that this does not turn out to be an acceptable distinction within the idea of judgment, but it at least shows that what Otto has in mind when he speaks of the feeling response in religion is not quite the purely animal thing that Oman understands by the term.

However, the main point of Oman's criticism still stands in that Otto does not show any clear point of differentiation between our personal response to the sense of the Holy as immanent in the world and a purely animal reaction to a strange situation and sometimes even gives the impression that he is quite oblivious to the distinction. It is just this distinctively personal element which constitutes the difference between the encounter with the Holy as immanent in nature and a purely animal reaction to a strange and unusual situation. In so far as our experience of the *mysterium tremendum et fascinans* is an encounter with the Holy, it is an encounter with intrinsic meaning, and not merely an emotional reaction; it has the character of a personal encounter, for it involves our personal response.

We can now form a clearer idea of what is meant when we speak of physical environment as standing in a personal relationship to us. Our personal life consists largely in the fact that we stand in a relationship of personal *rapport* with certain elements in the not-self. This appears obviously in our social relations with other persons. But we have also found that our relations with the purely physical can sometimes assume a personal character. We have found that what is not itself a person can enter into personal relations with us in terms of its intrinsic meaning for us. We illustrated this first of all from the physical gestures and dispositions of persons, and then from the work of

[1] Otto, *Philosophy of Religion*, p. 133.

art, and finally from the experience of the Holy in the face of nature.

If only all man's experience involved this element of intrinsic meaning and claimed from him this kind of personal response, then the whole problem of the diremption of his life into that which is personal and that which is impersonal would be overcome. Martin Buber expresses something of this longing and this hope when he says :

> If only we love the real world that will not let itself be extinguished, really in its horror, if only we venture to surround it with the arms of our spirit, our hands will meet hands that grip them.[1]

The language here is typical of Buber, and, however expressive, it is not very precise. But the least that such a statement can mean is that if only we will have the courage to enter into personal relationship with the world as it is, we shall find that it enters significantly into our personal life instead of merely obtruding upon it. This does depend partly on our willingness to respond in a personal way to our world. But if this relationship is to be possible, our experience of the world must come to us in a form which claims our personal response. We have seen that there are certain situations in which it does, but this is by no means always so, and Buber does not give sufficient weight to this difficulty.

Bertrand Russell states the other side of the case when he says :

> That man is the product of causes which had no prevision of the end which they were achieving ; that his origin, his growth, his hopes and fears, his loves and beliefs are but the outcome of accidental collocations of atoms ; that no fire, no heroism, no intensity of thought and feeling, can preserve an individual life beyond the grave ; that all the labour of the ages, all the devotion, all the

---

[1] *I and Thou*, p. 94.

inspiration, all the noon-day brightness of human genius, are destined to extinction in the vast death of the solar system, and that the whole temple of man's achievement must eventually be buried beneath the *debris* of a universe in ruins—all these things, if not quite beyond dispute, are yet so nearly certain that no philosophy which rejects them can hope to stand. Only within the scaffolding of these truths, only on the firm foundation of unyielding despair can the soul's inhabitations hence-forth be safely built.[1]

If this is not the whole truth about man's universe, it is at least an important aspect of the truth which, if we are not to give ourselves up to an unrealistic romanticism, we must recognise. This aspect of the world claims no response from us as persons. It does not look like the world of a personal God at all. If God loves man concretely and has conferred redemption upon him in his actual situation, then this aspect of the world must somehow be overcome and transfigured in the work of Christ. This is the modern form of the problem which the doctrine of cosmic redemption must answer.

The Tension Between the Personal and the Impersonal Considered in Relation to the Primitive Conception of the Conflict Between the Holy and the Demonic. How is all this related to the Biblical treatment of the problem in terms of the conflict between Christ and the demons? If we are to find any relationship at all, we must first of all reach a sympathetic appreciation of what was involved in this belief in a demon-possessed universe. We must see it not simply as a ridiculous illusion, but try to understand the experience which lies behind it.

The ideas of both the Holy and the demonic have suffered considerably from attempts to reduce them to the purely secular ideas of goodness and evil. Of the two, the idea of the demonic has suffered most in this respect. We have already referred to the great service rendered by

[1] *Mysticism and Logic*, p. 47.

Q

Rudolf Otto in rehabilitating the idea of the Holy as expressing an irreducible element in our experience. We criticised Otto for failing to recognise the element of personal response as well as the purely emotional reaction which is involved in the experience of the Holy. But this does not affect his main contention that the experience of the Holy always involves an element of what is quite appropriately called the experience of the *mysterium tremendum et fascinans* and cannot be described in purely ethical concepts.

However, because he describes this aspect of the encounter with the Holy as mere emotional reaction and not as personal response, and so severs it completely from the moral content of the idea of the Holy, he precludes at the outset any possibility of drawing moral distinctions within our experience of the *mysterium tremendum et fascinans*. He has to produce the moral content as an emergent factor at a later stage, like a magician producing a rabbit out of an empty hat. One serious consequence of this is that he falls into the error of thinking that, because all encounter with the Holy essentially involves the experience of the *mysterium tremendum et fascinans*, therefore all experience of the *mysterium tremendum et fascinans* is an encounterwith the Holy. This, of course, does not follow. The fact is that the primitive emotional elements into which Otto analyses the experience of the *mysterium tremendum et fascinans* may be associated with evil as much as with the personal values of righteousness and love which emerge as the moral element in the Holy. It is the encounter with impersonal evil in the setting of the *mysterium tremendum et fascinans* which constitutes the experience of the demonic, and lies behind the belief in this or that particular demon.

Otto is aware that the experience of the *mysterium tremendum et fascinans* can have this demonic aspect, at least in primitive religious experience. But he makes the mistake of treating it as simply a primitive interpretation of the element of *tremendum* in the Holy.   If, however, we recognise that both the demonic and the Holy are associated with the kind of experience that Otto describes as the *mysterium tremendum et fascinans*, but that each is distinct and *sui generis*, some of the main difficulties of Otto's argument are overcome.   We have already argued that in so far as the type of experience associated with the *mysterium tremendum et fascinans* is an encounter with the Holy, it must involve not merely an emotional reaction, but a personal response.   It is primarily in this aspect that the demonic is distinguished from and contrasted with the Holy.   The essence of the demonic is sheer enmity to the personal.   It is that which menaces the rational intentionality of the personal from within and frustrates and stultifies it from without.

It is only as a loose form of speech that we can say that the demons, as they are spoken of in the New Testament, for instance, are personal creatures inhabiting nature. They are rather sub-personal spirits.   It is when a man has descended to a sub-personal level of behaviour, as for example in madness, that he is said to be possessed by demons.   Or again, in the Epistles of St. Paul, the animal desires and passions, in so far as they over-ride the intentionality of persons and become compulsions and obsessions, are associated with the activities of demons. Disease, obtruding upon and frustrating personal life, is regarded as the work of demons.   Any force which is sub-personal in form and super-human in power has demonic associations for the primitive mind.   Whenever man encountered forces which were too great for him to control, yet too void of meaning for him to make a personal submission to them in worship, these forces came to be associated with the activities of demonic powers.

But the idea of the demonic is not to be thought of as simply equivalent to that of impersonal evil any more than the idea of the Holy can be simply equated with the values of personal righteousness. The thought of the impersonal structure of the world as it is described, for instance, in the passage from Bertrand Russell which we quoted above, may be depressing and even perturbing. But if it is no more than the thought of the impersonal, it does not terrify. In its demonic aspect, however, it has the awful and terrifying aspect of the *tremendum* as Otto describes it. But it is not merely the *mysterium tremendum* set over against the Holy as the *mysterium fascinans* ; for the Holy is also *tremendum* in its awful majesty and the demonic is also *fascinans* in its seductive and tempting way. It tempts us to abandon the effort to be a person and to realise the values of personal life. It tempts us to accept the meaninglessness of the world and to abandon ourselves to it, either accepting the destruction of self in subjection to sub-personal influences both of inward desire and outward pressure, or by a tyrannical assertion of self against all that is not-self without any regard to the intrinsic values of personal life.

Like the experience of the Holy, the experience of the demonic cannot be understood simply in terms of its analysis. It is only in so far as we can enter into a sympathetic understanding of it that we can appreciate its force. One can best understand how it figured in the mind of primitive peoples by a sympathetic appreciation of their art. There are certain characteristics which appear in all archaic forms of art which suggest the demonic element in experience. In a typical statue of the archaic period of Greek sculpture, for instance, when the Holy and the demonic had not yet begun to be clearly distinguished, the statues of the gods stand in an impassive, blank, sub-personal attitude, often wearing a fixed, mysterious smile on an otherwise expressionless face. Yet along with these sub-personal aspects, there is the suggestion of a super-human power—a suggestion that the statue dominates us rather than we it. One cannot walk round it as one can walk round the more personal statues of a later period. It faces front and must be approached from in front. The approach to it is like an act of submission. It is at once terrifying and fascinating, yet it stultifies all attempts to adopt a positive personal attitude towards it.[1]

When the demonic is thus considered as representing a living element in experience and not merely as a curious, out-moded belief in a host of unseen beings, its relevance to the serious problems of religion becomes apparent. In expressing both the terror and the tempting fascination which man feels in the face of forces which are sub-personal in character yet super-human in power, it represents essentially the same problem as that with which we have been dealing—namely the menace with which the impersonal structure of man's world threatens his personal life. Therefore when we say that the central problem which the doctrine of cosmic redemption must solve is that of the suffering arising out of the impersonal nature of man's environment, we have not moved so far from the Biblical conception of redemption which is expressed in the assertion that Christ has overcome the power of the demons. The concepts are different, as they must be if we are to interpret the idea in terms of our own culture. But it is essentially the same factors in experience that are involved. So in spite of the diversity of its various formulations, the problem is fundamentally a unity.

[1] Paul Tillich, who, more than any other modern theologian, has recognised the importance of the idea of the demonic, claims that it is chiefly from a study of archaic art that he has arrived at his appreciation of what is meant by the demonic. *Cf. The Interpretation of History,* pp. 77 ff.

CHAPTER XVII

THE FORM OF THE ANSWER

IT is now time to take another look about us and see where we stand in the argument as a whole.

(1) Right at the very outset we accepted the principle that :

> Once a community has accepted a redemptive faith, the impact of their environment upon them forces them either to narrow their concept of redemption by giving it an other-worldly interpretation, or to widen its reference so as to include the whole of their environment.

(2) We illustrated this principle from the development of Jewish eschatology, showing that it was the latter alternative which they preferred and how this led to the formulation of the Biblical doctrine of cosmic redemption.

(3) In Parts II and III we further illustrated the same principle from the fact that the church, in different ages, has been forced to choose between various forms of other-worldly dualism and a serious interpretation of the doctrine of cosmic redemption. We found that the modern form of this dualism is based on the conscious recognition of the tension between the impersonal, determinate world of physical environment and the world of personal activity and personal moral value.

(4) In the present section, turning back from this theological and philosophical analysis to our own experience, we found this same tension between the personal and the impersonal, appearing not merely as an academic problem, but as a source of personal anguish. We then proceeded to show the essential identity of this problem, expressed in

these modern terms, with the problem which the New Testament writers express in terms of the domination of the natural order by demons.

The apocalyptic promise, as we have interpreted it, and in so far as it relates to physical environment, was essentially that this element in environment, which threatens to overwhelm man's personal life, would somehow be overcome. There is no doubt that the faith of the New Testament did express the belief that these elements had been overcome or had begun to be overcome in and through the work of Christ. They expressed this by saying that He had broken the power of the demons. We must now enquire what such a faith means in terms of living experience.

When we see the belief in demons not as mere fantasy, but as giving recognition to an aspect of the world which is all too real and prominent in human experience, one thing becomes certain. Not even the Christians of the first century would have been so credulous as to believe that this painful and frustrating aspect of experience was overcome, simply because there was a tradition to that effect. There must have been something in their experience of Christ which confirmed this tradition or they could not have subscribed to it with such confidence and enthusiasm.

Now if we have been successful in our efforts to show that the problem, as it was stated by the early church in terms of demonic possession, is fundamentally the same as the problem as we now state it in terms of the tension between the personal and the impersonal, then the same problem will have the same solution. This means that those elements in the religious experience of the Christians of the first century, which confirmed them in the belief that Christ had overcome the demons, will also constitute our main evidence for believing that Christ has transformed the impersonal and meaningless nature of our environment.

They will thus constitute the basis in experience for any modern formulation of the doctrine of cosmic redemption, and will determine its meaning for us.   It seems reasonable to suppose that these elements will be duplicated in our experience, since it is the constant claim of the church that we continue to share in the faith of the New Testament.

But at this point we encounter a difficulty.   The fact that we share in the essentials of the faith of the New Testament does not mean that our religious experience is in all respects parallel to the experience of early Christians. Our experience of the various charismatic ministries that are listed by St. Paul (1 Corinthians 12/8–10) appears to be different from theirs.   And it may well be argued that it was just in the exercise of these very ministries—particularly the ministry of divine healing—that the first Christians found evidence of the universal efficacy of the work of Christ.   We are told that the blind saw, the lame walked, the lepers were cleansed, the deaf heard and the dead were raised.   This was the evidence which the first Christians claimed to have seen with their own eyes.

This, however, is just the kind of evidence which does not appear, at first sight, to be available to us.   Therefore it would seem that though there are elements in our experience which present essentially the same problem as that which was solved for the early church by the doctrine of cosmic redemption, the factors which confirmed their belief in this solution are absent from our experience.

But this is not quite the case.   The truth of the matter is that modern literature contains a far greater number of accounts of what are claimed to be divine healings than does the New Testament.   The written evidence in these cases is certainly no less convincing than the evidence of the New Testament.   And again, most of us who move about in church circles hear the personal testimony of one or two people who claim to have been healed through the influence of Christ.   I have seen with my own eyes several such healings. This seems to me to be very much the same kind of evidence as was available to the first Christians. The only real difference lies in the fact that, in a church which is two thousand years older and many times larger, these extraordinary incidents are immersed in a far more voluminous matrix of mediocrity, and are therefore not given the same general prominence.

Do we therefore argue from these unusual incidents, which a few people claim bear a direct relation to the saving work of Christ, to the truth of the doctrine of cosmic redemption ? I think not. As I say, I have witnessed one or two of these unusual healings. On the occasions when the medical assistance essential to the competent investigation of such cases was available, I have made an open inquiry into them. The only outcome of such investigation was to show that there are undoubtedly many puzzling factors associated with the phenomenon known as divine healing. Evidence so slight and inconclusive as this could never supply the foundation for an important theological doctrine. Yet the evidence available to us in this field is not essentially different from that available to the first Christians.

We are therefore forced to conclude that it was not the evidence of the charismatic ministries in themselves which inspired the first Christians with such confidence in the universal efficacy of the work of Christ. It is only to those who are already convinced that Christ is Lord of heaven and earth that these extraordinary events have corroborative significance. It is only to those who already believe that Christ has " overcome the demons " that these events are miraculous in the true sense of the word—a manifestation of the Divine. The strong conviction of the early church that Christ had established His rule throughout the whole universe was not based primarily on an inference from such specific evidences as these, but on the more immediate evidence of the personal religious encounter with the Christ Himself—either as the Christ in the flesh or as the resurrected Christ.

This encounter is the central factor in Christian religious experience, which we must assume remains fairly constant through the changing centuries of the church's life if there is any unity of the faith at all. The terms in which this encounter is described may vary, but the Christ Himself remains the same. Therefore, if the early church found evidence, in this encounter, for their belief that the Christ had fundamentally transformed those elements in man's experience which the demons symbolised, then that same evidence should be available to us in the same way.

We have already acknowledged that the experience of Christian redemption is primarily a personal religious encounter with the Christ. We have also argued that it is only in the light of this encounter that Christian redemption can be understood. Redemption must be " seen by its own light ". It is in this personal encounter with the Christ that the doctrine of cosmic redemption must have its foundation if it has any foundation at all.

Jesus cannot be known as the Christ at second hand. At second hand we can know Him only as an historical figure of high moral standing. To know Him as the Christ is to recognise in Him a claim upon our personal response and thus to stand in immediate personal correlation with Him. The question, " Whom do men say that I the Son of Man am ? " did not lead Peter to a confession of faith. But the question, " Whom do ye say that I am ? " did. The recognition of Jesus as the Christ is not merely the adoption of an opinion or the giving of assent to a dogma. It is an immediate response of the total personality to a claim which we encounter in Him to our loyalty and devotion.

We have already defined intrinsic meaning as that which claims from us such an immediate personal response. Therefore we are adding nothing new when we say that the recognition of Jesus as the Christ is the recognition of intrinsic meaning in Him. If the encounter with Jesus as the Christ could be described in terms of extrinsic meaning then it would be possible to know Him as such at second hand. But it is intrinsic meaning in a unique form, for its claim upon us is absolute. We have already discussed the various ways in which we encounter intrinsic meaning as an element to which we can respond personally in an otherwise impersonal world. But in all these cases the claim upon our response is relative in that we can distinguish degrees of more or less within it. In our encounter with other persons, for instance, we recognise some as claiming from us the personal response of respect in a greater degree than others. But in the recognition of Jesus as the Christ no room is left for such comparison of relative factors. The claim upon us is absolute and the only appropriate response is that of worship. We know Him to be the Christ because we recognise the absolute claim upon our personal response, which we encounter in Him, to be the same as that absolute claim which we experience in the face of God. The encounter with Jesus as the Christ is an encounter with God. Whoever has seen Him has seen the Father. This is the foundation in experience of the doctrine of the divinity of Christ. Apart from such foundation it is a meaningless formula.

To those who share it, the experience which I am here describing will be easily recognisable. With those who do not share it, there is no point in going on to discuss the doctrine of cosmic redemption until they know something of the living experience of personal redemption. Therefore, in this context, I make no apologetic for, or further analysis of, this account of our religious awareness of the living Christ. If we said anything more, it would be necessary to say a great deal more. This is not the place for such an apologetic.

How is this encounter with the Christ related to other

instances of intrinsic meaning such as we have described ?
It is characteristic of an absolute claim that it will brook
no rivals.   Therefore once we have recognised the absolute-
ness of the claim which we encounter in Christ, we must
either condemn all other such claims as distractions from
the one absolute claim, or else they must be subsumed
under it as particular and partial manifestations of the same
thing.   The intrinsic meaning which we encounter in Christ
must either deny all other intrinsic meaning or else it must
interpret and fulfil it.

Now these are the very alternatives with which we have
found the church to be faced throughout her history.   In
her efforts to interpret the significance of the Christ in
relation to the world, she has been forced to see in Him and
His work either the simple condemnation of the whole
natural order, or else the revelation and fulfilment of a
meaning already latent in the natural order, however
partial and obscured it may have been.   This is the choice,
with which we have by now become familiar, between
various forms of dualism on the one hand and the doctrine
of cosmic redemption on the other.   We have already
argued that any solution of the dualistic type is in fundamental contradiction with the essentials of Biblical Christianity.   Therefore we must see the work of Christ, not as
a condemnation of the elements of intrinsic meaning which
we already find in the natural order, but as confronting us
in its fulness with what they, in their partial way, suggest.
That is to say, we must stand by Irenaeus, who held that
in the residual goodness of the natural order we have a
foretaste of the same graciousness of God which calls us
" upwards from lesser things to those greater ones which
are in His own presence " ;[1] rather than with Augustine,
who maintained that the good things of this world " are
but solaces of man's miseries, in no way pertinent to his
glories ".[2]   We must see the Christ as conferring the ulti-

[1] *Supra*, p. 106.   [2] *Supra*, p. 127.

mate intrinsic meaning which we encounter in Him upon the whole, rather than as denying such meaning as there already is in nature.

This is the bare form of the answer, but it is not its substance. In terms of systematic, objective thought, which is the necessary vehicle of philosophical theology, we can express only the form of the answer. The perception of its substance is contingent upon personal spiritual insight. Like all recognition of the divine work of Christ, it is an act of faith in the strict sense of ecstatic knowledge. It cannot ultimately be expressed in objective propositions, but can only be shared in the active response of faith.

Systematic, objective thought can recognise only two interpretations of the phrase " cosmic redemption ". The first we might call the full-blooded interpretation, which looks for some objective change in the material constitution of the universe. The second and more anaemic interpretation looks for no such objective alteration in the universe, but claims that the subjective alteration in man's outlook, wrought by his inward experience of redemption, so alters his estimate of the world around him as to be tantamount to a renewal of the world. The one is entirely objective and the other is entirely subjective.

But neither of these interpretations is adequate to describe the kind of renewal of man and his world to which the New Testament bears witness. If the former were true, it would be a matter for investigation by the physical sciences. If the latter were true it would be a question for psychology.

The logical analysis of our consciousness of our situation in existence, which arose out of our criticism of Hegel, may have appeared at the time as a difficult and perhaps rather unnecessary digression. But it is quite fundamental to a proper understanding of the sense in which a serious doctrine of cosmic redemption is possible. We showed there that the assumption of a sharp disjunction between the subjective and the objective elements in human experience, however useful as an epistemological device, is not the ultimate truth of our situation in existence. The world cannot ultimately be described as object and the self as subject *simpliciter*. Self and world are correlative terms. The language of systematic, objective thought cannot express this correlation. We can only recognise our experience of it in the frustration of attempting so to describe it.

It is at the level of this existential correlation of self and world that the demonic—the menace of sub-personal meaninglessness—is experienced. It is at the same level that the overcoming of the demonic in Christ is experienced. Therefore in the full appreciation both of the problem and its solution, we are operating below the level of the convenient disjunction between subjective and objective which is the working basis of systematic objective thought.

Personal redemption and cosmic redemption are not two separate things, the one subjective and the other objective. They are correlative aspects of one and the same thing. The objectivity of both consists in the objectivity of the event wherein they are accomplished.

By systematic analysis we can elucidate both the problem and the answer. But we cannot express them. We can only show them forth. Therefore in the last resort we must always be driven back upon language which is no less symbolic than that of the New Testament.

CHAPTER XVIII

THE FULNESS OF HIM THAT FILLETH ALL IN ALL

THE Biblical symbols for cosmic fall and redemption also express the correlation of self and world. The fallen angels and demons express structures appearing in outward experience which are correlative with the structures of anxiety in inward experience. When the prophets of the Old Testament saw judgment as operative in history, they were perceiving structures in the outward form of experience which were correlative with their inward experience of guilt. When the early Church saw in Christ the breaking of the power of the demons they were perceiving in the outward form of experience structures which were correlative with their inward sense of liberation.

Although the forms of expression familiar in these times are now archaic, we have seen that the existential experience which led men to formulate such doctrines have their counterpart in modern life. Naturally men no longer express their existential concern in the same terms as they did two thousand years ago. Not only their language, but the very concepts which they employ are different. But the problem of translating these ideas into modern terms is more serious than that. Such has been the development of our mainly technical civilisation that we are often quite inarticulate where our forefathers in the faith had a rich and subtly varied vocabulary of religious concepts to draw upon. Thus, when we try to arrive at a really penetrating understanding of the primitive doctrine of cosmic redemption, we find our thoughts operating at a level where we have to attempt to create not merely new words but even new concepts. Modern theology, with all the returning insights of this century, is full of this kind of difficulty. Take the work of Nicholas Berdyaev, for instance, or Martin Buber or Karl Heim or any of the Existentialists. The difficulties and complexities arise from the need to find a medium of communication rather than from any inherent difficulty or complexity in the matter itself.

On our analysis of the primitive concept of the demonic as the menace of sub-personal forces of super-human power, the nearest analogy in modern terminology is that of the " I-it " relationship usurping the place of the " I-Thou " relationship. I have already referred to Nicholas Berdyaev's account of the " de-animation " of the demonic.[1] The essence of his argument is that, in the first place, we must recognise that Christ did effect a real liberation of mankind from his immersion in nature and set him up as an independent spiritual being, offering him a free solution for human destiny. It was this liberation of the human spirit which made possible the controlling attitude to nature which finally found expression in post-Renaissance science. But this new development had its negative side. The de-animation of the demonic involved also the de-animation of all nature so that mankind was still further denied the truly responsive relationship to environment which his personal spiritual nature demands. The world became more than ever a meaningless " It ".[2]

The early Church denied the power of the demonic, but they never denied its existence. They knew only too well that it described a real factor in their experience. Today its existence is denied, but the same menace to personal spirit still remains within the secular context of the de-animated " I-it " relationship to the world. This appears in the fact that science must continually struggle against the world, instead of revealing its glory. The enmity of

[1] *Supra*, p. 26 f.   [2] *The Meaning of History*, pp. 113–115.

the demonic to spontaneity and vitality—the living aspect of spirit—which was once expressed in terms of the corruption of nature by demons, is now expressed in the conception of a mechanistic universe indifferent to the destiny of living spirit. The determinism which was once expressed in terms of the domination of the world by astral demons is now expressed in the secular " determinisms " of the various sciences—physical, economic, psychological, etc. This is the enmity of the demonic to intentionality—the conscious aspect of spirit. The enmity of the demonic to the rational, once expressed in terms of demon-possession now appears in the madness with which the obstinate enmity of the world of " It " continually threatens personality, and which appears ever more frequently in the form of neurosis. The enmity of the demonic to God, which was once expressed in terms of the rebellion of the demons against God, is now expressed in terms of the assertion of the particular and the individual over against the Absolute, within the " I-it " relationship. This arises first of all as an epistemological and metaphysical problem. But in the course of our criticism of certain aspects of German Idealism, we saw the deeper, spiritual issues which arise out of it.

The Relations of " It " and " Thou " in the World. The demonic is essentially meaninglessness. (This meaninglessness is symbolised in the language of the Bible by the ideas of chaos and darkness.) For this reason the absolutely demonic can have no positive existence. The absolutely demonic would be absolute meaninglessness. But total meaninglessness is total chaos—sheer formlessness. And without form nothing can have being ; for a thing cannot " be " without " being something ". That is to say, a thing cannot be a " thing " without some minimum of determination by a form. Yet the very presence of form implies meaning. Therefore the demonic is continually in the dilemma that in denying meaning it denies

R

its own existence. Therefore the destiny of the pure demonic must always be that of self-annihilation.[1]

The secularised demonic—the impersonal " It "—is caught in the same ontological dilemma. The pure " It " implies the same denial of meaning as the demonic. For to be a simple and absolute " It " a thing must be a simple and absolute particular. The moment it becomes involved in reference beyond itself, its particularity becomes impaired and is conditioned by that which is beyond its own existence.[2] Now the meaning of a thing is that which refers beyond its own particular existence. Meaning, therefore, denies the absolute particularity of the " It ", and so denies the " It " as such. Conversely, the world of " It ", to maintain its own existence as " It ", must deny meaning. This is why the world, as set over against us in the " I-it " relationship, becomes mere gross, meaningless matter, inimical to the life of spirit.

In denying its own particular meaning the " It " also denies the absolute Meaning which is the ground of all things and under which every particular meaning is subsumed.

Yet the " It " can maintain its particularity only as conditioned by that which limits its existence. Its particularity rests on its separation from other things. It can be separated from other things only in so far as it is bounded by them, and therefore related to them. But as involved in this reference beyond itself, it is dependent on form and meaning. Therefore, like the demonic, the " It " depends for its existence on that which it denies. For example, the simplest kind of " It " one can imagine is a mathematical point in space. Such a point cannot become definite and particular until it is defined in terms of its axes. Then it is involved in a reference and a meaning which extends beyond itself. This means that it is no more a simple

---

[1] *Cf.* P. Tillich, *The Interpretation of History*, p. 80 f.
[2] *Cf.* F. H. Bradley, *Principles of Logic*, p. 3 ff.

" It " for its meaning cannot be contained within the thought of the " It ".

Thus the structure which the outward form of experience assumes under the " I-it " relationship is caught in the same dilemma as the demonic. It denies meaning, yet its existence rests upon meaning.

This problem is the basis of F. H. Bradley's metaphysical reasoning. He shows how the claim of every particular to self-existence—i.e. the claim of every " It " to be a simple " It "—implies an infinite regress from the conditioned to the less conditioned. This regress in its turn implies the Absolute as its terminal and as the unconditioned ground of all things and the ultimate meaning of all things.[1] This is what I mean when I say that just as the existence of the demonic is grounded in the God whom it is its nature to deny, so the world of " It ", in its demonic character, must deny the ultimate Meaning in which its existence is grounded.

In this, of course, I am identifying the Absolute with God. Bradley would differ from me here in that he holds that the Absolute is unknown and unknowable, and that as soon as we begin to characterise it in any way we immediately falsify it. From his own standpoint, Bradley is quite correct in reaching this negative conclusion. For Bradley's work remains within the confines of autonomous conceptual thought. Now autonomous conceptual thought is essentially objectifying thought in that it must assume the simple subject-object relationship between self and world. In this it is simply the subjective side of the " I-it " relationship. That is to say, that which constitutes the structure of " It " in experience as viewed under the outward form is also the structure of conceptual thought when it is viewed under the inward form of experience. Therefore when Bradley attempts to comprehend the Absolute in conceptual thought, he is attempting to

[1] F. H. Bradley, *Appearance and Reality*.

comprehend it as an " It ". As the ground of all things the Absolute is also the ultimate Meaning of all things, and as ultimate Meaning it cannot be comprehended within the thought of " It ". We cannot know the Absolute in this sense. We can only encounter it in total free response, and in this encounter we cannot say " It ", but only " Thou ", and at the same time we know that we are contained by that which we address.

Just as the structure of " It " is the denial of meaning, so the experience of true intrinsic meaning has always the characteristic of an " I-Thou " encounter.

There are two ways in which an object or situation in the world may evoke our response. It may be significantly related to our concern simply as something which we want to satisfy a desire. That is to say, it evokes our response at the sub-personal level of concupiscence. On the other hand an object or situation may have meaning for us not merely in the sense that we wish to take and use it, but rather in that it actually lays a claim upon us. There is in it that which *claims* to be an object of our concern. It lays the claim upon us ; we do not lay the claim upon it. This is truly intrinsic meaning and the claim which it lays upon us is the distinctive characteristic of the experience of " Thou ".

That which has meaning for us only in terms of our desire belongs entirely to the world of " It ". Just as objectifying thought is structurally the subjective side of the " I-it " relationship, so sheer concupiscence is its subjective side dynamically. This is why men prefer the demonic world of " It " to the encounter with " Thou " in the world. The world of " It " enslaves them just as lust and concupiscence must always enslave ; but even in their enslavement they can use the mere " It " for their purposes and pleasures. Men prefer to rape the universe rather than to be wedded in organic marriage with it. The whole structure of our technical civilisation, as distinct from our culture, is based upon this. In these terms we can see the deepest meaning of St. John's words :

> And this is the condemnation, that the light is come into the world, and men loved the darkness rather than the light, because their deeds were evil.[1]

When we encounter in the world that which has meaning not merely in terms of our concupiscence, we must either respond to its claim upon us or else be judged by it. For every time we encounter meaning in this sense, we encounter also its divine ground. Therefore it makes the claim of " Thou " upon us.

But while special meanings can maintain themselves in a partial way in the world, and thereby become in some degree transparent to the ultimate meaning of the world in God, they are continually threatened by the demonic meaninglessness of the " It ". A special meaning can maintain itself in the world only by being separated from the meaninglessness which surrounds it. For example, a painting must be put in a frame, which is the symbol of its separation from what surrounds it. By this insistence on its own particularity, the mode of its existence becomes hopelessly involved in the structure of the world of " It ". Therefore the element of " Thou " which we encounter in it is only ambiguously present and is always threatened with extinction. A special period of history may have meaning for us and therefore acquire a degree of transparency to the ultimate meaning of all history. This happened with the prophets of Israel. But this can only be so so long as we hold that period of history apart from what appears to be the general meaninglessness of history at large. But then, in particularising any special period of history in this way, we rob it of its ultimate significance within the whole.

This continual threat and domination which the structure

[1] John 3/19.

of " It " holds over every particular thing or situation in
the world which has meaning in its own right is the basis
of the apocalyptic despair. On the other hand every
special meaning which we encounter in the world, as
threatened by the dominance of " It ", refers us to an
ultimate meaning which includes the whole and therefore
is beyond all threat from the demonic meaninglessness of
" It ".[1] This is the basis of the unbounded hope which
exists alongside the despair of apocalyptic.

The Overcoming of the " It " in Christ. In Christ we
encounter the absolute Meaning which is the ground of
every special intrinsic meaning. This cannot be explained,
for that would be to subject it to objectifying thought, and
to try to comprehend intrinsic meaning within the thought
of " It ". We cannot comprehend Jesus as the Christ.
We can only encounter Him, and encountering Him thus
we encounter Him as *the* " Thou ", and we know that when
He said : " He that hath seen me hath seen the Father "
He spoke the truth. This is the paradox of the Word made
flesh, that the Absolute Meaning which is the ground and
end of the world—the Alpha and the Omega—should be
manifested in a particular in the world.

Jesus belongs to the world of " It " as much as any other
particular in the world. This was so much so that it was
possible to ravish Him just as one ravishes the whole world
of " It ". As a mere " It " He could be crucified and
pushed into a hole in the ground, and that was the end of
Him. But in this very act of allowing His existence to be
sacrificed to His Meaning, Christ overcomes the power of
the structure of " It " for ever, so that though His existence
was destroyed, His essential Meaning remained untouched.

The temptation of Jesus, described in the New Testament
in terms of the demonic suggestions of Satan, can also be
described in terms of the secularised demonic ideas with
which we have been dealing. The essence of the tempta-

[1] *Cf.* P. Tillich, *The Interpretation of History*, p. 221 ff.

tion of Jesus was that He should use the power which came
from His unity with God to establish His own particular
existence in the world. The significance of the temptations
to turn stone into bread, to cast Himself down from the
temple, and to fall down and worship Satan, is the same in
each case. If Jesus had compromised with the demonic
" It " to the extent of using the power of God to establish
His own power in existence, He could draw all men to Him,
and rule them as He wished. But in doing this He would
be limiting His Meaning to the boundaries of His existence
as a particular in the world—like the picture that establishes its meaningfulness in existence by putting a frame
round itself—and would thereby fall into bondage to the
structure of " It ". He would have meaning only in terms
of our concupiscence. We could use His good offices, but
we could not worship Him, for He would be no more
Absolute " Thou ", but for ever compromised with the world
of " It ".

When Jesus resisted the temptation to establish His own
existence in the world, He had already, right at the beginning of His ministry, chosen the way of the crucifixion.
He had already decided to sacrifice His existence to His
Meaning. In this decision, His Meaning is completely
victorious over the enslaving structure of " It ". The
demonic power of " It " was broken. Though we crucify
Him and hide Him in a hole in the ground, we cannot
destroy the Meaning which is His essential being. He rises
again to be encountered by us as " Thou ". In this encounter we must either worship Him or be judged by Him.
There is no other alternative.

This cannot be regarded as an account of the Person of
Christ. But it does serve to show the sense in which the
terminology I have been using can be applied to His person,
and how His person and work are relevant to the problem
of the impersonal structure of human environment and the
evils arising therefrom. In adopting these terms I am not

rejecting anything of the traditional Trinitarian terminology. I am merely attempting to show the relevance of
the traditional dogmatic to the problems I have raised.

We have shown the sense in which the Christ overcomes
the bondage of the impersonal, meaningless structure of
" It " in His own person. Now we must consider the
sense in which He overcomes it in the world at large.

As having been incarnate in the world, Christ entered
the realm of our experience. He belongs therefore to the
realm of " things "—to the realm of " It ". Yet since in
Him the integrity of the Ultimate Intrinsic Meaning
remained unimpaired by the structure of " It ", we meet
Him only as " Thou ". In this sense the first disciples,
who knew Him in the flesh, have no advantage over us who
know only that He was in the flesh. The encounter with
the Ultimate " Thou " is in both cases essentially the same.
When we have encountered Him as " Thou " nothing is
added to His Meaning by our being able to grasp Him as
an " It " within experience.

But once we have been brought face to face with the
complete ascendency of meaning over existence, of " Thou "
over " It ", nothing can ever be meaningless for us again
in the ultimate sense of the utter meaninglessness of the
" It ". Something has entered our experience which
breaks through the structure of " It ", revealing its ground
in that to which we can say only " Thou ". That is to say,
once we have encountered God in Christ we must encounter
God in all things. This is the sense in which the Kingdom
has already come, and the power of the demonic is already
broken in Christ, even though the course of cosmic history
has not been violated by any cataclysmic intrusion of the
Divine. (If God did so intrude upon the world with
violence, then it would be reduced for ever to the level of
" It "—a thing to be manipulated—and could never again
reveal the glory of the " Thou ".) Yet while the course of
history remains thus unviolated, its entire face, both before

and after Christ, has been altered by His presence and His work in the world.

For those raised in the Protestant tradition, this can best be understood first of all at the personal level on which we are accustomed to think our religious thoughts, and which we have learned to understand. The idea, that as a result of the presence of God in Christ in the world the status of every individual person has been altered, is well known to the extent of becoming theologically threadbare. Once we have encountered the " Thou " in Christ we must see the claim of every individual person upon our personal response as grounded in the eternal Meaning which is in Him. The ethical command of Jesus : " Thou shalt love thy neighbour as thyself ", is not additional to the significance of His person, but is contained within it. It is not a simple command to change our subjective attitude to others. This would be impossible to fulfil, and would only be an addition to the burden of the law, and not a release from it. Our Christian love for others does not and cannot arise from obedience to a command. It arises from the fact that once we have encountered Jesus as the Christ and felt the claim which He makes upon us, we encounter something of that claim in every person we meet. This is why Jesus could say, " In as much as ye have done it unto one of the least of these my brethren, ye have done it unto me." We do not encounter a claim to our worship in them, for it is only as potential bearers of the Ultimate Meaning that we meet them. But we encounter a claim to our absolute, unqualified respect—a respect which involves our ultimate concern, though it does not exhaust it as does the claim of Christ.

There is nothing subjective about this. It does not proceed from us in any sense. It is as objective as the claim of Christ for it is the claim of Christ. For those into whose experience the complete ascendancy of " Thou " over " It " in the person of Christ has entered, the whole structure of the world—the whole structure of the outward form of experience—has been so transformed that in all persons whom they meet they encounter something of this same special claim upon their personal response.

But when we say that this claim is objective, this has nothing to do with the characteristic objectivity of the world of " It ". It is precisely this structure of objectivity that has been overcome. The change is objective only in the sense that it is not dependent on any activity on our part but is a change in the form in which our experience comes to us. That is to say, it is a change appearing within the correlation of self and world.

However, this principle is applicable not merely to persons. I begin with this illustration simply because we are familiar with it. The extension of this principle from persons in the world to the world at large can best be seen if we move now to another instance of our encounter with the claim of Christ. This is in the sacraments of the Church. When the Word became flesh, not only His personality became the bearer of Ultimate Intrinsic Meaning, but His flesh itself—that is to say, His material situation in the world. Thus all His acts, while they remain real acts in the world, become also symbolic acts in which there is the same ascendancy of meaning over existence as we find in His person. This is the justification of the inextricable union of the historical and the symbolic in the New Testament. In all He does we encounter the same inexhaustible meaning as we encounter in His person. In any situation in which the Christ is involved, this is true.

This fact is expressed in the special sacraments of the Church. For example, in the sacrament of the Lord's Supper, we encounter the whole meaning of Christ. We are in the presence of the ultimate " Thou ". This is the meaning of the doctrine of the real presence. We meet the characteristic claim upon our decision. We must either acknowledge the " Thou " or be judged by it. That is to say, we must either partake worthily or we eat and drink to our own damnation.

The meaning of the sacrament of baptism is essentially the same. It confronts us with the whole meaning and claim of Christ. We must either acknowledge Him in the vows of submission or we must reject Him and be judged by Him. (It need hardly be said, of course, that this is not presented as the immediate meaning of the sacrament to the infant recipient. It is within the organism of the baptised community that this meaning encounters us and the absolute claim is laid upon us.)

This kind of sacramental experience shows us that we encounter the meaning, and therefore the claim of Christ, not only in persons in the world, but at least at some points in the material world itself. However, the moment we attempt to restrict the sacramental principle to these special points in experience, we bind their meaning to their special existence in such a way that we once more establish in them the domination of the structure of " It " and their sacramental power becomes lost in its demonic meaninglessness.

The sacramental principle has been subjected to so much misunderstanding and distortion of this kind that neither the meaning nor the truth of this proposition becomes immediately clear. We can see its meaning best if we look for a moment at the history of sacramentalism in the Roman Catholic Church.

Bethune-Baker says, in his account of the original meaning of the word " sacrament " :

At first there were many sacraments : the term was used in a wider sense. It represented the Greek word " mystery " as used in the New Testament of a secret, long hidden, and still hidden from the mass of men, but revealed to Christians.[1]

[1] *The Early History of the Christian Doctrine*, p. 376.

This mystery—this open secret—was the Ultimate Meaning of all things as manifested in Christ. It was the manifestation of the " Thou " in Christ. Every situation in which this Meaning was encountered in its power was an encounter with Christ. Every such situation was a mystery—a sacrament. Baptism and the Lord's Supper were the two traditional signs in which this encounter with the sacramental presence of Christ in the world was focused. Certain spiritual benefits were known to accrue from the practice of these rites, but they were simply the benefits of the one mystery of our salvation. They did not constitute additional mysteries with additional saving power of their own. It was not in their own existence, but simply as a point of focus that they had saving power.

However, at the very outset of the Church's life, these special sacramental acts came to be misunderstood. The fundamental error for which Luther condemned the Catholic Church in his criticism of its sacramental doctrine has its source in the action of the first Christian who postponed his baptism to the end of his life in order that it might wash away *all* his sins.[1] This action implied that there was a special power in the particular sacramental act other than its transparency to the Christ. Rightly understood, a sacrament is not something that we can use. We can only approach it, for in approaching it we are approaching the " Thou ". But when we come to regard baptism as a rite which we can use at whatever date we please as a means of blotting out our transgressions, then there is nothing more of " Thou " in it. It has become a calculable factor—a mere " It ". Its meaning has become bound within the limits of its existence and has no more depth. This is seen from the fact that when baptism was regarded in this light in the early Church its meaning and power were thought to be exhausted in the exercise of the rite.

---

[1] By the end of the second century, this attitude was almost universal in the Church. *Cf.* Bethune-Baker, *loc. cit.*

That is to say, once a man had received baptism he had exhausted its power, and it had no meaning for his post-baptismal sins. With the truly sacramental, we cannot exhaust its meaning. It is sacramental simply because its meaning goes beyond the bounds of its particular existence and is inexhaustible in its depth. This is the meaning of Luther's statement that " the ship of our baptism never sinks ".

Once the Church had made this error in its interpretation of the sacrament of baptism, their view of the Lord's Supper soon became affected, and the conception of the sacraments as a kind of alchemy of the soul became firmly established. When this step was taken and the meaning of the sacrament bound to the existence of a special rite, the Church succumbed to the same temptation as that which Jesus resisted—namely that of binding His Meaning to His own existence—the temptation to place a frame round His meaning and thereby compromise with the world of " It ". When the Church bound the meaning of the sacramental principle to special rites it was forced to introduce this frame in the form of the rood screen, separating the sacred from the secular.

But when Luther made his startling re-discovery of the ascendancy of meaning over existence in the sacramental principle, this sacramental encounter with Christ in the depth of His Meaning became released from its bondage to the existence of special rites. When Luther said of the term " sacrament " : " To be sure, if I cared to use the term in its scriptural sense, I should allow but a single sacrament with three sacramental signs "[1], he had no longer any basis on which to limit the sacramental principle to three special signs other than an authoritarian view of Scripture which is no longer tenable. The Meaning of Christ could no longer be bound to any particular existence,

[1] *Works*, Vol. 2, p. 77. (At this stage in his thought Luther recognised also Penance as a special sacramental sign, though with some hesitation.)

for the sacramental principle was once more recognised as the complete ascendancy of meaning over the particular existence of the " It " in Christ.[1] The rood screen had to be taken away, just as the veil of the temple was rent when Christ died on the Cross. The distinction between the common bread and the bread of the holy table can no longer be maintained as a radical distinction. In this sense the Quakers are perfectly true to the sacramental principle in making a sacrament of every meal—though their practice remains open to criticism in that their rejection of all special signs leaves them without the necessary focus for sacramental worship.

When the sacramental principle is thus freed from its distortion in Roman Catholicism, we see that we cannot place any limit upon it. For when we limit it, we bind it to a particular existent and in doing this we contradict the " mystery " which is Christ—namely the complete ascendancy of Ultimate Meaning in Him over His particular existence.

The momentous significance of this has not been fully realised within Protestantism, largely because theological attention has been so intensely concentrated on the moral significance of salvation. But what it in fact means is that just as our encounter with the Christ as Ultimate Meaning, the " Thou ", the Son of God, implies an encounter with the claim of the " Thou " in every individual person whom we meet, so in every encounter with the material world we meet the same claim upon our ultimate concern in terms of the sacramental principle. This is more than a change in our inward being. It alters the whole correlation of self and world. It is the claim of God in Christ.

We found in Hegel the suggestion that the problem of

---

[1] When considered in relation to this context, the Lutheran doctrine of the *communicatio idiomatum* is not the piece of arid scholasticism which it is sometimes taken to be. It is a formal, dogmatic expression of the sacramental ubiquity and universal ascendancy of the Christ, which is an implicate of Luther's fundamental insight into the sacramental principle.

" unhappy consciousness "—the correlation of a personal self with an impersonal world—could be overcome only when all encounter with the world becomes in some sense also an integral part of our personal encounter with God. We found in Martin Buber the expression of a similar longing when we quoted him as saying :

> If only we love the real world that will not let itself be extinguished, really in its horror, if only we venture to surround it with the arms of our spirit, our hands will meet hands that grip them.

But we found that such a response to the world is impossible so long as it confronts us with the blank impersonal meaninglessness of the demonic " It ". The solution cannot lie simply in man's subjective willingness to respond in a truly personal way to his world. It is only in correlation with intrinsic meaning that such a response is possible. Man's world must *claim* his personal response and claim it absolutely before he can fully give himself to it and find the ultimate security of his personal being.

This is precisely what we find to be accomplished in the work of Jesus as the Christ. When we encounter in Him the complete ascendancy of meaning over existence—of " Thou " over " It "—the whole structure of our experience as it comes to us is altered. We are no more in bondage to the demonic—the meaningless " It ". For the ascendance of " Thou " over " It " in Christ sacramentally pervades the whole of our experience so that it no longer comes to us dominated by the structure of the meaningless " It ", but encounters us with the claim of " Thou ". Our personal response is claimed in a way which makes such response possible. The unhappy diremption of self into self and obstinately impersonal not-self has been overcome. A condition has been established in which personal spirit is no longer hopelessly stultified, but can freely grow in response to the grace of God. The world is no longer the object of our concupiscence which we ravish, and thereby put ourselves in bondage to it ; but, even in its horror, it reveals to us the glory of the image of God.   The Kingdom is indeed come in Christ, and the Christian Church may sing its hymns with full joy, for that which was spoken by the prophets is come to pass, and " the knowledge of the Lord covers the earth as the waters cover the sea".

The question immediately raises, however : How is it possible that a world in which we still encounter evil can reflect the image of God ?   But this actually raises no new problem.   It is simply an extension of the problem with which we are familiar on the personal level, namely : How is it possible that we, as sinners, are yet justified ? Indeed, the traditional answer to this question when it is asked at the personal level—that we are justified because Christ died for our sins—cannot be understood in its depth until it is understood as answering also the question about cosmic evil.   When Christ sacrificed His existence to the integrity of His Ultimate Meaning on the Cross, He over-came all meaninglessness.   In so doing He restored all evil to a place within the intrinsic meaning of the world, so that it is no more radical, fallen evil, but evil as conform-able to the forgiveness of God—and therefore, even in the midst of its pain to the peace of God.   If this were not so, then the crucifixion of the Christ, which is the pivotal point of all evil, could reflect nothing of the Divine and salvation—personal as well as cosmic—would be a vain thing.

But this, in its turn, raises another question : Is there then no place for the Christian struggle against evil in the world ?   This again is a question which is familiar at the personal level.   It was raised and answered by St. Paul when he said, " Shall we then sin that grace may the more abound ? "   Since the encounter with Christ in the world is always an encounter with an absolute claim upon our personal response, the life of the Church must always be one of striving, spurred on by the existence of evil as by a thorn in the flesh.

All this, however, becomes actual only within the fellowship of the Church. For those who are without, the structure of experience as it comes to them remains unchanged. Their world is still in bondage to the demonic meaninglessness of " It ". In this sense the Church is quite literally in the world, but not of it, for the world of the Church is a different world from that of those who are still in darkness. Just as for St. Paul it was the bondage of mankind to the arch-demons of sin and death that gave such tremendous urgency to the missionary enterprise, so today it is still the bondage of men to the demonic—the meaningless " It "—which gives the same urgency to the missionary enterprise.

This is the sense in which the redemption of the cosmos depends just as much on the redemption of man as man's redemption depends on the redemption of the whole. This is the truth of St. Paul's picture of the whole cosmos groaning and travailing in pain together until now, *waiting with earnest expectation for the manifestation of the sons of God.* The ultimate destiny of the Church is to become the whole cosmos, so that there shall be no more Church:

For there shall be no temple therein : for the Lord God Almighty and the Lamb are the temple of it. And the city shall have no need of the sun, neither of the moon, to shine in it ; for the glory of God shall lighten it, and the Lamb shall be the light thereof.[1]

So Christ shall be truly " the fulness of Him that filleth all in all."[2]

[1] Revelation 21/22–23.   [2] Ephesians 1/23.

S

CRITICISM OF HEGEL'S ARGUMENT

HEGEL'S argument, as we have set it forth on the basis of his statement of it in *The Phenomenology of Mind*, begins from the problem of the epistemological relationship of the knower to the known. Kant had already shown the relevance of this formal problem to the material problem of the relation of phenomenal environment to a personal subject of moral and religious experience. The dualistic form of his solution to this latter problem, as expressed by him in the antinomy of practical reason, was determined chiefly by his answer to the formal, epistemological problem. The new science had raised both the material and the formal problem in a new way. The Newtonian development of the Copernican astronomy had raised the material question of the relation of man as a moral and religious being to such an environment. At the same time, it raised the formal problem of the epistemological relation of the knowing subject to the world as known in this scientific way. In answering the epistemological problem in terms of a sharp distinction between *phenomena* and *noumena*, Kant made the material problem all the more acute, and could hold out a hope of the final fulfilment of personal and moral life only in the eventual escape of our immortal souls from the realm of phenomenal experience. But while the formal, epistemological problem and the material, moral problem are closely associated in Kant, they are never identified. In Hegel, they do eventually become identified, and this identification of a formal problem with a material problem which involves human desire and concern, in itself gives ground for the suspicion that there is serious confusion of thought in Hegel's argument.

The formal problem with which he begins is the logical anlaysis of objectivity. The transition from this to the material problem is made possible only by the fact that he abandons the attempt to describe objectivity in terms of formal relations and begins to speak in dynamic terms. Because of the contradictions into which the formal problem leads him, he finds it necessary to describe the relation of subject and object in knowledge in terms of contrary forces seeking a synthesis. What is one to make of such a solution to the formal problem ? What kind of meaning can we attach to propositions which describe logical relations as though they were dynamic movements ? Judgment, as a psychological event, might be meaningfully described in dynamic terms. But it is not *qua* psychological event that a judgment has meaning and reference. The problem of objectivity is not a psychological problem. It is a logical problem.

But it is easier to recognise the absurdity of speaking of logical relations as though they were dynamic movements than it is to *explain* why this is absurd. If one could give a simple analysis of the nature of " meaning ", " reference " and " relation ", then one could explain the absurdity. But if such a simple analysis of these terms were possible, then by that very same analysis one could also give a simple account of the relation of subject and object in knowledge, and the Hegelian problem would not arise at all. Perhaps the best illustration of the absurdity of speaking of logical relations as though they were moving forces is the *reductio ad absurdum* suggested by the Neo-Hegelian, F. H. Bradley. A force is a particular thing which can stand in relation to other particular things. Therefore if logical relations are forces of some kind, they must be particular things which exist. Now Bradley has pointed out that if relations exist as particulars in the same way as their terms exist, then we require relations to relate the relations to their terms, and so on *ad infinitum*.[1] Bradley, of course, has his own reasons for drawing attention to this difficulty in the idea of relations. But the point serves our purpose in showing the kind of absurdity that arises when we treat a formal problem as though it were a material one—when we treat logical relations as though they were entities of the same order as the terms which they relate. This is the absurdity involved in Hegel's description of the contradiction into which his epistemological analysis leads him in terms of the opposition of two forces.

The philosopher, of course, is not to be denied the use of metaphor if he should find that this is the best form in which he can express his thought. But Hegel does not use these dynamic concepts as metaphors. He uses them literally, and his argument depends on their literal interpretation. It is only

---

[1] *Appearance and Reality*, pp. 25 ff.   *Principles of Logic*, pp. 12 ff.

because he employs these concepts literally, that he is able to identify the whole process of history and the whole of cosmic evolution with the self-development of the Idea. The essence of the argument is as follows :

(1) All self-consciousness and all knowledge is described in terms of this three-fold dynamic process of thesis, antithesis and synthesis.

(2) All teleological process involves (*a*) an abstract idea which is to be realised, (*b*) a concrete process in which it is realised, and (*c*) the end of the process which unites the abstract idea and the concrete actuality, in that it realises the idea in concrete actuality.

(3) Hegel treats all process as teleological in this sense. Therefore all process can be described in terms of the same three-fold dynamic process as was used to describe the epistemological form of self-consciousness. Therefore when we describe the self-development of the Idea, we are describing the whole process of reality. The fulfilment of this process is in the person and work of Christ and in the gift of the Holy Spirit which comes through Him.

But all this rests on the fundamental error of treating logical relations as though they were dynamic movements. Once you grant Hegel this point, it is only too true that one can describe every and any process as the self-development of the Idea. Indeed, the whole issue is so vague that it is almost impossible to conceive of anything which could not be so described. And for this very reason, the description adds nothing whatever to our understanding of the process concerned. This makes sympathetic, internal criticism of Hegel extremely difficult. If we consent to ignore this fundamental confusion of thought in identifying a formal and a material problem, then we very soon find ourselves saying the same kind of thing as Hegel. If, on the other hand, we recognise this fundamental error at the outset, then his whole argument is undermined. It is undermined to such an extent that it becomes impossible to offer any further sympathetic criticism of the argument as it stands. For if we are correct in asserting that Hegel has made this fundamental error, then we have not merely raised an objection to the argument, but have denied that it is an argument at all, and have reduced what purports to be an argument to sheer nonsense.

The truth of this is reflected in the actual history of philo-

sophy since Hegel.   Either one is a philosopher of the Hegelian
type and accepts the vagaries on which this type of philosophy
rests ; or else one insists on the necessity of clear analysis at
the outset and then the whole Hegelian argument becomes
irrelevant.   This cannot, of course, be said to have held as an
absolute rule.   But in the main, it is true to say that philosophers have been so divided, and that controversy between
those two main groups has never gone and never can go beyond
this fundamental issue.

All this would appear to bring us face to face with the same
deadlock.   If the whole Hegelian argument is undermined by
this fundamental point of criticism, there seems little point in
going ahead to inquire whether the interpretation of the cosmic
significance of the work of Christ at which he arrives can be
called a Christian doctrine of cosmic redemption.   This remains
true so long as we treat his argument as what it purports to
be—namely a linear argument beginning from a formal question about the relation of subject and object in knowledge and
leading to a material conclusion about the ultimate destiny of
the universe.

BIBLIOGRAPHICAL NOTE

*Throughout this book quotations are made by kind
permission of the publishers from editions as here listed.*

London : unless otherwise stated.

ABBOTT, T. K. *Kant's Theory of Ethics*. Longmans, 1883.

Ante-Nicene Christian Library. ed. Roberts and Donaldson.
Edinburgh, Clark, 1867–72.

ARISTOTLE, *Works*. ed. Ross. Oxford, Clarendon Press, 1908–
1931.

AQUINAS, ST. THOMAS. *Summa Theologica*. Literally translated by Fathers of the English Dominican Province.
Burns, Oates & Washbourne, 1911–22.

AULEN, GUSTAV. *Christus Victor*. S.P.C.K., 1931.

BERDYAEV, NICHOLAS. *The Meaning of History*. Bles, 1936.

— *Freedom and the Spirit*. New York, Scribners, 1935.

— *Slavery and Freedom*. New York, Scribners, 1944.

— *Spirit and Reality*. New York, Scribners, 1939.

BETHUNE-BAKER, J. F. *An Introduction to the Early History
of Christian Doctrine*. Methuen, 1942.

BEVAN, EDWYN. *Stoics and Sceptics*. Oxford, Clarendon Press,
1913.

BIGG, CHARLES. *The Christian Platonists of Alexandria*. Oxford,
Clarendon Press, 1886.

BOEHME, JACOB. *Of the Incarnation of Jesus Christ*. tr. J. R.
Earle. Constable, 1934.

BOUSSET, WILHELM. *Die Religion des Judentums*. Berlin,
Reuter u. Reichard, 1906.

NEUEN. *Hauptprobleme der Gnosis :* Forschungen zur Religion u.
Literatur des Alten u. Neuen Testaments. Göttingen,
Vandenhoek u. Ruprecht Verlag, 1907.

BRADLEY, FRANCIS H. *Appearance and Reality*. Swann, Som-
merschein, 1906.

—. *Essays on Truth and Reality*. Oxford, Clarendon Press,
1914.

—. *The Principles of Logic*. Kegan Paul, 1883.

BRANSCOMB, B. HARVIE. *The Gospel of Mark*. Hodder &
Stoughton, 1937.

BUBER, MARTIN. *I and Thou.* Edinburgh, Clark, 1937.

BURKITT, F. C. *Jewish and Christian Apocalypses.* Oxford University Press, 1914.

—. *The Church and Gnosis.* Cambridge University Press, 1932.

BUTTERWORTH, W. *Origen on First Principles.* S.P.C.K., 1936.

CADIOU, RÉNÉ. *Introduction au Système d'Origène.* Paris, Les Belles Lettres, 1932.

CAMPBELL, JOHN McLEOD. *The Nature of the Atonement.* Macmillan, 1878.

CAVE, SIDNEY. *The Doctrine of the Work of Christ.* Hodder & Stoughton, 1937.

CHARLES, R. H. *Apocrypha and Pseudepigrapha of the Old Testament.* Oxford, Clarendon Press, 1914.

—. *Eschatology : Hebrew, Jewish and Christian.* Black, 1913.

—. *The Religious Development Between the Old and the New Testaments.* Williams & Norgate, 1913.

CLARK, H. W. *The Cross and the Eternal Order.* Lutterworth Press, 1940.

DAVIDSON, A. B. *The Theology of the Old Testament.* Edinburgh, Clark, 1904.

DENIS, J. M. *La Philosophie d'Origène.* Paris, Impresse Nationale, 1884.

DIBELIUS, MARTIN. *Die Geisterwelt im Glauben des Paulus.* Göttingen, Vandenhoek u. Ruprecht Verlag, 1909.

Dictionary of the Bible. ed. J. Hastings. New York, Scribners, 1889–1902.

Die Griechischen Christlichen Schriftsteller der Ersten Drei Jahrhunderte. Leipzig, Der Königliche Prussische Akademie der Wissenschaft, 1897–1936.

DILLMAN, A. *Genesis Critically and Exegetically Expounded.* tr. Stephenson. Edinburgh, Clark, 1897.

DOBSCHUTZ, ERNST VON. *The Eschatology of the Gospels.* Hodder & Stoughton, 1910.

DODD, C. H. *The Parables of the Kingdom.* Nisbet, 1935.

—. *The Apostolic Preaching.* Hodder & Stoughton, 1936.

EISLER, ROBERT. *Weltenmantel und Himmelszelt.* München, Beck, 1910.

Encyclopedia of Religion and Ethics. ed. J. Hastings. New York, Scribners, 1908–22.

Excerpta ex Theodoto. tr. & ed. R. P. Casey. Christophers, 1934.

FARMER, HERBERT H. *The World and God.* Nisbet, 1943.

FAYE, EUGÈNE DE. *Gnostiques et Gnosticism.* Paris, Presses
Universitaires de France, 1913.
—. *Origen and His Work.* auth. tr. Fred. Rothwell. Oxford,
Clarendon Press, 1929.

GRESSMANN, HUGO. *Der Messias.* "Forschungen zur Religion
u. Literatur des Alten u. Neuen Testaments." Göttingen,
Vandenhoek u. Ruprecht Verlag, 1929.

HARNACK, ADOLF VON. *History of Dogma.* Williams & Nor-
gate, 1894–9.
HEGEL, G. W. F. *The Phenomenology of Mind.* tr. J. B.
Baillie, Allen & Unwin, 1931.

IRENAEUS. *Quinque Libres Adversus Haereses.* ed. W. Harvey.
Cambridge University Press, 1857.

JACKSON, F. J. FOAKES and LAKE, KIRSOPP, ed. *The Beginnings
of Christianity.* Macmillan, 1920–1936.

KNOX, W. L. *St. Paul and the Church of the Gentiles.* Cambridge
University Press, 1939.
KREBS, E. *Der Logos als Heiland im Ersten Jahrhundert.*
"Freiburg Theologische Studien." 1910.

LIETZMANN, HANS. *Der Weltheiland.* Bonn, Marcus u. Weber's
Verlag, 1909.
LIGHTFOOT, J. B. *St. Paul's Epistles to the Colossians and to
Philemon.* Macmillan, 1882.
LUTHER, MARTIN. *Works.* Philadelphia, United Lutheran
Publication House, 1915–1932.

MACGREGOR, G. H. C. *St. John's Gospel.* Hodder & Stoughton,
1936.
MANSEL, HENRY LONGVILLE. *Gnostic Heresies of the Second and
Third Centuries.* Murray, 1875.
MANSON, T. W. *The Teaching of Jesus.* Cambridge University
Press, 1931.
MONTEFIORE, C. G. *The Hibbert Lectures, 1892.* Williams &
Norgate, 1892.
MOORE, GEORGE FOOT. *Judaism.* Cambridge University Press,
1927.

NORDEN, EDUARD. *Die Geburt des Kindes.* Leipzig, Teubner,
1924.

OMAN, JOHN. *The Idea of the Holy.* " The Journal of Theological Studies," Vol. XXV, N. 99, April, 1924. Oxford, Clarendon Press.

OTTO, RUDOLF. *The Idea of the Holy.* tr. Harvey. Oxford University Press, 1923.

—. *Philosophy of Religion.* Williams & Norgate, 1931.

PHILO. *Works.* Heinemann, 1921–41.

—. *Pistis Sophia.* tr. Mead. Watkins, 1921.

PLATO. *The Republic.* tr. Jowett. Macmillan, 1924.

RAVEN, CHARLES E. *Apollinarianism.* Cambridge University Press, 1923.

ROBINSON, H. WHEELER. *Inspiration and Revelation in the Old Testament.* Oxford, Clarendon Press, 1946.

—. *Redemption and Revelation.* Nisbet, 1942.

RUSSELL, BERTRAND. *Mysticism and Logic.* Longmans, 1918.

SCHWEITZER, ALBERT. *The Mysticism of the Apostle Paul.* tr. Montgomery. New York, Holt, 1931.

—. *The Quest of the Historical Jesus.* Black, 1936.

Science, Religion and Reality. ed. Needham. Macmillan, 1926.

SMITH, W. ROBERTSON. *The Religion of the Semites.* Black, 1927.

Theologisches Worterbuch zum Neuen Testament. ed. G. Kittell. Stuttgart, 1933–38.

TILLICH, PAUL. *The Interpretation of History.* New York, Scribners, 1936.

VERGIL. *Eclogues and Georgics.* tr. Royds. Dent, n.d.

WAGNER, W. *Uber σώζω und seine Derivata im Neuen Testament.* " Zeitschrift für die Neutestamentliche Wissenschaft." 1905.

WEISS, JOHNNES. *History of Primitive Christianity.* Macmillan, 1937.

WELCH, A. C. *The Religion of Israel.* Edinburgh, Clark, 1912.

WELLHAUSEN, J. *History of Israel.* Edinburgh, Black, 1885.

WILLEY, BASIL. *The Seventeenth Century Background.* Chatto & Windus, 1934.

WILLIAMS, NORMAN POWELL. *The Ideas of the Fall and Original Sin.* Longmans, 1927.

WITTGENSTEIN, LUDWIG. *Tractetus Logico-Philosophicus.* Allen & Unwin, 1922.

INDEX OF NAMES

INDEX OF SUBJECTS

271

C. Tinling & Co., Ltd., Liverpool, London, and Presco